Yii Project Blueprints

From conception to production, learn how to develop real-world applications with the Yii framework

Charles R. Portwood II

BIRMINGHAM - MUMBAI

Yii Project Blueprints

Copyright © 2014 Packt Publishing

All rights reserved. No part of this book may be reproduced, stored in a retrieval system, or transmitted in any form or by any means, without the prior written permission of the publisher, except in the case of brief quotations embedded in critical articles or reviews.

Every effort has been made in the preparation of this book to ensure the accuracy of the information presented. However, the information contained in this book is sold without warranty, either express or implied. Neither the author, nor Packt Publishing, and its dealers and distributors will be held liable for any damages caused or alleged to be caused directly or indirectly by this book.

Packt Publishing has endeavored to provide trademark information about all of the companies and products mentioned in this book by the appropriate use of capitals. However, Packt Publishing cannot guarantee the accuracy of this information.

First published: September 2014

Production Reference: 1190914

Published by Packt Publishing Ltd.
Livery Place
35 Livery Street
Birmingham B3 2PB, UK.

ISBN 978-1-78328-773-4

www.packtpub.com

Cover Image by Pratyush Mohanta (tysoncinematography@gmail.com)

Credits

Author
Charles R. Portwood II

Reviewers
Amirsaman Memaripour
Atsushi Sakurai
Jonathan Weatherhead

Commissioning Editor
Antony Lowe

Acquisition Editor
Joanne Fitzpatrick

Content Development Editor
Dayan Hyames

Technical Editor
Venu Manthena

Copy Editors
Sarang Chari
Insiya Morbiwala
Alfida Paiva
Stuti Srivastava

Project Coordinator
Harshal Ved

Proofreaders
Simran Bhogal
Maria Gould
Ameesha Green
Paul Hindle

Indexers
Hemangini Bari
Mariammal Chettiyar

Graphics
Ronak Dhruv

Production Coordinator
Komal Ramchandani

Cover Work
Komal Ramchandani

About the Author

Charles R. Portwood II has over 10 years of experience in developing modern web applications and is well versed in integrating PHP with native mobile applications. An avid proponent for the Yii framework and open source software, Charles has contributed multiple guides, extensions, and applications to the Yii community. In addition to being a programmer, he is also a Linux system administrator. When not in front of a computer, he can be found writing stories, photographing nature, or spending time with his wife.

About the Reviewers

Amirsaman Memaripour is a second year PhD student at the Department of Computer Science and Engineering of University of California, San Diego. Along with his studies as an undergraduate and Master's student, he has been developing web applications using PHP and ASP.NET. For the past 3 years, he has been actively using the Yii framework to develop medium- and large-scale web applications.

> I would like to thank my family for their invaluable presence and continued support.

Atsushi Sakurai has been working on the design of microprocessors — including a 32-bit CISC, RISC, and a 64-bit VLIW processor — for over 25 years at Fujitsu. In the past, he has been the manager of the support project for ARM processors. He started this project 13 years ago and built the support site using plain PHP, and then rebuilt the system using Yii 5 years ago. He is a founder of the Japanese users group of Yii, named Yii-Jan. He left Fujitsu in 2013, and then started a consulting company named FS-Micro Corp that helps automotive suppliers in terms of the functional safety based on the ISO 26262. Naturally, he built a website for the company by himself using Yii, as Yii is a powerful framework that can reduce the development cost of the portal site greatly.

Jonathan Weatherhead is a code scientist, software developer, Internet enthusiast, and coffee addict. Specializing in web-driven technologies and object-oriented architectures, he has been working with PHP since 2003 and maintains his blog at `planetjon.ca`.

He passionately feels that, "The great thing about software development is that you get to play God with your very own sandbox."

www.PacktPub.com

Support files, eBooks, discount offers, and more

You might want to visit www.PacktPub.com for support files and downloads related to your book.

Did you know that Packt offers eBook versions of every book published, with PDF and ePub files available? You can upgrade to the eBook version at www.PacktPub.com and as a print book customer, you are entitled to a discount on the eBook copy. Get in touch with us at service@packtpub.com for more details.

At www.PacktPub.com, you can also read a collection of free technical articles, sign up for a range of free newsletters and receive exclusive discounts and offers on Packt books and eBooks.

http://PacktLib.PacktPub.com

Do you need instant solutions to your IT questions? PacktLib is Packt's online digital book library. Here, you can access, read and search across Packt's entire library of books.

Why subscribe?

- Fully searchable across every book published by Packt
- Copy and paste, print and bookmark content
- On demand and accessible via web browser

Free access for Packt account holders

If you have an account with Packt at www.PacktPub.com, you can use this to access PacktLib today and view nine entirely free books. Simply use your login credentials for immediate access.

Table of Contents

Preface	**1**
Chapter 1: A Task-management Application	**7**
Describing the project	**7**
Tasks	8
Projects	8
Users	8
The database	**8**
The tasks table	8
The projects table	9
Users	10
Choosing a database technology	10
The tasks table	10
The projects table	10
The database overview	11
Initializing the project	**11**
Creating the database with migrations	**14**
Creating models with Gii	**16**
Enhancing the models	16
Updating the default validation rules	17
Defined relations	18
Removing tasks when a project is deleted	19
Retrieving the project metadata	19
Automatically setting the created and updated time	20
Creating the presentation layer	**21**
Managing projects	21
Creating the layout	22
Creating the project index action	24
Changing a project's completion state	26
Deleting projects	27
Creating and updating projects	27
Viewing tasks	30

Managing tasks	31
Preventing unauthorized access to our application	34
Requiring authentication with filters and access rules	34
Creating a controller for the authentication	35
Creating a login layout	36
Creating a login view	37
Identifying our users with the UserIdentity CUserIdentity class	38
Creating the login model	39
Finishing touches	**40**
Disabling Gii	41
Defining a default route	41
Adding extra routes	41
Summary	**42**
Chapter 2: Discovering What's Nearby	**43**
Describing the project	**43**
Searching nearby locations	43
Showing locations	44
Storing locations	44
Importing locations	44
Designing the database	**44**
Locations	44
Initializing the project	**45**
Creating the configuration file	46
Retrieving the sample data	47
Creating the database	**47**
Creating the locations model	**48**
Importing the data feed	**49**
Google APIs	**51**
Enabling Google APIs	51
Generating an API key	52
Storing the API key	53
Creating the presentation layer	**53**
Interacting with the Google Maps JavaScript API	55
Searching nearby locations	59
Selecting a location	60
Showing locations on a map	61
Optimizing the performance with caching	63
Summary	**65**

Chapter 3: Scheduled Reminders	67
Prerequisites	**67**
Describing the project	**68**
Users	68
Events	69
Reminders	69
The task runner	70
Initializing the project	**70**
Create a MySQL user and database	70
Creating a Yii configuration file	71
Creating a parameters configuration file	72
Adding Composer dependencies	72
Creating the database	**73**
The users migration	73
The reminders and events migration	74
Creating models	**76**
Model behaviors	76
The Users model	77
Bcrypt password hashing	78
The Reminders model	78
The Events model	79
Searching for events and displaying them	**80**
Custom routing for dates	81
Creating the controller for events	81
Creating the reminders controller	83
Creating the layout	85
Creating the main view	86
Creating the item view	87
Creating the event list view	87
Creating and saving events	91
Creating the controller to manage users	**94**
Creating users	94
Deleting users	95
Changing the user's password	96
Authenticating with Bcrypt	97
Requiring authentication	99
Sending e-mail reminders	**99**
Summary	**102**

Chapter 4: Developing an Issue-tracking Application — 103
Prerequisites — 103
Describing the project — 104
Users — 105
Roles — 105
Issues — 105
Statuses — 106
Updates — 106
Receiving e-mails — 106
Initializing the project — 107
Managing users — 108
Roles and authentication — 108
Listing users — 110
Deleting users — 112
Creating and updating users — 112
Viewing users and associated issues — 114
Implementing the issue-management component — 115
The Issues model — 116
The Issues Update model — 118
Showing issues that belong to the user — 119
Searching for issues — 120
Creating issues — 121
Viewing and updating issues — 123
E-mail views — 125
Testing our application — 127
Handling inbound e-mail parsing — 127
Sending e-mails to SendGrid — 127
Adjusting SendGrid Parse settings — 128
Creating and updating issues over e-mail — 129
Summary — 132

Chapter 5: Creating a Microblogging Platform — 133
Prerequisites — 134
Describing the project — 135
Users — 135
Followers — 135
Likes — 136
Shares — 136
Initializing the project — 136
Making a better Yii bootstrap file — 137

Enabling users to manage their information	**140**
Upgrading our UserIdentity class	140
Defining user relations	141
Determining whether a user is following another user	142
Implementing a secure registration process	142
Handling forgotten passwords	149
Resetting a forgotten password	151
Enabling users to manage their details	153
Verifying a new e-mail address	158
Viewing a timeline of shares	**160**
Retrieving shares	162
Sharing new content	**166**
Resharing	167
Liking and unliking shares	168
Viewing shares	170
Searching for shares	**171**
Sharing on Twitter with HybridAuth	**172**
Setting up a Twitter application	172
Configuring HybridAuth	174
Implementing HybridAuth social sign-on and sharing	176
Summary	**179**

Chapter 6: Building a Content Management System — 181

Prerequisites	**182**
Describing the project	**183**
Users	183
Content	184
Categories	184
Search engine optimizations	185
Initializing the project	**185**
Exploring the skeleton project	**186**
Extending models from a common class	186
Creating a custom validator for slugs	187
View management with themes	188
Truly dynamic routing	189
Telling Yii to use our custom UrlManager	189
Displaying and managing content	**193**
Rendering the sitemap	194
Displaying a list view of content	196

Displaying content by ID	197
Adding comments to our CMS with Disqus	199
Searching for content	202
Managing content	203
Viewing and managing categories	**205**
Viewing entries in a category	206
Viewing an RSS feed for categories	206
Managing categories	208
Social authentication with HybridAuth	**210**
Validating remote identities	210
Remote registrations	211
Linking a social identity to an existing account	212
Authenticating with a social identity	214
Creating a Yii CWebUser object from a remote identity	216
Putting it all together	217
Exploring other HybridAuth providers	224
Summary	**225**
Chapter 7: Creating a Management Module for the CMS	**227**
Prerequisites	**228**
What are modules?	**228**
Describing the project	**228**
Initializing the module	229
Routing with a module	229
Moving the management functionality into the module	229
Adding file upload capabilities	229
Deploying modules	230
Initializing the project	**230**
Creating the module	**231**
Registering the module with Yii	232
Adding custom routes to a module	**235**
Creating the controllers	**236**
Migrating the functionality to the module	**238**
Migrating content management	238
Migrating categories	244
Implementing user management	247
Uploading files	**250**
Creating the File class	250
Creating the FileUploader class	251
Creating the FileUpload class	254
Creating the controller for the file manager	256

Strategies for deploying our application	260
Deploying as the application	261
Deploying as a submodule	261
Deploying as a Composer dependency	261
Summary	**262**
Chapter 8: Building an API for the CMS	**263**
Prerequisites	264
Describing the project	264
Configuring the module	265
Extending Yii to render JSON or XML in a RESTful way	265
Handling data input	265
Authenticating users to the API	266
Handling API exceptions	266
Handling data responses	266
Implementing actions	267
Initializing the project	267
Extending Yii to return data	268
Rendering data	271
Calling actions in a RESTful way	274
Authenticating users	274
Overloading CAccessControlFilter	277
Processing the incoming data	279
Handling errors	280
Exception handling	280
Custom error handling	280
Testing whether everything works	281
Authenticating users	282
Testing the authentication	284
Sending authenticated requests	286
Implementing CRUD actions	287
Deleting users	288
Retrieving users	289
Creating and updating users	291
Implementing other controller actions from the main application	292
Implementing categories and content API controllers	293
Documenting our API	293
Summary	**294**
Index	**295**

Preface

The Yii framework is a high-performance, fast, open source, and a rapid development PHP framework that can be used to develop modern web applications. It provides the toolkit for developing both personal projects and enterprise applications.

This book is a step-by-step guide to develop eight reusable real-world applications using the Yii framework. *Yii Project Blueprints* will guide you through several projects, from project conception to planning your project and finally implementing it. You will explore the key features of the Yii framework and learn how to use it efficiently and effectively to build solid core applications that you'll be able to reuse in real-world projects. You'll also learn how to integrate Yii with third-party libraries and services, create your own reusable code bases, and discover many more Yii features that will expand your knowledge and expertise of Yii.

What this book covers

Chapter 1, *A Task-management Application*, covers developing a simple task-management application from the ground up using SQLite and basic database migrations. This chapter will cover all the moving parts of Yii and prepare you for working with more complex applications.

Chapter 2, *Discovering What's Nearby*, covers how to integrate the Yii framework with the Google Maps API to display information about what is near a given user. You'll also learn how to create command-line tools to handle importing and processing data.

Chapter 3, *Scheduled Reminders*, focuses on developing a multiuser web-based scheduling and reminders application that can notify users via e-mail when a scheduled event is about to occur.

Chapter 4, *Developing an Issue-tracking Application*, covers how to create a multiuser issue-tracking and management system, complete with an e-mail notification system using MySQL as a database backend. This chapter will also cover handling input from e-mail submissions to trigger actions within the application.

Chapter 5, *Creating a Microblogging Platform*, covers how to create your own microblogging platform similar to Twitter, complete with a robust user authentication and registration system. You'll also learn how to integrate your application with third-party social networks using HybridAuth, as well as how to streamline your headless development time with Composer.

Chapter 6, *Building a Content Management System*, covers how to create a feature-complete content management system and blogging platform that expands using the knowledge built upon in the previous chapters. This chapter will also demonstrate how to integrate with even more third-party open source libraries.

Chapter 7, *Creating a Management Module for the CMS*, focuses on the development of a management module for the content management system built in the previous chapter. In this chapter, you'll learn how to migrate data from controllers to a Yii module that can be reused and managed independently of the content management system.

Chapter 8, *Building an API for the CMS*, covers how to create a JSON REST API module for the content management system that can be used for both client-side web applications and native development. This chapter will cover the basics of creating a secure and authenticated JSON REST API, and will demonstrate how to adapt controller actions for JSON responses rather than web view responses.

What you need for this book

To ensure that you can run the examples provided on any operating system and to ensure the accuracy of command-line entries, this book will use VirtualBox and Vagrant to establish a common development platform. Provided with this book are instructions on how to set up this cross-platform development environment. For this book, you'll need the following:

- VirtualBox 4.3.x
- Vagrant 1.3.x
- Ubuntu Server 14.04 LTS
- MySQL 5.6.x
- PHP 5.5.x
- Yii framework 1.1.x
- Composer

Who this book is for

This book is for you if you are a PHP developer with a good knowledge of PHP5 and some experience with the Yii framework and want to jump-start your knowledge of Yii and start building reusable real-world applications and tools.

Conventions

In this book, you will find a number of styles of text that distinguish between different kinds of information. Here are some examples of these styles and an explanation of their meaning.

Code words in text, database table names, folder names, filenames, file extensions, pathnames, dummy URLs, user input, and Twitter handles are shown as follows: "We'll also need to modify our UserIdentity class to allow for socially authenticated users to sign in."

A block of code is set as follows:

```
<?php
// change the following paths if necessary
$config=dirname(__FILE__).'/config/main.php';
$config = require($config);
require_once('/opt/frameworks/php/yii/framework/yiic.php');
```

When we wish to draw your attention to a particular part of a code block, the relevant lines or items are set in bold:

```
<div class="form-group">
<?php $selected = array('options' => array(isset($_
GET['id']) ? $_GET['id'] : NULL => array('selected' => true))); ?>
<?php echo CHtml::dropDownList('id', array(), CH
tml::listData(Location::model()->findAll(),'id','name'),
CMap::mergeArray($selected, array('empty' => 'Select a Location')));
?>
</div>
<button type="submit" class="pull-right btn btnprimary">Search</
button>
</form>
```

Any command-line input or output is written as follows:

```
$ php protected/yiic.php migrate up
```

New terms and **important words** are shown in bold. Words that you see on the screen, in menus or dialog boxes for example, appear in the text like this: "Click on the link titled **Model Generator**, and then fill in the form on the page that appears."

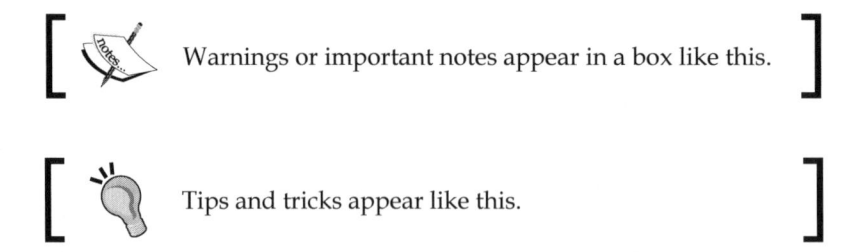

> Warnings or important notes appear in a box like this.

> Tips and tricks appear like this.

Reader feedback

Feedback from our readers is always welcome. Let us know what you think about this book—what you liked or may have disliked. Reader feedback is important for us to develop titles that you really get the most out of.

To send us general feedback, simply send an e-mail to feedback@packtpub.com, and mention the book title via the subject of your message. If there is a topic that you have expertise in and you are interested in either writing or contributing to a book, see our author guide on www.packtpub.com/authors.

Customer support

Now that you are the proud owner of a Packt book, we have a number of things to help you to get the most from your purchase.

Downloading the example code

You can download the example code files for all Packt books you have purchased from your account at http://www.packtpub.com. If you purchased this book elsewhere, you can visit http://www.packtpub.com/support and register to have the files e-mailed directly to you.

Downloading the color images of this book

We also provide you a PDF file that has color images of the screenshots/diagrams used in this book. The color images will help you better understand the changes in the output. You can download this file from: https://www.packtpub.com/sites/default/files/downloads/7734OS_ColoredImages.pdf.

Errata

Although we have taken every care to ensure the accuracy of our content, mistakes do happen. If you find a mistake in one of our books — maybe a mistake in the text or the code — we would be grateful if you would report this to us. By doing so, you can save other readers from frustration and help us improve subsequent versions of this book. If you find any errata, please report them by visiting http://www.packtpub.com/submit-errata, selecting your book, clicking on the **errata submission form** link, and entering the details of your errata. Once your errata are verified, your submission will be accepted and the errata will be uploaded on our website, or added to any list of existing errata, under the Errata section of that title. Any existing errata can be viewed by selecting your title from http://www.packtpub.com/support.

Piracy

Piracy of copyright material on the Internet is an ongoing problem across all media. At Packt, we take the protection of our copyright and licenses very seriously. If you come across any illegal copies of our works in any form on the Internet, please provide us with the location address or website name immediately so that we can pursue a remedy.

Please contact us at copyright@packtpub.com with a link to the suspected pirated material.

We appreciate your help in protecting our authors, and our ability to bring you valuable content.

Questions

You can contact us at questions@packtpub.com if you are having a problem with any aspect of the book, and we will do our best to address it.

1
A Task-management Application

One of the best ways to get started with the Yii framework is by making useful applications. The first application that will be covered in this book is a simple task management application. In this chapter, we will cover the planning of the development of this project, developing the application, and creating useful components that we will reuse in later chapters.

Describing the project

One of the most important steps in starting a new project is planning it. By planning the project before we begin programming, we can easily identify most (if not all) models that our application will use, key features that we'll need to implement, as well as any areas that may cause us problems while developing our applications. Breaking down the project beforehand also helps us estimate how long it will take to develop each part of our applications as well as the application as a whole. While requirements and expectations for our application will most likely change during its development, identifying the core components of your application will help ensure that the core functionality of our application works as we intend.

For our task management application, there are two main components: tasks and projects. Let's break each of these components down.

Tasks

The first component of our application is tasks. A task is an item that needs to be done by our user and usually consists of a brief, concise title, and a description of what needs to be done to complete that task. Sometimes, a task has a due date or time associated with it that lets us know when the task needs to be completed. Tasks also need to indicate whether they have been completed or not. Finally, a task is usually associated with a group or project that contains similar or related tasks.

Projects

The second component of our application is projects. Projects group related tasks together and usually have a descriptive name associated with them. Projects may also have a due date or time associated with them, which indicates when all tasks in a project need to be completed. We also need to be able to indicate whether or not a project is completed.

Users

By breaking down our project, we've also identified a third component of our application: users. Users in our application will have the ability to create and manage both projects and tasks as well as view the statuses and due dates of any given task. While this component of our application may seem obvious, identifying it early on allows us to better understand the interaction that our users will have with the various components of our application.

The database

With the core components of our application identified, we can now begin to think about what our database is going to look like. Let's start with the two database tables.

The tasks table

By looking at our requirements, we can identify several columns and data types for our `tasks` table. As a rule, each task that we create will have a unique, incrementing ID associated with it. Other columns that we can quickly identify are the task name, the task description, the due date, and whether or not the task has been completed. We also know that each task is going to be associated with a project, which means we need to reference that project in our table.

There are also some columns we can identify that are not so obvious. The two most useful columns that aren't explicitly identified are timestamps for the creation date of the task and the date it was last updated on. By adding these two columns, we can gain useful insights into the use of our application. It's possible that in the future, our imaginary client may want to know how long an unresolved task has been open for and whether or not it needs additional attention if it has not been updated in several days.

With all the columns and data types for our table identified, our `tasks` table written with generic SQL data types will look as follows:

```
ID INTEGER PRIMARY KEY
name TEXT
description TEXT
completed BOOLEAN
project_id INTEGER
due_date TIMESTAMP
created TIMESTAMP
updated TIMESTAMP
```

The projects table

By looking at our requirements for projects, we can easily pick out the major columns for our `projects` table: a descriptive name, whether or not the project has been completed, and when the project is due. We also know from our `tasks` table that each project will need to have its own unique ID for the task to reference. When the time comes to create our models in our application, we'll clearly define the one-to-many relationship between any given project and the many tasks belonging to it. If we keep a created and updated column, our `projects` table written in generic SQL will look as follows:

```
ID INTEGER PRIMARY KEY
name TEXT
completed BOOLEAN
due_date TIMESTAMP
created TIMESTAMP
updated TIMESTAMP
```

Downloading the example code
You can download the example code files for all Packt books you have purchased from your account at http://www.packtpub.com. If you purchased this book elsewhere, you can visit http://www.packtpub.com/support and register to have the files e-mailed directly to you.

Users

Our application requirements also show us that we need to store users somewhere. For this application, we're going to store our users in a flat file database. In *Chapter 3, Scheduled Reminders*, we will expand upon this and store users in their own database table.

Choosing a database technology

Now that we have decided what our database is going to look like, it's time to start thinking about where we're going to store this information. To help familiarize yourself with the different database adapters Yii natively supports, for this project, we will be using SQLite. Since we now know where we're going to store our data, we can identify all the correct data types for database tables.

The tasks table

Since SQLite only supports five basic data types (NULL, INTEGER, REAL, TEXT, and BLOB), we need to convert a few of the data types we initially identified for this table into ones that SQLite supports. Since SQLite does not support Boolean or timestamps natively, we need to find another way of representing this data using a data type that SQLite supports. We can represent a Boolean value as an integer either as 0 (false) or 1 (true). We can also represent all of our timestamp columns as integers by converting the current date to a Unix timestamp.

With our final data types figured out, our tasks table now will look like this:

```
ID INTEGER PRIMARY KEY
name TEXT
description TEXT
completed INTEGER
project_id INTEGER
due_date INTEGER
created INTEGER
updated INTEGER
```

The projects table

By applying the same logic to our projects table, we can derive the following structure for this table:

```
ID INTEGER PRIMARY KEY
name TEXT
completed INTEGER
due_date INTEGER
```

```
created INTEGER
updated INTEGER
```

The database overview

By spending a few minutes thinking about our application beforehand, we've successfully identified all the tables for our application, how they interact with one another, and all the column names and data types that our application will be using. We've done a lot of work on our application already without even writing a single line of code. By doing this work upfront, we have also reduced some of the work we'll need to do later on when creating our models.

Initializing the project

With our final database structure figured out, we can now start writing code. Using the instructions in the official guide (http://www.yiiframework.com/doc/guide/), download and install the Yii framework. Once Yii is installed, navigate to your webroot directory, and create a new folder called tasks. Next, navigate inside the tasks folder, and create the following folder structure to serve as our application's skeleton:

```
tasks/
    assets/
    protected/
            commands/
            components/
            config/
            controllers/
            data/
            migrations/
            models/
            runtime/
            views/
                    layouts/
                    projects/
                    tasks/
                    site/
```

> Yii has a built-in tool called yiic, which can automatically generate a skeleton project. Refer to the quick start guide (http://www.yiiframework.com/doc/guide/1.1/en/quickstart.first-app) for more details.

A Task-management Application

Depending upon the web server you are using, you may also need to create a .htaccess file in the root directory of your tasks folder. Information about how to set up your application for the web server you are using can be found in the quick start guide (http://www.yiiframework.com/doc/guide/1.1/en/quickstart.apache-nginx-config).

After setting up our skeleton structure, we can first create our configuration file located at protected/config/main.php. Our configuration file is one of the most important files of our application as it provides Yii with all the critical information necessary to load and configure our application. The configuration file informs Yii about the files to be preloaded by Yii's built-in autoloader, the modules to be loaded, the component to be registered, and any other configuration options we want to pass to our application.

For this application, we will be enabling the Gii module, which will allow us to create models based upon our database structure. We will also enable two components, urlManager and db, which will allow us to set up custom routes and access our SQLite database. Have a look at the following code snippet:

```php
<?php
return array(
    'basePath'=>dirname(__FILE__).DIRECTORY_SEPARATOR.'..',
    'name'=>'Task Application',
    'import'=>array(
        'application.models.*',
        'application.components.*',
    ),
     'modules'=>array(
        // Include the Gii Module so that we can
//generate models and controllers for our application
        'gii'=>array(
            'class'=>'system.gii.GiiModule',
            'password'=>false,
            'ipFilters'=>false
        ),
    ),
    'components'=>array(
        'urlManager'=>array(
            'urlFormat'=>'path',
            'showScriptName'=>false,
            'rules'=>array(
                '<controller:\w+>/<id:\d+>'=>'<controller>/view',
                '<controller:\w+>/<action:\w+>/<id:\d+>'=>
                  '<controller>/<action>',
```

```
                    '<controller:\w+>/<action:\w+>'=>
                        '<controller>/<action>',
                ),
            ),
            // Define where our SQLite database is going to be
            // stored, relative to our config file
            'db'=>array(
                'connectionString' =>
                    'sqlite:'.dirname(__FILE__).'/../data/tasks.db',
            )
        )
    );
```

Next, we can create our `index.php` file as follows, which will serve as our bootstrap endpoint for our web application:

```
<?php
// change the following paths if necessary
$yii='/opt/frameworks/php/yii/framework/yii.php';
$config=dirname(__FILE__).'/protected/config/main.php';

// remove the following lines when in production mode
defined('YII_DEBUG') or define('YII_DEBUG',true);
// specify how many levels of call stack should be shown in each log
message
defined('YII_TRACE_LEVEL') or define('YII_TRACE_LEVEL',3);

require_once($yii);
Yii::createWebApplication($config)->run();
```

Finally, we can create our applications `yiic` file in `protected/yiic.php` as follows, which will allow us to run console commands native to Yii from our application:

```
<?php
// change the following paths if necessary
$config=dirname(__FILE__).'/config/main.php';
$config = require($config);
require_once('/opt/frameworks/php/yii/framework/yiic.php');
```

Creating the database with migrations

Now that our application can be bootstrapped, we can create our database. To do this, we are going to create a migration. Migrations are a feature of Yii that allow the creation and modification of your database to be a part of your application. Rather than creating schema modifications in pure SQL, we can use migrations to grow our database as a part of our application. In addition to acting as a revision system for our database schema, migrations also have the added benefit of allowing us to transmit our database with our application without having to worry about sharing data that would be stored in our database.

To create our database, open up your command-line interface of choice, navigate to your tasks directory, and run the following command:

```
$ php protected/yiic.php migrate create tasks
```

The `yiic` command will then prompt you to confirm the creation of the new migration:

```
Yii Migration Tool v1.0 (based on Yii v1.1.14)


Create new migration '/var/www/tasks/protected/migrations/m131213_013354_tasks.php'? (yes|no) [no]:yes
New migration created successfully.
```

> To prevent naming conflicts with migrations, `yiic` will create the migration with the following naming structure: `m<timestamp>_<name>`. This has the added benefit of allowing us to sequentially apply or remove specific migrations based upon the order in which they were added. The exact name of your migration will be slightly different than the one listed in the preceding command.

After confirming the creation of the migration, a new file will be created in the `protected/migrations` folder of our application. Open up the file, and add the following to the `up` method:

```
$this->createTable('tasks', array(
    'id' => 'INTEGER PRIMARY KEY',
    'title' => 'TEXT',
    'data' => 'TEXT',
    'project_id' => 'INTEGER',
    'completed' => 'INTEGER',
    'due_date' => 'INTEGER',
    'created' => 'INTEGER',
```

```
        'updated' => 'INTEGER'
    ));

    $this->createTable('projects', array(
        'id' => 'INTEGER PRIMARY KEY',
        'name' => 'TEXT',
        'completed' => 'INTEGER',
        'due_date' => 'INTEGER',
        'created' => 'INTEGER',
        'updated' => 'INTEGER'
    ));
```

Notice that our database structure matches the schema that we identified earlier in the chapter.

Next, replace the contents of the down method with instructions to drop the database table if we call migrate down from the yiic command. Have a look at the following code:

```
    $this->dropTable('projects');
    $this->dropTable('tasks');
```

Now that the migration has been created, run migrate up from the command line to create the database and apply our migration. Run the following commands:

```
$ php protected/yiic.php migrate up
Yii Migration Tool v1.0 (based on Yii v1.1.14)
Total 1 new migration to be applied:
    m131213_013354_tasks

Apply the above migration? (yes|no) [no]:yes
*** applying m131213_013354_tasks
*** applied m131213_013354_tasks (time: 0.009s)
Migrated up successfully.
```

Now, if you navigate to protected/data/, you will see a new file called tasks.db, the SQLite database that was created by our migrations.

> Migration commands can be run non-interactively by appending --interactive=0 to the migrate command. This can be useful if you want to automate deployments of your code to remote systems or if you run your code through an automated testing service.

Creating models with Gii

Now that our database has been created, we can create models for our database table. To create our models, we are going to use Gii, Yii's built-in code generator.

Open up your web browser and navigate to `http://localhost/gii` (in this book, we will always use `localhost` as our working hostname for our working project. If you are using a different hostname, replace `localhost` with your own). Once loaded, you should see the **Yii Code Generator**, as shown in the following screenshot:

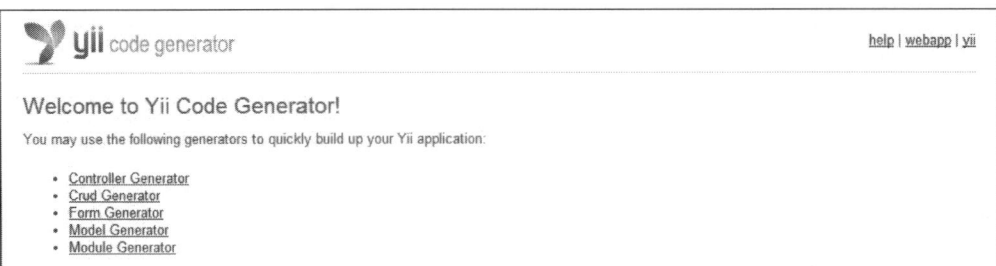

 If you aren't able to access Gii, verify that your web server has rewriting enabled. Information about how to properly configure your web server for Yii can be found at (`http://www.yiiframework.com/doc/guide/1.1/en/quickstart.apache-nginx-config`).

Click on the link titled **Model Generator**, and then fill in the form on the page that appears. The table name should be set to `tasks`. The model name should prepopulate. If it doesn't, set the model name to `Tasks`, and then click on preview. Once the page has reloaded, you can preview what the model will look like before clicking on the **Generate** button to write your new model to your `protected/models/` directory. Once you have generated your model for `tasks`, repeat the process for `projects`.

Enhancing the models

Now that our models have been created, there are several sections that should be modified.

Updating the default validation rules

The first part of our model that needs to be modified is the validation rules. Validation rules in Yii are stored in the model's `rules()` method and are executed when the model's `validate()` method is called. Starting with our `tasks` model, we can see that Gii has already prepopulated our validation rules for us based upon our database.

There are several fields of this model that we would like to always have set, namely, `project_id`, `title`, the task itself, and whether or not it has been completed. We can make these fields required in our model by adding a new array to our rules section, as follows:

```
array('project_id, title, data, completed', 'required')
```

By making these fields required in our model, we can make client- and server-side validation easier when we start making forms. Our final method for this model will look as follows:

```
public function rules()
{
        return array(
            array('project_id, completed, due_date, created, updated',
'numerical', 'integerOnly'=>true),
             array('project_id, title, data, completed', 'required'),
            array('title, data', 'safe'),
            array('id, title, data, project_id, completed, due_date,
created, updated', 'safe', 'on'=>'search'),
        );
}
```

Our project's models should also be changed so that the project name and its completed status are required. We can accomplish this by adding the following to our validation rules array:

```
array('name, completed', 'required')
```

> Additional validation rules can be found in the Yii wiki at http://www.yiiframework.com/wiki/56/

Defined relations

Another component of our model that we should change is the `relations()` method. By declaring model relations in Yii, we can take advantage of the ability of ActiveRecords to automatically join several related models together and retrieve data from them without having to explicitly call that model for its data.

For example, once our model relations are set up, we will be able to retrieve the project name from the Tasks model, as follows:

```
Tasks::model()->findByPk($id)->project->name;
```

Before we can declare our relations though, we need to determine what the relations actually are. Since SQLite does not support foreign key relations, Gii was unable to automatically determine the relations for us.

In Yii, there are four types of relations: BELONGS_TO, HAS_MANY, HAS_ONE, and MANY_MANY. Determining the relation type can be done by looking at the foreign key for a table and asking which relational type fits best based upon the data that the table will store. For this application, this question can be answered as follows:

- Tasks belong to a single project
- A project has one or many tasks

Now that we have determined our relationship types between our two tables, we can write the relations. Starting with the `tasks` table, replace the `relations()` method with the following:

```
public function relations()
{
return array(
      'tasks' => array(self::HAS_MANY, 'Task', 'project_id')
    );
}
```

The syntax for the relations array is as follows:

```
'var_name'=>array('relationship_type', 'foreign_model', 'foreign_key',
[... other options ..])
```

For our projects model, our `relations()` method looks like this:

```
public function relations()
{
    return array(
        'tasks' => array(self::HAS_MANY, 'Tasks', 'project_id')
    );
}
```

Removing tasks when a project is deleted

In our model's current state, whenever a project is deleted, all the tasks associated with it become orphaned. One way of dealing with this edge case is to simply delete any tasks associated with the project. Rather than writing code to handle this in the controller, we can have the model take care of it for us by referencing the project's model's `beforeDelete()` method as follows:

```php
public function beforeDelete()
{
    Tasks::model()->deleteAllByAttributes(array('project_id' => $this->id));
    return parent::beforeDelete();
}
```

Retrieving the project metadata

There is also metadata about a project that we cannot obtain directly from the `projects` database table. This data includes the number of tasks a project has, as well as the number of completed tasks a project has. We can obtain this from our model by creating two new methods in the project's model, as follows:

```php
public function getNumberOfTasks()
{
    return Tasks::model()->countByAttributes(array('project_id' => $this->id));
}

public function getNumberOfCompletedTasks()
{
    return Tasks::model()->countByAttributes(array('project_id' => $this->id, 'completed' => 1));
}
```

Additionally, we can determine the progress of a project by getting a percentage of completed tasks versus the total number of tasks, as follows:

```php
public function getPercentComplete()
{
    $numberOfTasks = $this->getNumberOfTasks();
    $numberOfCompletedTasks = $this->getNumberOfCompletedTasks();

    if ($numberOfTasks == 0)
        return 100;
    return ($numberOfCompletedTasks / $numberOfTasks) * 100;
}
```

Automatically setting the created and updated time

The last change needed to be made to the models is to enable them to automatically set the created and updated timestamp in the database every time the model is saved. By moving this logic into the models, we can avoid having to manage it either in the forms that submit the data or in the controllers that will process this data. This change can be made by adding the following to both models:

```
public function beforeSave()
{
    if ($this->isNewRecord)
        $this->created = time();

    $this->updated = time();

    return parent::beforeSave();
}
```

In the `beforeSave()` method, the updated property is always set every time the model is saved, and the created property is only set if ActiveRecord considers this to be a new record. This is accomplished by checking the `isNewRecord` property of the model. Additionally, both properties are set to `time()`, the PHP function used to get the current Unix timestamp.

The last piece of code that is important in this method is `return parent::beforeSave();`. When Yii's `save()` method is called, it checks that `beforeSave()` returns true before saving the data to the database. While we could have this method return true, it's easier to have it return whatever the parent model (in this case `CActiveRecord`) returns. It also ensures that any changes made to the parent model will get carried to the model.

> Since the `beforeSave()` method is identical for both models, we could also create a new model that only extended `CActiveRecord` and only implemented this method. The tasks and projects model will then extend that model rather than `CActiveRecord` and will inherit this functionality. Moving shared functionality to a shared location reduces the number of places where code needs to be written and, consequently, the number of places a bug can show up in.

Creating the presentation layer

Up until this point, all the code that has been written is backend code that the end user won't be able to see. In this section, we will be creating the presentation layer of our application. The presentation layer of our application is composed of three components: controllers, layouts, and views. For this next section, we'll be creating all the three components.

As a developer, we have several options to create the presentation layer. One way we can create the presentation layer is using Gii. Gii has several built-in tools that can assist you in creating new controllers, forms for our views, and even full create, read, update, and delete (CRUD) skeletons for our application. Alternatively, we can write everything by hand.

Managing projects

The first part of the presentation layer we are going to work on is the projects section. To begin with, create a new file in `protected/controllers/` called `ProjectControllerProjectController.php` that has the following class signature:

```
<?php
class ProjectControllerProjectController extends CController {}
```

For our controllers, we will be extending Yii's base class called `CController`. In future chapters, we will create our own controllers and extend the controllers from them.

Before we can start displaying content from our new action, we'll need to create a layout for our content to be rendered in. To specify our layout, create a public property called `$layout`, and set the value to `'main'`:

```
public $layout = 'main';
```

Next, let's create our first action to make sure everything is working:

```
public function actionIndex()
{
    echo "Hello!";
}
```

Now, we should be able to visit `http://localhost/projects/index` from our web browser and see the text `Hello` printed on the screen. Before we continue defining our actions, let's create a layout that will help our application look a little better.

Creating the layout

The layout that we specified references the file located in `protected/views/layouts/main.php`. Create this file and open it for editing. Then, add the following basic HTML5 markup:

```
<!DOCTYPE html>
<html>
    <head>
    </head>
    <body>
    </body>
</html>
```

Then add a title within the `<head>` tag that will display the application name we defined in `protected/config/main.php`:

```
<title><?php echo Yii::app()->name; ?></title>
```

Next, let's add a few meta tags, CSS, and scripts. To reduce the number of files we need to download, we'll be including styles and scripts from a publicly available **Content Distribution Network (CDN)**. Rather than writing markup for these elements, we're going to use `CClientScript`, a class made to manage JavaScript, CSS, and meta tags for views.

For this application, we'll be using a frontend framework called **Twitter Bootstrap**. This framework will style many of the common HTML tags that our application will use, providing it with a cleaner overall look.

> When you're ready to go live with your application, you should consider moving the static assets you are using to a CDN, referencing popular libraries such as Twitter Bootstrap and jQuery from a publicly available CDN. CDNs can help to reduce hosting costs by reducing the amount of bandwidth your server needs to use to send files. Using a CDN can also speed up your site since they usually have servers geographically closer to your users than your main server.

First, we're going to call `CClientScript`, as follows:

```
<?php $cs = Yii::app()->clientScript; ?>
```

Secondly, we're going to set the `Content-Type` to `text/html` with a `UTF-8` character set, as follows:

```
<?php $cs->registerMetaTag('text/html; charset=UTF-8', 'Content-Type'); ?>
```

Next, we're going to register the CSS from Twitter Bootstrap 3 from a popular CDN, as follows:

```php
<?php $cs->registerCssFile( '//netdna.bootstrapcdn.com/bootstrap/3.0.3/css/bootstrap.min.css' ); ?>
```

Then we'll register the JavaScript library for Twitter Bootstrap:

```php
<?php $cs->registerScriptFile( '//netdna.bootstrapcdn.com/bootstrap/3.0.3/js/bootstrap.min.js' ); ?>
```

Finally, we're going to register jQuery 2.0 and have Yii placed at the end of the `<body>` tag, as follows:

```php
<?php $cs->registerScriptFile( '//code.jquery.com/jquery.js', CClientScript::POS_END ); ?>
```

`CClientScript` also supports method chaining, so you could also change the preceding code to the following:

```php
<?php Yii::app()->clientScript
        ->registerMetaTag('text/html; charset=UTF-8', 'Content-Type')
        ->registerCssFile( '//netdna.bootstrapcdn.com/bootstrap/3.0.3/css/bootstrap.min.css' )
        ->registerScriptFile( '//netdna.bootstrapcdn.com/bootstrap/3.0.3/js/bootstrap.min.js' )
        ->registerScriptFile( 'https://code.jquery.com/jquery.js', CClientScript::POS_END); ?>
```

For the last part of our layout, let's add a basic header within our `<body>` tag that will help with navigation, as follows:

```html
<div class="row">
    <div class="container">
        <nav class="navbar navbar-default navbar-fixed-top" role="navigation">
            <div class="navbar-header">
                <a class="navbar-brand" href="/"><?php echo CHtml::encode(Yii::app()->name); ?></a>
            </div>
        </nav>
    </div>
</div>
```

After the closing `</div>` tag, add the following:

```
<div class="row" style="margin-top: 100px;">
    <div class="container">
        <?php echo $content; ?>
    </div>
</div>
```

The `$content` variable that we've added to our layout is a special variable that contains all the rendered HTML markup from our view files and is defined by the `CController` class in the `render()` method. Yii will automatically populate this variable for us whenever we call the `render()` method from within our controllers.

Creating the project index action

With our layout defined, we can get back to creating actions. Let's start by modifying our `actionIndex()` method so that it renders a view.

First, create a variable to store a searchable copy of our model. Have a look at the following code:

```
$model = new Projects('search');
```

Next, render a view called `index`, which references `protected/views/projects/index.php`, and pass the model we created to this view, as follows:

```
$this->render('index', array('model' => $model));
```

Now, create the view file in `protected/views/projects/index.php` and open it for editing. Begin by adding a button in the view as follows, which will reference the `save` action that we will create later on:

```
<?php echo CHtml::link('Create New Project', $this->createUrl('/projects/save'), array('class' => 'btn btn-primary pull-right')); ?>
<div class="clearfix"></div>
```

Then add a descriptive title so that we know what page we are on. Have a look at the following line of code:

```
<h1>Projects</h1>
```

Finally, create a new widget that uses `CListView`, a built-in Yii widget designed for displaying data from `CActiveDataProvider`. In Yii, widgets are frontend components that help us to quickly generate commonly used code, typically for presentation purposes. This widget will automatically generate pagination for us as necessary and will allow each of our items to look the same. Have a look at the following code:

```php
<?php $this->widget('zii.widgets.CListView', array(
    'dataProvider'=>$model->search(),
    'itemView'=>'_project',
)); ?>
```

The new widget that we created consists of two parts. The first is the `dataProvider`, which provides data to the widget. This data comes from our project's model's `search()` method, a piece of code automatically generated by Gii.

The second part of the widget is the `itemView`, which references the specific view file that our items will be rendered out of. In this case, the view references a file in the same directory of `protected/views/projects` called `_project.php`. Create this file and then add the following code to it:

```php
<div>
    <div class="pull-left">
        <p><strong><?php echo CHtml::link(CHtml::encode($data->name), $this->createUrl('/projects/tasks', array('id' => $data->id))); ?></strong></p>
        <p>Due on <?php echo date('m/d/Y', $data->due_date); ?></p>
<?php if ($data->completed): ?>
            Completed
        <?php else: ?>
            <?php if ($data->numberOfTasks == 0): ?>
                <p>No Tasks</p>
            <?php else: ?>
                <p><?php echo $data->getPercentComplete(); ?>% Completed</p>
            <?php endif; ?>
        <?php endif; ?>
    </div>
    <div class="pull-right">
        <?php echo CHtml::link(NULL, $this->createUrl('/projects/save', array('id' => $data->id)), array('title' => 'edit', 'class' => 'glyphicon glyphicon-pencil')); ?>
```

```
            <?php echo CHtml::link(NULL, $this->createUrl('/projects/
complete', array('id' => $data->id)), array('title' => $data-
>completed == 1 ? 'uncomplete' : 'complete', 'class' => 'glyphicon
glyphicon-check')); ?>
            <?php echo CHtml::link(NULL, $this->createUrl('/projects/
delete', array('id' => $data->id)), array('title' => 'delete', 'class'
=> 'glyphicon glyphicon-remove')); ?>
    </div>
    <div class="clearfix"></div>
</div>
<hr/>
```

If we refresh our browser page now, our view will show us that no results were found. Before we can see data, we need to create an action and view to create and update it. Before we start creating new records, let's create two other actions that we outlined in our item's view: complete and delete.

Changing a project's completion state

First, let's create an action to mark a project as completed or uncompleted. This action will only be responsible for changing the completed field of the projects table to 0 or 1, depending on its current state. For simplicity, we can just XOR the field by 1 and save the model. Have a look at the following code:

```
public function actionComplete($id)
{
    $model = $this->loadModel($id);
    $model->completed ^= 1;
    $model->save();
    $this->redirect($this->createUrl('/projects'));
}
```

Additionally, we'll create another private method called `loadModel()`, which will load our appropriate model for us and throw an error if it cannot be found. For this method, we'll use `CHttpException`, which will create an HTTP exception with the error message we provide if a model with the specified ID cannot be found. Have a look at the following code:

```
private function loadModel($id)
{
    $model = Projects::model()->findByPk($id);
    if ($model == NULL)
        throw new CHttpException('404', 'No model with that ID could
be found.');
    return $model;
}
```

Deleting projects

Next, we'll create a method to delete the project. This method will use the `loadModel()` method we defined earlier. Additionally, if we encounter an error deleting the model, we'll throw an HTTP exception so that the user knows something went wrong. Here's how we go about it:

```
public function actionDelete($id)
{
    $model = $this->loadModel($id);

    if ($model->delete())
        $this->redirect($this->createUrl('/projects'));

    throw new CHttpException('500', 'There was an error deleting the model.');
}
```

Creating and updating projects

With the two other methods defined, we can now work on creating and updating a project. Rather than creating two actions to handle both these tasks, we're going to create one action that knows how to handle both by checking the ID that we'll pass as a GET parameter. We can do that by defining a new action that looks as follows:

```
public function actionSave($id=NULL) {
```

We can then either create a new project or update a project based upon whether or not we were provided with an ID by the user. By taking advantage of `loadModel()`, we also take care of any errors that would occur if an ID was provided but a project with that ID didn't exist. Have a look at the following code:

```
if ($id == NULL)
    $model = new Projects;
else
    $model = $this->loadModel($id);
```

Next, we can detect whether the user submitted data by checking the $_POST variable for an array called `Projects`. If that array is defined, we'll assign it to our `$model->attributes` object. Before saving the model, however, we'll want to convert whatever the user entered into a Unix timestamp. Have a look at the following code:

```
if (isset($_POST['Projects']))
{
    $model->attributes = $_POST['Projects'];
```

A Task-management Application

```
            $model->due_date = strtotime($_POST['Projects']['due_date']);
            $model->save();
    }
```

Finally, we'll render the view and pass the model down to it, as follows:

```
$this->render('save', array('model' => $model));
```

Create a new file in protected/views/projects/ called save.php and open it to edit. Begin by adding a header that will let us know whether we are editing a project or creating a new one, as follows:

```
<h1><?php echo $model->isNewRecord ? 'Create New' : 'Update'; ?>
Project</h1>
```

Next, we'll create a new widget with CActiveForm, which will take care of the hard tasks of creating and inserting form fields into our view file (such as what the names and IDs of form fields should be):

```
<?php $form=$this->beginWidget('CActiveForm', array(
    'id'=>'project-form',
    'htmlOptions' => array(
        'class' => 'form-horizontal',
        'role' => 'form'
    )
)); ?>
<?php $this->endWidget(); ?>
```

Between the beginWidget and endWidget call, add an error summary if the user encounters an error:

```
<?php echo $form->errorSummary($model); ?>
```

Then, after the error summary, add the form fields and their associated styles, as follows:

```
<div class="form-group">
    <?php echo $form->labelEx($model,'name', array('class' => 'col-sm-2 control-label')); ?>
    <div class="col-sm-10">
        <?php echo $form->textField($model,'name', array('class' => 'form-control')); ?>
    </div>
</div>

<div class="form-group">
```

```
        <?php echo $form->labelEx($model,'completed', array('class' =>
'col-sm-2 control-label')); ?>
    <div class="col-sm-10">
        <?php echo $form->dropDownList($model,'completed', array('0'
=> 'No','1' => 'Yes'), array('class' => 'form-control')); ?>
    </div>
</div>

<div class="form-group">
    <?php echo $form->labelEx($model,'due_date', array('class' =>
'col-sm-2 control-label')); ?>
    <div class="col-sm-10">
        <div class="input-append date"> 
MM/DD/YYYY
            <?php $this->widget('zii.widgets.jui.CJuiDatePicker',
array(
                    'model' => $model,
                    'attribute' => 'due_date',
                    'htmlOptions' => array(
                        'size' => '10',
                        'maxlength' => '10',
                        'class' => 'form-control',
                        'value' => $model->due_date == "" ? "" :
date("m/d/Y", $model->due_date)
                    ),
                )); ?>
</div>
    </div>
</div>

<div class="row buttons">
    <?php echo CHtml::submitButton($model->isNewRecord ? 'Create' :
'Save', array('class' => 'btn btn-primary pull-right')); ?>
</div>
```

> Did you notice how we're taking advantage of the Yii widget called CJuiDatePicker? This widget will provide us with a clean interface for selecting dates from a calendar view, rather than requiring our end user to type in the date manually and in the specified format we've requested.

Now we can create, update, view, and delete projects. Additionally, we've created an easy action to mark them as completed. Before we're done with this controller, we need to add an action that allows us to view tasks in our project.

Viewing tasks

Our `tasks` action for this controller will function in the same manner as our `index` action but will instead use a view called `tasks`:

```
public function actionTasks($id=NULL)
{
    if ($id == NULL)
        throw new CHttpException(400, 'Missing ID');

    $project = $this->loadModel($id);
    if ($project === NULL)
        throw new CHttpException(400, 'No project with that ID exists');

    $model = new Tasks('search');
    $model->attributes = array('project_id' => $id);

    $this->render('tasks', array('model' => $model, 'project' => $project));
}
```

The `tasks.php` view in `protected/views/projects/tasks.php` will look as follows:

```
<?php echo CHtml::link('Create New Task', $this->createUrl('/tasks/save?Tasks[project_id]=' . $project->id), array('class' => 'btn btn-primary pull-right')); ?>
<div class="clearfix"></div>
<h1>View Tasks for Project: <?php echo $project->name; ?></h1>
<?php $this->widget('zii.widgets.CListView', array(
    'dataProvider'=>$model->search(),
    'itemView'=>'_tasks',
)); 
?>
```

The `_tasks.php` item view in `protected/views/projects/tasks.php` will look as follows:

```
<div>
    <div class="pull-left">
        <p><strong><?php echo CHtml::link(CHtml::encode($data->title), $this->createUrl('/tasks/save', array('id' => $data->id))); ?></strong></p>
```

[30]

```
        <p>Due on <?php echo date('m/d/Y', $data->due_date); ?></p>
    </div>
    <div class="pull-right">
        <?php echo CHtml::link(NULL, $this->createUrl('/tasks/save',
array('id' => $data->id)), array('class' => 'glyphicon glyphicon-
pencil')); ?>
        <?php echo CHtml::link(NULL, $this->createUrl('/tasks/
complete', array('id' => $data->id)), array('title' => $data-
>completed == 1 ? 'uncomplete' : 'complete', 'class' => 'glyphicon
glyphicon-check')); ?>
        <?php echo CHtml::link(NULL, $this->createUrl('/tasks/delete',
array('id' => $data->id)), array('class' => 'glyphicon glyphicon-
remove')); ?>
    </div>
    <div class="clearfix"></div>
</div>
<hr/>
```

Managing tasks

Now that we can manage projects, let's work on managing tasks. Our `TasksController` is going to be nearly identical to our project's controller with only a few differences. Start by creating a new file in `protected/controllers` called `TasksController.php` that has the following signature:

```
<?php class TasksController extends CController {}
```

By only making a small change to our `loadModel()` method, we can reuse the delete and complete action from our projects controller, as follows:

```
private function loadModel($id)
{
    $model = Tasks::model()->findByPk($id);
    if ($model == NULL)
        throw new CHttpException('404', 'No model with that ID could
be found.');
    return $model;
}
```

A Task-management Application

Our `save` action is almost identical to our project's `save` action. Have a look at the following code:

```php
public function actionSave($id=NULL)
{
    if ($id == NULL)
        $model = new Tasks;
    else
        $model = $this->loadModel($id);

    if (isset($_GET['Tasks']))
        $model->attributes = $_GET['Tasks'];

    if (isset($_POST['Tasks']))
    {
        $model->attributes = $_POST['Tasks'];
        $model->due_date = strtotime($_POST['Tasks']['due_date']);
        $model->save();
    }

    $this->render('save', array('model' => $model));
}
```

The view file for this action is almost the same as well. If you haven't already, create a file called `save.php` in `protected/views/tasks/`, and then add the following lines of code to finish the view:

```php
<ol class="breadcrumb">
  <li><?php echo CHtml::link('Project', $this->createUrl('/projects')); ?></li>
  <li class="active"><?php echo $model->isNewRecord ? 'Create New' : 'Update'; ?> Task</li>
</ol>
<hr />
<h1><?php echo $model->isNewRecord ? 'Create New' : 'Update'; ?> Task</h1>
<?php $form=$this->beginWidget('CActiveForm', array(
    'id'=>'project-form',
    'htmlOptions' => array(
        'class' => 'form-horizontal',
        'role' => 'form'
    )
)); ?>
    <?php echo $form->errorSummary($model); ?>
```

[32]

```php
    <div class="form-group">
        <?php echo $form->labelEx($model,'title', array('class' => 'col-sm-2 control-label')); ?>
        <div class="col-sm-10">
            <?php echo $form->textField($model,'title', array('class' => 'form-control')); ?>
        </div>
    </div>

    <div class="form-group">
        <?php echo $form->labelEx($model,'data', array('class' => 'col-sm-2 control-label')); ?>
        <div class="col-sm-10">
            <?php echo $form->textArea($model,'data', array('class' => 'form-control')); ?>
        </div>
    </div>

    <div class="form-group">
        <?php echo $form->labelEx($model,'project_id', array('class' => 'col-sm-2 control-label')); ?>
        <div class="col-sm-10">
            <?php echo $form->dropDownList($model,'project_id', CHtml::listData(Projects::model()->findAll(), 'id', 'name'), array('empty'=>'Select Project', 'class' => 'form-control')); ?>
        </div>
    </div>

    <div class="form-group">
        <?php echo $form->labelEx($model,'completed', array('class' => 'col-sm-2 control-label')); ?>
        <div class="col-sm-10">
            <?php echo $form->dropDownList($model,'completed', array('0' => 'No','1' => 'Yes'), array('class' => 'form-control')); ?>
        </div>
    </div>

    <div class="form-group">
        <?php echo $form->labelEx($model,'due_date', array('class' => 'col-sm-2 control-label')); ?>
        <div class="col-sm-10">
            <div class="input-append date">
                <?php $this->widget('zii.widgets.jui.CJuiDatePicker', array(
                    'model' => $model,
                    'attribute' => 'due_date',
                    'htmlOptions' => array(
```

```
                            'size' => '10',
                            'maxlength' => '10',
                            'class' => 'form-control',
                            'value' => $model->due_date == "" ? "" : 
date("m/d/Y", $model->due_date)
                        ),
                    )); ?>                   </div>
            </div>
        </div>

        <div class="row buttons">
            <?php echo CHtml::submitButton($model->isNewRecord ? 'Create'
: 'Save', array('class' => 'btn btn-primary pull-right')); ?>
        </div>

<?php $this->endWidget(); ?>
```

Preventing unauthorized access to our application

Our tasks application can now do everything we defined in our requirements. However, it is open to the world. Anyone who wants to edit our tasks could simply visit our website and change anything without our knowledge. Before finishing up, let's create a simple authentication system to protect our data.

Requiring authentication with filters and access rules

The first part in protecting our application is making sure that only authorized people can visit our application. We can do this by adding a filter to our controller called `accessControl` and defining access rules to access our content.

A filter is a piece of code that gets executed before (and/or after) a controller action runs, which means that the user will be required to be authenticated before accessing our content. To add the `accessControl` filter, add the following to both `TasksController` and `ProjectsController`:

```
public function filters()
{
    return array(
        'accessControl',
    );
}
```

Next, create a new method called `accessRules()`, which will define what users can access our application. For our application, we want to deny access to anyone who isn't authenticated. Have a look at the following code snippet:

```
public function accessRules()
{
    return array(
        array('allow',
            'users'=>array('@'),
        ),
        array('deny',  // deny all users
            'users'=>array('*'),
        ),
    );
}
```

In the preceding array, `@` is a shorthand reference to an authenticated user. Now if we try to visit our web page, we'll be redirected to `/site/login`, the default `login` action in Yii.

Creating a controller for the authentication

Create a file called `SiteController.php` in `protected/controllers`, and then create `login` and `logout` actions as follows:

```
<?php
class SiteController extends CController
{
    public $layout = 'signin';

    public function actionLogin()
    {
        $model = new LoginForm;

        if (isset($_POST['LoginForm']))
        {
            $model->attributes = $_POST['LoginForm'];
            if ($model->login())
                $this->redirect($this->createUrl('/projects'));
        }
        $this->render('login', array('model' => $model));
    }
```

```
        public function actionLogout()
        {
            Yii::app()->user->logout();
            $this->redirect($this->createUrl('/site/login'));
        }
    }
```

Creating a login layout

For this controller, we're going to create a new layout called `login.php` in `protected/views/layouts`. Copy the markup from `protected/views/layouts/main.php` to our new layout, and replace the contents of the `<body>` tag with the following:

```
<div class="row">
    <div class="container">
        <?php echo $content; ?>
    </div>
</div>
```

To make our login page look more like a login page, add the following CSS to the layout either as an inline style or as a separate file in `/css/signup.css`:

```
body {
  padding-top: 40px;
  padding-bottom: 40px;
  background-color: #eee;
}

.form-signin {
  max-width: 330px;
  padding: 15px;
  margin: 0 auto;
}
.form-signin .form-signin-heading,
.form-signin .checkbox {
  margin-bottom: 10px;
}
.form-signin .checkbox {
  font-weight: normal;
}
.form-signin .form-control {
  position: relative;
```

```css
    font-size: 16px;
    height: auto;
    padding: 10px;
    -webkit-box-sizing: border-box;
       -moz-box-sizing: border-box;
            box-sizing: border-box;
}
.form-signin .form-control:focus {
  z-index: 2;
}
.form-signin input[type="text"] {
  margin-bottom: -1px;
  border-bottom-left-radius: 0;
  border-bottom-right-radius: 0;
}
.form-signin input[type="password"] {
  margin-bottom: 10px;
  border-top-left-radius: 0;
  border-top-right-radius: 0;
}
```

Creating a login view

Create a new form in `protected/views/site/login.php` that will hold our login model, as follows:

```php
<?php $form=$this->beginWidget('CActiveForm', array(
    'id'=>'login-form',
    'enableClientValidation'=>true,
    'htmlOptions' => array(
            'class' => 'form-signin',
            'role' => 'form'
    ),
    'clientOptions'=>array(
        'validateOnSubmit'=>true,
    ),
)); ?>

    <?php if (!Yii::app()->user->isGuest): ?>
        <h2 class="form-signin-heading">You are already signed in! Please <?php echo CHtml::link('logout', $this->createUrl('/site/logout')); ?> first.</h2>
    <?php else: ?>
```

```
        <h2 class="form-signin-heading">Please sign in</h2>
        <?php echo $form->errorSummary($model); ?>
        <?php echo $form->textField($model,'username', array('class'
=> 'form-control', 'placeholder' => 'Username')); ?>
        <?php echo $form->passwordField($model,'password',
array('class' => 'form-control', 'placeholder' => 'Password')); ?>
        <?php echo CHtml::tag('button', array('class' => 'btn btn-lg
btn-primary btn-block'), 'Submit'); ?>
    <?php endif; ?>
<?php $this->endWidget(); ?>
```

Identifying our users with the UserIdentity CUserIdentity class

Before we create our login model, we need to create a way to identify our users. Fortunately, Yii has a built-in class to handle this called `CUserIdentity`. By easily extending `CUserIdentity`, we can create a key-value login pair that will ensure that only authenticated users can log in to our application.

Create a new file called `UserIdentity.php` in `/components`, and add the following:

```
<?php
class UserIdentity extends CUserIdentity
{
    public function authenticate()
    {
        $users=array(
            'demo'=>'demo',
            'admin'=>'admin',
        );
        if(!isset($users[$this->username]))
            $this->errorCode=self::ERROR_USERNAME_INVALID;
        elseif($users[$this->username]!==$this->password)
            $this->errorCode=self::ERROR_PASSWORD_INVALID;
        else
            $this->errorCode=self::ERROR_NONE;
        return !$this->errorCode;
    }
}
```

The `authenticate()` method of `UserIdentity` is what we'll use in our login model to ensure that we have valid credentials. In this class, we are simply checking whether the `username` that will be sent to this class by our login model matches the key associated with it. If a user's password does not match the key in our `$users` array, or if the user is not defined in our `$users` array, we return an error code.

Creating the login model

The last component we need to authenticate our users is to create a generic model to authenticate the user against. Begin by creating a new file called `LoginForm.php` in `protected/models`. This class will extend `CFormModel`, a generic model in Yii for forms, as follows:

```
<?php class LoginForm extends CFormModel {
```

Since `CFormModel` doesn't connect to a database, we defined attributes as public properties, as follows:

```
public $username;
public $password;
private $_identity;
```

Our model also needs validation rules to verify that we have a valid user. In addition to making sure `username` and `password` are provided, we're going to provide an additional validation rule called `authenticate`, which will validate that we have a valid username and password. Have a look at the following lines of code:

```
public function rules()
{
    return array(
        array('username, password', 'required'),
        array('password', 'authenticate'),
    );
}
```

Because our `authenticate()` method is a custom validator, its method signature has two parameters, `$attribute` and `$params`, which have information about the attribute and parameters that may have been passed from the validator. This method will determine whether our credentials are valid. Have a look at the following code:

```
public function authenticate($attribute,$params)
{
    if(!$this->hasErrors())
    {
        $this->_identity=new UserIdentity($this->username,$this->password);
        if(!$this->_identity->authenticate())
            $this->addError('password','Incorrect username or password.');
    }
}
```

Finally, we'll create the `login()` method that our `SiteController` calls. In addition to validating our credentials, it will do the heavy lifting of creating a session for the user. Have a look at the following code:

```
public function login()
{
    if (!$this->validate())
        return false;

    if ($this->_identity===null)
    {
        $this->_identity=new UserIdentity($this->username,$this->password);
        $this->_identity->authenticate();
    }

    if ($this->_identity->errorCode===UserIdentity::ERROR_NONE)
    {
        $duration = 3600*24*30;
        Yii::app()->user->login($this->_identity,$duration);
        return true;
    }
    else
        return false;
}
```

Now you can visit our site and log in with the credentials provided in our `UserIdentity.php` file.

Finishing touches

Before completing our project, there are a few things we need to take care of in our `protected/config/main.php` file to enhance the security of our application and to make our application easier to use.

It would be nice to also add some pictures of the final application.

Disabling Gii

At the beginning of our project, we enabled the Gii module to assist us in creating models for our application. Since Gii has the ability to write new files to our project, we should remove the following section from our `config` file:

```
'gii'=>array(
    'class'=>'system.gii.GiiModule',
    'password'=>false,
    'ipFilters' => false
),
```

Defining a default route

Presently, if we try to visit the root URL of our application, we are presented with an error. To avoid this, we can add a route in to the routes array of our URL Manager component. With this addition, whenever we visit the root URL of our application, we will be presented with the `index` action of the project's controller. Have a look at the following code:

```
'components'=>array(
    [...]
    'urlManager'=>array(
        [...]
        'rules'=>array(
            [...]
            '/' => 'projects/index'
        ),
    )
)
```

Adding extra routes

Finally, add two more routes to our URL Manager routes array. These routes will help us more easily access the `login` and `logout` actions for our site. Have a look at the following code:

```
'login' => 'site/login',
'logout' => 'site/logout'
```

Summary

In this chapter, we covered quite a lot of information. We created an automated way of creating and distributing our database, models to represent the tables in the database, and a few controllers to manage and interact with our data. We also created a simple key-value authentication system to protect our data. Many of the methods we used in this chapter, and the code we wrote, can be reused and expanded upon in later chapters. Before continuing, be sure to take a look at all the classes we referenced in the chapter, in the official Yii documentation, so that you can better understand them.

2
Discovering What's Nearby

When developing an application, we are often presented with the geolocation data for a particular point of interest. Whether it's a business location or a job that the end user is applying to, knowing what's around that particular location can provide immediate value to the user when making a decision about that location. For example, a user may want to know what restaurants are near a particular location or what public services or public transportation options are near a particular job the user is interested in. With the help of third-party location APIs, we can inform the user what is near a given point of interest. For our second application, we develop a web application that shows the user what is near a particular point of interest using information from the Google Places API. In this chapter, we also cover how to integrate third-party libraries into our application and how to improve the performance of our application with caching.

Describing the project

As with our tasks application that was outlined in *Chapter 1, A Task-management Application*, we begin the development by getting a high-level overview of what the project will do and how our application will behave.

Searching nearby locations

The core component of this application is its ability to find other locations near an existing location. The easiest way to find this information is to take advantage of a third-party API. For this application, we'll be using the Google Places API, a web API that can provide nearby locations from given latitude and longitude coordinates.

Showing locations

Rather than simply telling our users what locations are near a given point of interest, we can enhance user experience by showing them the points of interest and nearby locations on a map. Many different mapping sources exist to show a map. For this application, we'll take advantage of another Google API, the Google Maps API.

Storing locations

To show the user the locations that are available for them to search nearby, we need to store these locations first. For storing these locations, we'll need a database that we can store imported locations into. Like our tasks application that we developed in *Chapter 1, A Task-management Application*, we'll use SQLite as our primary database again.

Importing locations

Finally, we're going to need a command-line tool to import locations from a data feed. To accomplish this, we're going to create a console task that can be run from the command line. This task will fetch information from the provided JSON feed and import it into our database. By making this a command-line task, we can automate and schedule the import via scheduled tasks on Windows or a Unix crontab.

Designing the database

With the core components of our application identified, we can now get started with developing the database. Let's start with creating our `locations` table.

Locations

When developing applications that import data from an external source, you can often take advantage of the structure of the external feed to determine what your own database tables should look like. Provided with the chapter resources at `protected/data/` is a file called `parks.json` that serves as our external data source. Since the data in this feed is consistent, let's take a look at a single item in the feed:

```
{
    "name" : "Cancer Survivors' Garden",
    "lat" : "41.884242",
    "long" : "-87.617404",
    "city" : "Chicago",
    "state" : "IL"
}
```

A single element in our data feed is composed of the name of the location, its latitude and longitude coordinates, and the city and state of the location. To make things simple, we can represent each of these attributes as a `TEXT` attribute in our table. Once we have added an `ID` column and `created` and `updated` columns, our `locations` table will look as follows:

```
ID INTEGER PRIMARY KEY
name TEXT
lat TEXT
long TEXT
city TEXT
state TEXT
created INTEGER
updated INTEGER
```

Initializing the project

As we did in our tasks project, we begin the development by creating a few folders in our application web root:

```
nearby/
    assets/
    js/
    protected/
        commands/
        config/
        controllers/
        data/
        extensions/
        migrations/
        models/
        runtime/
        views/
```

In this application, we added two new folders, `commands` and `extensions`. The `commands` folder is a special folder in Yii that `yiic` will reference when running console commands. The `extensions` folder is a special folder in Yii, where Yii extensions or third-party classes can be placed.

Next, let's go ahead and add our Yii Bootstrap file, index.php, to the root of our application. We need to be sure to change the Yii path to the location on the system:

```php
<?php

// change the following paths if necessary
$yii='/path/to/yii/framework/yii.php';
$config=dirname(__FILE__).'/protected/config/main.php';

error_reporting(E_ALL);
ini_set('display_errors', '1');
// remove the following lines when in production mode
defined('YII_DEBUG') or define('YII_DEBUG',true);
// specify how many levels of call stack should be shown in each log message
defined('YII_TRACE_LEVEL') or define('YII_TRACE_LEVEL',3);

require_once($yii);
Yii::createWebApplication($config)->run();
```

Now, let's create our yiic.php file within our protected folder that will run both our migrations and console commands. Once again, we need to be sure to adjust the path to the Yii framework in the require statement:

```php
<?php

// change the following paths if necessary
$config=dirname(__FILE__).'/config/main.php';

$config = require($config);

require_once('/path/to//yii/framework/yiic.php');
```

Creating the configuration file

Next, we need to create the configuration file that our Yii application will use. Let's add the following to protected/config/main.php:

```php
<?php
return array(
    'basePath'=>dirname(__FILE__).DIRECTORY_SEPARATOR.'..',
    'name'=>'Places Nearby',
    'import'=>array(
        'application.models.*',
    ),
```

```
    'components'=>array(
        'db'=>array(
            'connectionString' => 'sqlite:'.dirname(__FILE__).'/../
data/locations.db',
        ),
        'urlManager'=>array(
            'urlFormat'=>'path',
            'showScriptName'=>false,
            'rules'=>array(
            '<controller:\w+>/<id:\d+>'=>'<controller>/view',
'<controller:\w+>/<action:\w+>/<id:\d+>'=>'<controller>/<action>','<co
ntroller:\w+>/<action:\w+>'=>'<controller>/<action>',
            ),
        )
    )
);
```

In comparison to the configuration file we made in *Chapter 1, A Task-management Application*, the only parts of the file that were changed are the location of the database file for SQLite to use and the name of the application.

Retrieving the sample data

Provided with the chapter resources within the `protected/data` folder is a file called `parks.json`; it contains the sample data that we will use for our application. Let's go ahead and grab this file from the project resources and add it to the `protected/data` folder.

Creating the database

To create the database, we again use migrations. From the command line, let's navigate to the project root and create the migration using `yiic`:

```
$ php protected/yiic.php migrate create locations
```

After confirming the creation, we open up the new migration file in `protected/migrations` and replace the `contents up()` method with the following:

```
    return $this->createTable('locations', array(
        'id' => 'INTEGER PRIMARY KEY',
        'name' => 'TEXT',
        'lat' => 'TEXT',
        'long' => 'TEXT',
```

```
        'city' => 'TEXT',
        'state' => 'TEXT',
        'created' => 'INTEGER',
        'updated' => 'INTEGER'
));
```

Then, we replace the contents of the `down()` method with the following:

```
return $this->dropTable('locations');
```

From the command line, let's now apply the new migration:

```
$ php protected/yiic.php migrate up
```

Creating the locations model

To interact with our data, we need to create a model that once again references our new database table. Using the instructions outlined in *Chapter 1, A Task-management Application*, we enable the `Gii` module and create a new model called Location to interact with the `locations` table in our database.

Once created, we add a `beforeSave()` method to the generated file (`protected/modules/Location.php`) to automatically set the created and updated time:

```
public function beforeSave()
{
   if ($this->isNewRecord)
      $this->created = time();

   $this->updated = time();

   return parent::beforeSave();
}
```

Then, we modify the `rules()` method:

```
public function rules()
{
    return array(
        array('created, updated', 'numerical', 'integerOnly'=>true),
        array('name, lat, long, city, state', 'required'),
        array('title, data', 'safe'),
        array('name, lat, long, city, state, created, updated', 'safe', 'on'=>'search'),
    );
}
```

Importing the data feed

Before creating the frontend controllers to display our data, we need to create a tool to import our data feed. To create this tool, we create a class in our commands directory that extends `CConsoleCommand`; this will enable us to import data from the command line and automate it if we so choose.

To begin, we need to create a new class called `ImportLocationsCommand` inside of our `commands` directory at `/protected` that extends `CConsoleCommand`. The filename inside the commands directory should be `ImportLocationscommand.php`:

```
<?php
class ImportLocationsCommand extends CConsoleCommand {}
```

Next, we add a method to handle the retrieval of the data we want to import. To provide the greatest amount of flexibility, we create two methods: the first will fetch the data from our external data source and the second will actually import the data into our database.

In a real-world application, the first method that we build might fetch the data from a web resource via CURL. Alternatively, the data might be uploaded and provided to us via FTP. Since our data is stored locally, however, our method will simply fetch the contents of the file:

```
private function getData()
{
    $file = __DIR__ . '/../data/parks.json';
    return CJSON::decode(file_get_contents($file));
}
```

By moving this functionality into its own method, we can easily change this method in future to fetch this data from another location, without having to change other parts of our code.

Next, we create a new method called `actionImportLocations()` that will perform the import:

```
public function actionImportLocations() {}
```

For simplicity, we assume that our `getData()` method will always return valid data to this method. Inside the method, we add the following:

```
echo "Loading Data...\n";
$data = $this->getData();
```

An important consideration when importing data is to make sure that we don't accidentally create duplicate data within our application. There are several ways to handle this.

The easiest way to handle this edge case is to simply truncate the database table and perform a fresh import. While this type of import is incredibly simple, with larger datasets, it could cause our application not to function properly while the import is running.

A more reliable method would be to import this data into a temporary database table and then delete the active table and rename the temporary one to the active table's name. In addition to ensuring that we don't have duplicate data, this method also ensures that if we have a problem importing the data, we can simply abort the import with an error and not worry about having a corrupted database. Additionally, this method should also reduce the downtime associated with importing the raw data.

The most complex way of importing the data would be to compare your existing database with the data from the feed and import only the difference between the two. While significantly more complex, this method can reduce the overhead needed to retrieve the data, and when put in combination with the previous method, should reduce almost all of the downtime associated with an import.

To keep things simple, we're going to opt for the first method, which we can easily implement, as follows. First, we're going to truncate the existing data in our database:

```
echo "Truncating old data...\n";
Location::model()->deleteAll();
```

Since our database matches our data feed, we'll simply iterate through the results and import them row by row:

```
echo "Importing Data...\n";
foreach($data as $id=>$content)
{
    $model = new Location;
    $model->attributes = $content;
    $model->save();
}
```

From the command line, we can now import our data by running the `importlocations` command we just created. Running command-line tasks takes the following format:

```
$ php protected/yiic.php <command_name> <action_name>
```

In our case, the full command looks as follows:

`$ php protected/yiic.php importlocations importlocations`

If the import went well, we will see the debug output that we added to the command without any errors:

```
$ php protected/yiic.php importlocations importlocations
Loading Data...
Truncating old data...
Importing Data...
```

> You can read more about CConsoleCommand from the official guide at http://www.yiiframework.com/doc/guide/1.1/en/topics.console or from the Yii class reference at http://www.yiiframework.com/doc/api/1.1/CConsoleCommand.

Google APIs

Before we begin work at the frontend of our application, we need to create an API key to interact with Google Maps and the Google Places API.

Enabling Google APIs

To enable the Google APIs our project is using, open up a web browser and navigate to the Google API Console located at https://console.developers.google.com/project. Once we have logged in to a Google account, we click on the **Create Project** button and fill out the form with a unique project name and project ID, as shown in the following screenshot:

Discovering What's Nearby

Once the project has been created, we navigate to the newly created project and click on the **APIs & auth** link in the sidebar. From the list of APIs, we toggle both **Google Maps JavaScript API v3** and **Places API** to **ON**, as shown in the following screenshot:

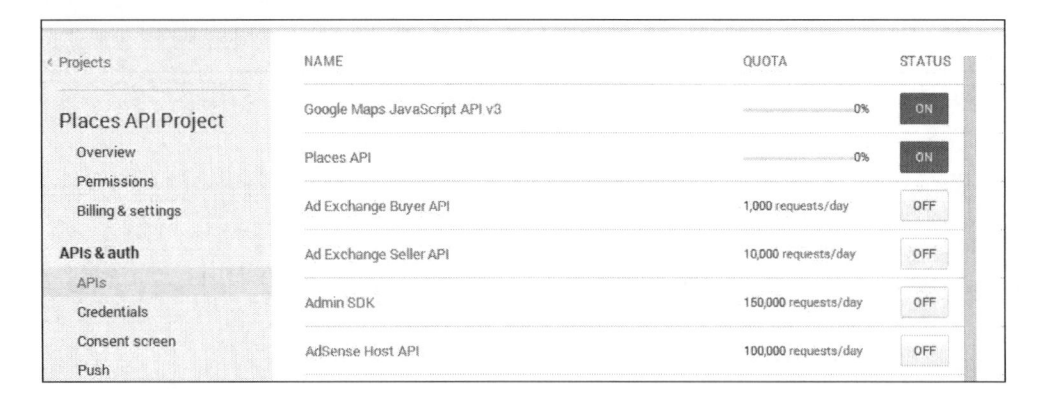

Generating an API key

With both APIs enabled for the project, we click on the **Credentials** link in the sidebar. From this menu, we can create a new API key for our application to use. Once on this page, we are presented with two options, either an OAuth Client ID or a Public API key. Click on **Create new Key** under **Public API access**, as shown in the following screenshot:

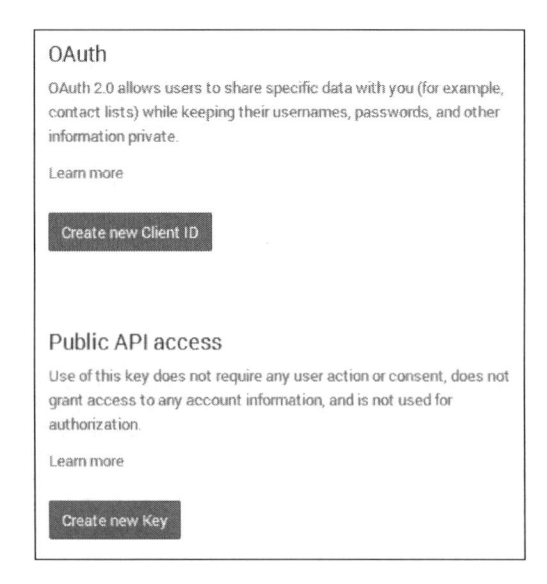

Then, from the next menu select **Server key**, which will generate a new client API key for us to use in our application:

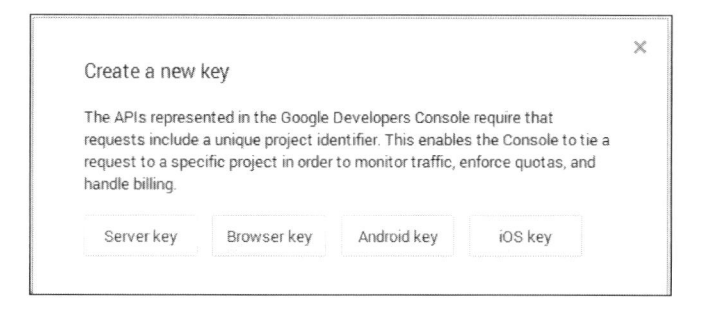

Once the page reloads, we copy the full API key to our clipboard.

Storing the API key

Next, we need to store our API in our application so that we can use it. Fortunately, Yii provides a setting for static parameters in `protected/config/main.php` called `params` that we can store our API key in. Let's add the following as a root element to our configuration file and replace `<your_api_key_here>` with the actual API key:

```
'params' => array(
    'PlacesApi' => array(
        'apiKey' => '<your_api_key_here>'
    )
)
```

This data is then available as an array through `Yii::app()->params`, which we can query against, as follows:

```
$apiKey = Yii::app()->params['PlacesApi']['apiKey'];
```

Creating the presentation layer

Now, we're ready to start displaying content. To get started, we create a new controller called `SiteController.php` in the `protected/controllers` directory that contains the following:

```
<?php
class SiteController extends CController
{
    public function actionIndex()
    {
```

```
            $this->render('index');
        }
}
```

Next, let's create our main layout in `protected/views/layouts/main.php`. For simplicity, we're once again going to use the jQuery and Twitter Bootstrap styles from publicly available CDNs, as follows:

```
<!DOCTYPE html>
<html>
    <head>
        <title><?php echo CHtml::encode(Yii::app()->name); ?></title>
        <?php Yii::app()->clientScript
                ->registerMetaTag('text/html; charset=UTF-8', 'Content-Type')
                ->registerCssFile( '//netdna.bootstrapcdn.com/bootstrap/3.0.3/css/bootstrap.min.css' )
                ->registerScriptFile( 'https://code.jquery.com/jquery.js' )
                ->registerScriptFile( '//netdna.bootstrapcdn.com/bootstrap/3.0.3/js/bootstrap.min.js')
                ->registerScriptFile( 'https://maps.googleapis.com/maps/api/js?sensor=false&key=' . Yii::app()->params['PlacesApi']['apiKey']);
        ?>
    </head>
    <body>
        <div class="row">
            <div class="container">
                <nav class="navbar navbar-default navbar-fixed-top navbar-inverse" role="navigation">
                    <div class="navbar-header">
                        <a class="navbar-brand" href="/"><?php echo CHtml::encode(Yii::app()->name); ?></a>
                    </div>
                </nav>
            </div>
        </div>
        <div class="row" style="margin-top: 100px;">
            <div class="container">
                <?php echo $content; ?>
            </div>
        </div>
    </body>
</html>
```

Since our application will have only one page, we will register the Google Maps JavaScript API directly in our layout, as shown in the preceding code. Note that when we registered this JavaScript file, we included our Google API key, which we added to the `params` section of our configuration file:

```
->registerScriptFile( 'https://maps.googleapis.com/maps/api/
js?sensor=false&key=' . Yii::app()->params['PlacesApi']['apiKey']);
```

Next, let's create a simple view file for our `site/index` action in `protected/views/sites/index.php` to hold our maps container:

```
<div class="col-xs-12 col-sm-9">
   <div id="map-canvas" style="width: 100%; min-height: 500px"></div>
</div>
```

Interacting with the Google Maps JavaScript API

Since Google Maps is a JavaScript API, we need to write some JavaScript code to interact with it.

To begin, create a new file in `/js` called `Main.js`. This JavaScript file will store all of our JavaScript methods to create and interact with Google Maps. The utility functions we create here will make interacting with the map easier later on.

Before we start writing any JavaScript, we need to load our JavaScript file from our layout. To do this, we can register a new script from `CClientScript` by adding the following to our call to `CClientScript` in our `main.php` file at `protected/views/layouts`:

```
->registerScriptFile(Yii::app()->baseUrl .'/js/Main.js');
```

Now that our JavaScript file will be loaded, we open up our `Main.js` file and create a new JavaScript object called `Main`:

```
var Main = {}
```

Within this object, we need to create three properties: a property to store the Google Maps object, a property to store any options Google Maps may require, and a property to store any marker we add to the map:

```
map : null,
mapOptions : {},
markers : [],
```

[55]

Next, we create a function that will actually load the Google Maps object. This function will need to handle two separate loading cases.

The first case this function will need to handle is the loading of Google Maps without any map markers. In this situation, we assume the user has arrived at the page for the first time and has not selected the point of interest that they want to see nearby locations for. The second case this function will need to handle is the initialization of the map with a given point of interest centered and focused on.

To handle these two cases, our function will accept a latitude and longitude location. If the latitude and longitude positions are given to the method, we will center the map on that location. If they are not provided, we will center the map on a zoomed-out location of where our data generally lies, which in this case is the downtown Chicago area:

```
loadMap : function(lat, lng) {
zoom = 16;
    if (lat == undefined && lng == undefined)
    {
        // Lat long of downtown Chicago area
        lat = "41.878114";
        lng = "-87.629798";
        zoom = 13;
    }
}
```

Then, within the same function, we're going to set our map options and load the map in the placeholder that we set in our `index.php` file at `protected/views/site`:

```
Main.mapOptions = {
   zoom: zoom,
   center: new google.maps.LatLng(lat, lng),
};

Main.map = new google.maps.Map(document.getElementById("map-canvas"), Main.mapOptions);
```

So that we can see our map in action, we add the following to our `index.php` file at `protected/views/site` and refresh the page:

```
<?php $cs->registerScript('loadMap', "Main.loadMap();"); ?>
```

Once the page loads, we should see the Google Maps object displayed, as shown in the following screenshot:

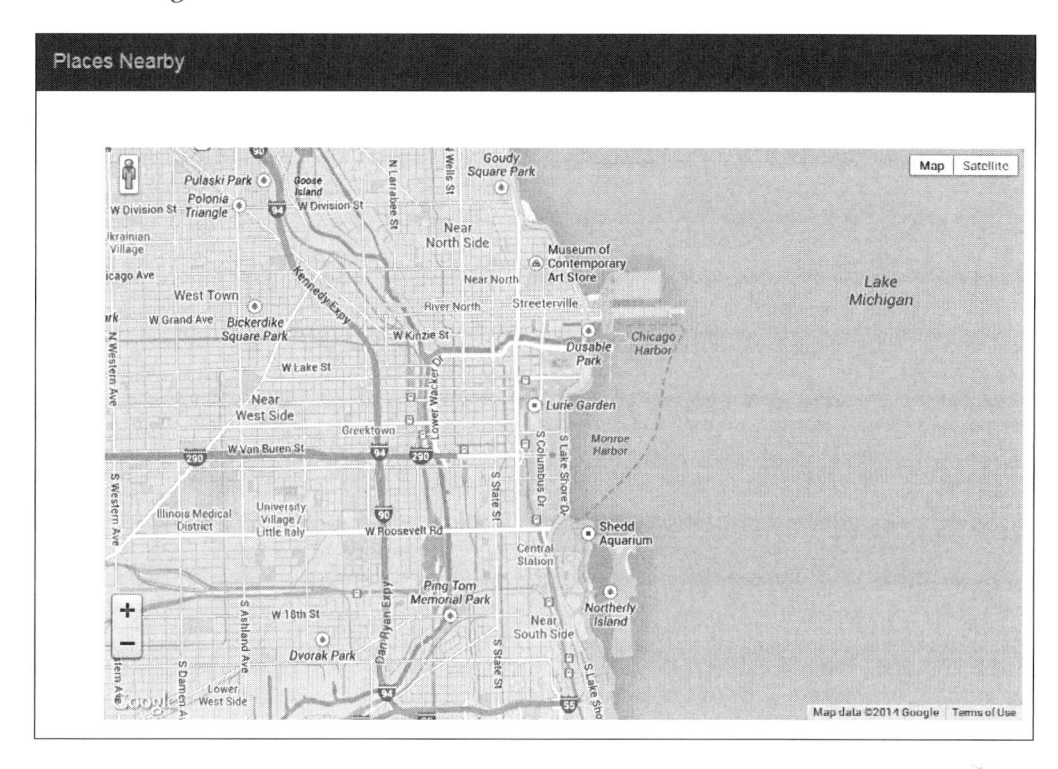

After verifying that our map has loaded, let's head back to our `Main.js` file and add a few more utility functions.

First, let's add a simple wrapper to create the Google Maps latitude and longitude coordinates. This method will help ensure that our Google Maps object loads when we want to interact with it:

```
createLocation : function(lat,lng) {
   return new google.maps.LatLng(lat,lng);
},
```

Secondly, let's create a function to add map markers. This function will need to display two types of markers, the first being the selected point of interest and the second being the nearby points of interest:

```
addMarker : function(position, title, icon) {
   if (icon == true)
   {
```

```
            var pinColor = "2F76EE"; // a random blue color that i picked
            var icon = new google.maps.MarkerImage("http://chart.apis.
google.com/chart?chst=d_map_pin_letter&chld=%E2%80%A2|" + pinColor,
                new google.maps.Size(21, 34),
                new google.maps.Point(0,0),
                new google.maps.Point(10, 34));
    }
}
```

Within the function, we create a new `marker` object:

```
var marker = new google.maps.Marker({
position: position,
    title: title,
    icon: icon
});
```

Then, we push this `marker` object onto the map:

```
Main.markers.push(marker);
```

Then, we add the `marker` object to the `markers` variable that we defined earlier. This allows us to clear the map if we want to make our application more dynamic:

```
marker.setMap(Main.map);
```

Finally, let's create a function that will clear the map. This function will iterate through all of the markers in the `markers` variable that we defined earlier and remove the map marker we set with `addMarker()`:

```
clearMarkers : function() {
    $(Main.markers).each(function() {
        this.setMap(null);
    });

    Main.markers = [];
}
```

> More information on how to interact with the Google Maps JavaScript API v3 is located at https://developers.google.com/maps/documentation/javascript/tutorial.

Searching nearby locations

To search nearby locations, we're going to take advantage of the Google Places API. Rather than implementing the API documentation ourselves, as outlined in `https://developers.google.com/places/documentation/`, we're going to take advantage of an open source wrapper for the API located at `https://github.com/joshtronic/php-googleplaces`.

To take advantage of this wrapper, we download the repository to our `extensions` folder, which should look as follows, once we have downloaded the repository:

```
protected/
    extensions/
        GooglePlaces.php
```

With the wrapper downloaded, we reopen `SiteController.php` and create a new private method called `getPlaces()`, which takes a location from our database as an argument:

```
private function getPlaces($location) {}
```

To make Yii aware of this class, we need to first import it using `Yii::import()`. This method is preferred over a `require` or `include` statement because it both registers the class with Yii's autoloader and only loads the class once if we use it multiple times. Since this class wasn't autoloaded in our configuration file, we need to manually import it here:

```
Yii::import('ext.GooglePlaces');
```

> How does Yii know that `ext.GooglePlaces` represents `protected/extensions/GooglePlaces.php`? Yii uses path aliases to easily identify where files and folders are located within our application root. This enables us to easily reference these files and folders without having to specify an absolute path. You can read more about path aliases at `http://www.yiiframework.com/doc/guide/1.1/en/basics.namespace`.

Next, we instantiate the class with the API key that we created earlier:

```
$places = new GooglePlaces(Yii::app()->params['PlacesApi']['apiKey']);
```

Then, we specify the radius and location that we want to search around:

```
$places->radius = 200;
$places->location = array($location->lat, $location->long);
```

> In a densely populated area with many different shops, it's safe to assume that we'd find several results within a 200-meter radius. In a less densely populated area, it would be wise to adjust our radius to something much larger to find nearby results better.

Then, we search for nearby locations:

```
return $places->search();
```

With a method in place to perform the search, we now need to update our `index` action to call our new method. To do this, we assume that the client is going to specify which location they want to search around by selecting a location from a drop-down list and sending us the unique ID we created for the record when we imported it. Within `SiteController.php`, we add the following action:

```
public function actionIndex()
{
    $location = $places = array();

    if (isset($_GET['id']))
    {
        $location = Location::model()->findByPk($_GET['id']);
        $places = $this->getPlaces($location);
    }

    $this->render('index', array('location' => $location, 'places' => $places));
}
```

Selecting a location

Now that our controller can search nearby locations, we need to update our view, `protected/views/site/index.php`, with a form to allow the user to select a location they're inserted in:

```
<div class="col-xs-6 col-sm-3 sidebar-offcanvas">
    <h3>Locations</h3>
    <hr />
    <form role="form">
```

```
            <div class="form-group">
                <?php $selected = array('options' => array(isset($_
GET['id']) ? $_GET['id'] : NULL => array('selected' => true))); ?>
                <?php echo CHtml::dropDownList('id', array(), CH
tml::listData(Location::model()->findAll(),'id','name'),
CMap::mergeArray($selected, array('empty' => 'Select a Location')));
?>
            </div>
            <button type="submit" class="pull-right btn btn-
primary">Search</button>
        </form>
        <div class="clearfix"></div>
    </div>
```

In the previous code sample, we used `CHtml::listData()` to simultaneously retrieve a list of locations from our database and populate the drop-down menu with the appropriate ID name pairs to be displayed. Using `CHtml::listData()`, we can ensure that our data is fetched and displayed dynamically based on what we have in our database.

Showing locations on a map

While our form is functional, we still need to update our view to actually display the locations on the map. This is where we use the JavaScript code we created earlier. Before the closing `</div>` tag of our sidebar, let's load `CClientScript` to dynamically register the JavaScript with Yii:

```
<?php $cs = Yii::app()->getClientScript(); ?>
```

Now, there are two cases we need to handle. In the first case, the user has arrived at our site for the first time and simply needs to be shown the map. In the second case, we need to show a map that is centered around our point of interest. Since our `$places['results']` array will be empty in the first case, we can express this as follows:

```
<?php
if (!empty($places['results']))
{
$cs->registerScript('loadMap', "Main.loadMap({$location->lat},
{$location->long});");

    // Center the map with the origin marker
    $lat = $location->lat;
    $long = $location->long;
```

Discovering What's Nearby

```
        $name = $location->name;
        $cs->registerScript('origin', "
            Main.addMarker(
                Main.createLocation('{$lat}', '{$long}'),
                \"{$name}\",
                true
            );
        ");
    }
    else
    {
    $cs->registerScript('loadMap', "Main.loadMap();");
    }
```

Let's reload the page and try it out. If a location is selected, a blue marker will indicate the position on the map. Otherwise, no marker will be shown.

Next, we need to add the nearby locations to the map. To do this, we simply iterate through the `$places['results']` array and register a unique script that will place a marker on the map. For added clarity for the end user, we also add the item as a text entry in the sidebar:

```
<hr />
<h3>What's Nearby?</h3>
<ul>
    <?php foreach ($places['results'] as $place): ?>
        <li><?php echo $place['name']; ?></li>
        <?php
            // Add the nearby POI's
            $lat = $place['geometry']['location']['lat'];
            $long = $place['geometry']['location']['lng'];
            $name = $place['name'];
            $icon = $place['icon'];
            $cs->registerScript('loadMarker-' . $place['id'], "
                Main.addMarker(
                    Main.createLocation('{$lat}', '{$long}'),
                    \"{$name}\"
                    );
            ");
        ?>
    <?php endforeach; ?>
</ul>
```

With everything in place, we can now search our `locations` database and see nearby locations displayed on the map:

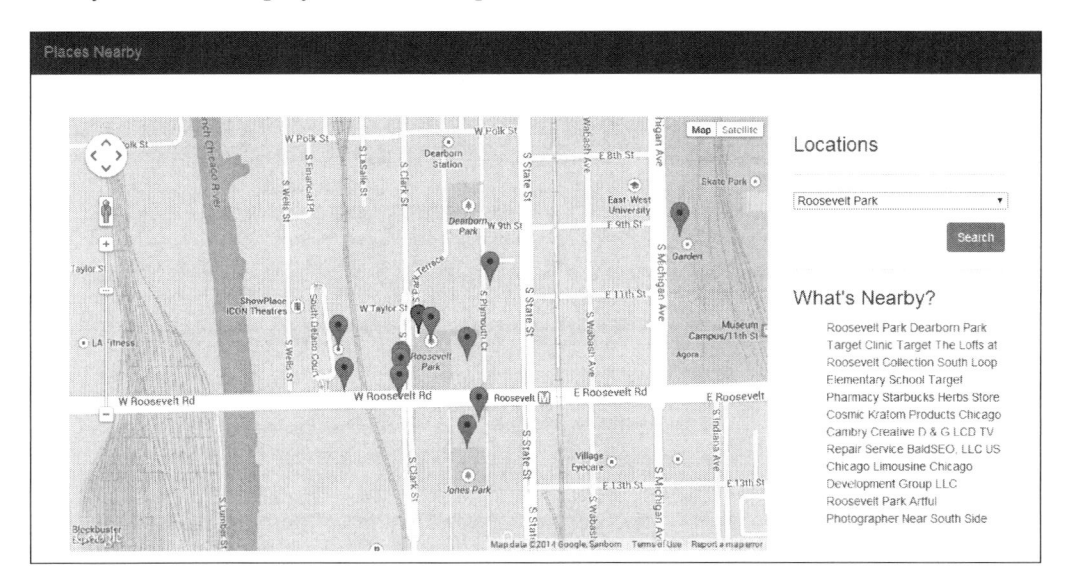

Optimizing the performance with caching

As is often the case with third-party APIs, the Google Places API is a paid-for resource that comes with a daily courtesy limit (currently at 1,000 requests per day), which means that every time a user makes a request to our application, we're paying for it.

However, since the likelihood of a new point of interest being created within the next few hours, days, or even weeks is pretty small, we can cache this data locally rather than making a request to Google each time the page is requested. Doing this will not only save us money, but it will also speed up our application since this data can be retrieved from a local resource rather than a third-party one.

To do this, we first need to enable a cache in our configuration file. There are several different caches available for use in Yii, including file-based caches, memcache-based caching, and a Redis cache. For this application, we'll keep things simple and use file-based caching. To enable the cache, we add the following to the components section of our configuration file:

```
'cache' => array(
    'class' => 'CFileCache'
),
```

Discovering What's Nearby

With the cache enabled, we start using it within our application. Let's open up `SiteController.php` and replace the `getPlaces()` method with the following:

```
private function getPlaces(&$location)
{
    // Generate a hash
    $hash = md5($location->lat . '-' . $location->long);

    // Retrieve data from the cache
    $cache = Yii::app()->cache->get($hash);

    // If we don't have any cached data, perform a search
    // against the API
    if ($cache === false)
    {
        Yii::import('ext.GooglePlaces');
        $places = new GooglePlaces(Yii::app()->params['PlacesApi']['apiKey']);
        $places->radius = 200;
        $places->location = array($location->lat, $location->long);
        $cache = $places->search();
        // And store the result in the cache
        Yii::app()->cache->set($hash, $cache);
    }

    return $cache;
}
```

Let's walk through what we just did. First, we're going to generate a unique hash that we'll store our hashes against. To do this, we're going to store the latitude and longitude of any given location as an md5 hash, which should provide sufficient search space for us to store our results:

```
$hash = md5($location->lat . '-' . $location->long);
```

Next, we're going to retrieve the cache result from the cache. In the event that data is not returned, this method will return false:

```
$cache = Yii::app()->cache->get($hash);
```

If we don't have any value presently stored in the cache, we'll perform a search against the API:

```
if ($cache === false) {}
```

After retrieving the results from the API, we then store it against the md5 hash that we generated earlier:

```
$cache = $places->search();
Yii::app()->cache->set($hash, $cache);
```

Finally, we return the data:

```
return $cache;
```

By adding this cache, our application should perform much better when multiple users are searching against it, and we reduce the risk of hitting our daily API limit. If we do need to upgrade our application to one that needs more requests, we can be confident that we're only paying for what we absolutely need, rather than for each request.

Summary

Throughout this chapter, we covered a lot of ground. We went over how to integrate console commands into our application with CConsoleCommand as well as how to import data into our database from an external source. We also went over how to integrate with two popular Google APIs: Google Maps and the Google Places API. Additionally, we covered caching the responses of these APIs. Finally, we went over importing third-party code into our application.

In this chapter and in Chapter 1, *A Task-management Application*, we went over almost all the basic components of building a Yii application. In the next chapter, we will create a scheduling application that will automatically remind the user of events before they occur'. We'll also expand on all of the topics we covered so far to build and work with more complex topics. Before continuing, be sure to take a look at all the classes we referenced in this chapter, in the official Yii documentation, so that you can better understand them.

3
Scheduled Reminders

In the previous two chapters, we developed simple reactionary applications that went over the basic components of the Yii framework. For our next project, we will expand upon the concepts previously covered by creating a scheduled reminders application that will allow our users to search for, create, and schedule both events and reminders for themselves. This application will also send the user notifications automatically when the reminder is scheduled to occur.

Prerequisites

Before we start, there are a couple of things that we'll need to install and acquire:

- Install the latest version of MySQL (at the time of writing this, MySQL 5.6). MySQL is the most popular open source database and is a key part of LAMP (Linux, Apache, MySQL, and PHP). Because of its popularity with web hosting providers, MySQL is often the de facto choice for modern web applications.

  > MySQL can be installed from either your distributions package management system or downloaded from `mysql.com`. More details can be found at `http://dev.mysql.com/doc/refman/5.6/en/installing.html`.

- Acquire an SMTP server or credentials to an SMTP server for our application to send e-mails with. The key details that we will need are a SMTP host, port, username, and password. Depending on the server, you may also need to know the type of security your server uses (such as SSL or TLS). If you do not have a SMTP server available, there is an abundant number of options available, ranging from setting up a Postfix SMTP server, using Gmail as an SMTP relay, or even obtaining a free SMTP account from SendGrid (`http://www.sendgrid.com`).

- Verify that our PHP instance has mcrypt libraries installed so that we can properly hash the passwords we'll be using. If your PHP instance already supports mcrypt, you should see an mcrypt section listed in `phpinfo()`. If mcrypt is not enabled in your PHP instance, install it either from your upstream provider, by enabling the mcrypt module, or by recompiling PHP.
- Finally, we'll need to download and install Composer from `https://getcomposer.org/`. Composer is a PHP dependency manager that will allow us to declare and automatically install libraries that our application will use.

Once we've obtained all of the prerequisites for our application, we can get started with development.

Describing the project

Our scheduled reminders project can be broken down into four main components:

- Users who will create events and reminders
- Events that the user wants to be reminded of
- Reminders for the actual event (of which there could be many)
- A command-line task to process and send out the reminders to the user via e-mail

Users

The first component of our application is the users who will be using it. Users will be responsible to create both events and reminders for themselves. The users will also be the recipients of the reminder e-mails that they created. Using this information, we can simplify our database schema to the following structure:

```
ID INTEGER PRIMARY KEY
email STRING
password STRING
created INTEGER
updated INTEGER
```

In *Chapter 1, A Task-management Application*, we created a very primitive user authentication system that we'll be reusing and expanding upon and reusing in later chapters. In this chapter, we'll develop a system to create, delete, and manage the passwords of users with our application. We'll also cover several basic guidelines for properly securing, storing, and working with our users' credentials.

Events

The second component of our application is events. Events are things that a particular user wants to be reminded of and will occur at a given time on a given date. Events should be easy to search through and intuitive to find. Additionally, events can have one, many, or no reminders associated with them. We can express this in our database schema, as follows:

```
ID INTEGER PRIMARY KEY
user_id INTEGER
title STRING
data TEXT
time INTEGER
created INTEGER
updated INTEGER
```

A new concept that we'll be introducing in this chapter is the concept of database relations. Many times, data in our database will be associated with an attribute or data in another table of our database. In this case, an event is something that belongs to a given user. The relations that we create in this application will allow us to easily represent data in our tables without having to store that data in multiple places.

Reminders

A reminder is a time-sensitive event that belongs to a user-created event and acts as an indicator to our task runner to notify the user of the details of the event itself. This can be expressed in our simplified database schema, as follows:

```
ID INTEGER PRIMARY KEY
event_id INTEGER
title STRING
offset INTEGER
time INTEGER
created INTEGER
updated INTEGER
```

When we set up our Reminders model, we'll define a relationship between a reminder and the event. As events are already bound to a user, we can transitively determine the user a reminder should be sent to without having to add the user_id field to the reminder itself.

Scheduled Reminders

The final piece of our reminders has to do with how we handle timestamps. In previous chapters, timestamps served only as metadata to specific records. Our reminders, however, will have to take into account the time that an event will be triggered, which means that we'll be involving time zones. While using UTC solves a lot of the issues when dealing with time, our reminders have to be aware of what the time offset is for a particular reminder.

For our application, that means we'll need to store the time that the end user will see in addition to either the time zone offset of the user or a conversion of that time into the real UTC time.

The task runner

The final component of our application is the task runner that will find reminders that need to be sent out and actually send them out to the user. While there are many ways to go about creating this task runner, we will be creating a command-line task that will run repeatedly after *n* minutes and will process all events between the trigger time and the provided interval in minutes. This approach will allow us to define how frequently or infrequently we want our reminders to be processed without having to rewrite code.

Initializing the project

At this point, you should be fairly familiar with how to initialize a basic Yii framework project. Go ahead and create the base folder structures, and create the `index.php`, `yiic`, `yiic.bat`, and `yiic.php` files. Then in the `webroot` directory of our application, create a folder called `vendors`. This folder will be used for all of our Composer dependencies for us.

Create a MySQL user and database

If you haven't already created a MySQL user, password, and database for the project, do so now. From the MySQL command line, you can run the following commands to do this:

```
CREATE USER 'ch3_reminders'@'localhost' IDENTIFIED BY 'ch3_reminders';
CREATE DATABASE IF NOT EXISTS `ch3_reminders`;
GRANT ALL PRIVILEGES ON `ch3\_reminders` . * TO 'ch3_reminders'@'localhost';
```

Creating a Yii configuration file

Our Yii configuration file will be slightly different than our previous configuration files due to the use of our MySQL database. We'll start off with the base configuration `protected/config/main.php` and add the new components afterwards:

```php
<?php return array(
    'basePath'=>dirname(__FILE__).DIRECTORY_SEPARATOR.'..',
    'name'=>'Scheduled Reminders',
    'import'=>array(
       'application.models.*',
    ),
    'components'=>array(

       'errorHandler'=>array(
            'errorAction'=>'site/error',
         ),
        'urlManager'=>array(
          'urlFormat'=>'path',
          'showScriptName'=>false,
          'rules'=>array(
             '/' => 'event/index',
             'event/date/<date:[\w-]+>' => 'event/index',
'<controller:\w+>/<action:\w+>/<id:\d+>'=>'<controller>/<action>',
 <controller:\w+>/<action:\w+>'=>'<controller>/<action>')
        )
    )
);
```

In order for our application to interact with MySQL, we'll need to update the database component so that Yii knows how to use the MySQL PDO adapter. We can do this by adding the following to our components array:

```php
'db' => array(
    'class' => 'CDbConnection',
    'connectionString' => 'mysql:host=127.0.0.1;dbname=ch3_reminders',
    'emulatePrepare' => true,
    'username' => 'ch3_reminders',
    'password' => 'ch3_reminders',
    'charset' => 'utf8',
    'schemaCachingDuration' => '3600'
),
```

> In this configuration, we've added `schemeaCachingDuration`, which outlines how long Yii will cache our MySQL schema. This will prevent unnecessary SQL commands, such as `DESCRIBE TABLE`, which will slow down our application. It's important to note that if you are using this option, you'll need to clear Yii's internal cache. You can find out more about MySQL-specific database configuration at http://www.yiiframework.com/doc/api/1.1/CDbConnection.

Creating a parameters configuration file

Many times, we have sensitive information we'd like to store in our configuration file that we wouldn't necessarily want to store with our version control software for security reasons. One way we can get around this is by storing this information in a separate file and then excluding it from being committed to source control. When we deploy our application to our production servers, we can manually add this file.

In Yii, we can accomplish this by adding the following to our base array of our configuration file:

```
'params' => array(
    'smtp' => require __DIR__ . '/params.php'
)
```

Next, create a new file in the `config` folder called `params.php`. This file will store our SMTP credentials for our application. Have a look at the following code:

```
<?php return array(
    'host' => '',
    'username' => '',
    'password' => '',
    'from' => '',
    'port' => ''
);
```

At this time, go ahead and add your SMTP credentials to the `params.php` file.

Adding Composer dependencies

The last configuration change we'll need to make is the inclusion of a file called `composer.json` in our `webroot` directory. For this project, we'll be using a dependency called `PHPMailer` that will help us send e-mails from our application. We'll also include a package called `password-compat`, which will provide us with the necessary userland functions for working with Bcrypt, a password hashing library that we'll cover in more detail when we start working with users and authentication.

This file should look as follows:

```
{
    "minimum-stability" : "dev",
    "require": {
        "phpmailer/phpmailer": "dev-master"
        "ircmaxell/password-compat": "dev-master"
    }
}
```

With our Composer dependencies defined, we can now install them by running the following from our command line:

`cd /path/to/project`

`php /path/to/composer.phar`

If everything goes well, you should see something similar outputted to your screen. If not, Composer will return and notify you of the error for you to correct:

```
Loading composer repositories with package information
Installing dependencies (including require-dev) from lock file
  - Installing phpmailer/phpmailer (dev-master f9d229a)
    Cloning f9d229af549d28d4c9fdd3273bf6525cde3bc472
Generating autoload files
```

Finally, we need to load the dependencies into Yii. The easiest way to do this is to add the following to our `index.php` file before `require_once($yii)`:

```
require_once(__DIR__ . '/vendor/autoload.php');
```

Creating the database

With our dependencies and configuration files in place, we can now create our database. Using the `yiic` command, create a migration called users and a migration called reminders.

The users migration

The users migration will create the `users` database and ensure that no duplicate e-mail address can be entered at the database level. Within the `protected/migrations` folder, open up the users migration:

In the `up()` method, add the following:

```
$this->createTable('users', array(
    'id'        => 'pk',
    'email'     => 'string',
    'password'  => 'string',
    'created'   => 'integer',
    'updated'   => 'integer'
));
```

> You may notice that the column types we selected do not match up with MySQL column types. This is because we are allowing Yii to determine the appropriate column type for the database adapter we are using. This allows interoperability between multiple database drivers, meaning that we could seamlessly swap the underlying database technology from a MySQL database to a SQLite or Postgres database without having to change our migrations. The Yii manual has more information about valid column types at http://www.yiiframework.com/doc/api/1.1/CDbSchema#getColumnType-detail.

Next, we want to create a unique index on the `email` column, which we can do as follows:

```
$this->createIndex('email_index', 'users', 'email', true);
```

Finally, in the `down()` method, add a call to drop the `users` table:

```
$this->dropTable('users');
```

The reminders and events migration

Now, we'll create reminders and events migrations that will create the `reminders` and `events` table in our database. These two tables will store the bulk of the data for our application.

1. In our reminders migration, add the following to the `up()` method to create the `events` table:

    ```
    $this->createTable('events', array(
        'id'       => 'pk',
        'user_id'  => 'integer',
        'title'    => 'string',
    ```

```
    'data'      => 'text',
    'time'      => 'integer',
    'created'   => 'integer',
    'updated'   => 'integer'
));
```

2. Then create a foreign key relationship between `events` and `users`:

   ```
   $this->addForeignKey('event_users', 'events', 'user_id', 'users',
   'id', NULL, 'CASCADE', 'CASCADE');
   ```

3. Then create the `reminders` table, as follows:

   ```
   $this->createTable('reminders', array(
       'id'         => 'pk',
       'event_id'   => 'integer',
       'offset'     => 'integer',
       'time'       => 'integer',
       'created'    => 'integer',
       'updated'    => 'integer'
   ));
   ```

4. Finally, create a foreign key relationship between `reminders` and `events`:

   ```
   $this->addForeignKey('reminder_events', 'reminders', 'event_id',
   'events', 'id', NULL, 'CASCADE', 'CASCADE');
   ```

Notice that for both foreign keys, we want everything to be removed if a parent record is removed. For instance, if we delete an event, all reminders associated with that event should be removed as well. And if a user is deleted, all events and all reminders associated with those events should also be removed.

Then, to the `down()` method, add the following to drop the foreign keys and the tables. Once data has been added to our database, we won't be able to drop the tables until the foreign key relationships have been removed:

```
$this->dropForeignKey('event_users', 'events');
$this->dropForeignKey('reminder_events', 'reminders');
$this->dropTable('events');
$this->dropTable('reminders');
```

Once everything has been added, apply the migrations.

Creating models

By now, you should be familiar with using the Gii tool to create models for our newly created tables. Go ahead and create the models for `Users`, `Reminders`, and `Events`. After creating each model, there are several changes we need to make to each of them.

Model behaviors

The first change that will need to be made to our newly created models is the automatic setting of the created and updated timestamp. In previous chapters, we modified the `beforeSave()` method to do this; however, Yii provides an easier way to implement this feature that is database-agnostic and reduces the amount of code we have to add to our models. To do this, we are going to attach a behavior to each of our models.

Behaviors in Yii are objects that have methods that can be attached to a component (in our case, a model). These behaviors then listen for certain events on the attached component (such as the `beforeSave()` method) and execute when that event is triggered.

The behavior that we'll be adding to each of our models is called `CTimestampBehavior` and provides the necessary tools to automatically set the created and updated time. To attach this behavior, simply add the following method to our `Users.php`, `Events.php`, and `Reminders.php` files within the `protected/models` directory:

```php
public function behaviors()
{
    return array(
        'CTimestampBehavior' => array(
            'class'           => 'zii.behaviors.CTimestampBehavior',
            'createAttribute' => 'created',
            'updateAttribute' => 'updated',
            'setUpdateOnCreate' => true
        )
    );
}
```

> More information about `CTimestampBehavior` can be found in the Yii documentation available at http://www.yiiframework.com/doc/api/1.1/CTimestampBehavior/.

The Users model

The first change we'll need to make to our Users model is the definition of the relations between users and events. If you used Gii to generate the models, it must have prepopulated the `relations()` method for you. Otherwise, add the following method to the `Users.php` model at `protected/models/`:

```
public function relations()
{
   return array(
      'events' => array(self::HAS_MANY, 'Events', 'user_id'),
   );
}
```

Next, we'll need to add a private attribute to our model that will store the old attributes of our model so that we can compare previous values to changed values without having to requery the database. Have a look at the following line of code:

```
private $_oldAttributes = array();
```

We can automatically populate this attribute by adding an `afterFind()` method to our model:

```
public function afterFind()
{
   if ($this !== NULL)
      $this->_oldAttributes = $this->attributes;
   return parent::afterFind();
}
```

Finally, we'll want to add a `beforeSave()` method to our model that will not modify the user's password if we change the user's e-mail address, and that will properly encrypt the password if we do change it:

```
public function beforeSave()
{
   if ($this->password == NULL)
      $this->password = $this->_oldAttributes['password'];
   else
      $this->password = password_hash($this->password, PASSWORD_BCRYPT, array('cost' => 13));

   return parent::beforeSave();
}
```

Bcrypt password hashing

When storing passwords in a database, it is extremely important that you store those passwords in such a way that makes it easy for us to verify that the user provided the right password but makes it difficult for attackers to guess the password. Since most users use the same e-mail address and password for all their online identities, it's extremely important that we keep that information as secure as possible.

One way of doing this is by using a symmetric block cipher cryptographic algorithm, such as Bcrypt. Bcrypt converts plain text passwords into a hash with a salted value, iterated multiple times as defined by a cost factor. When using Bcrypt, the cost factor increased the work effector required to both generate and verify a password. By increasing the time it takes to generate and verify passwords, we can make a brute force attack very costly to a potential attacker. This cost factor also allows us as developers to adjust the difficulty of the password over time as computing power increases.

> You can read more about the password functions that were introduced in PHP 5.5 at http://us2.php.net/manual/en/ref.password.php.

The Reminders model

Next, we need to make a few changes to our Reminders model. First, let's verify that the relations have been properly set up. In protected/models/Reminders.php, add the following:

```
public function relations()
{
   return array(
      'event' => array(self::BELONGS_TO, 'Events', 'event_id'),
   );
}
```

Then, add a beforeValidate() method to convert the user submitted time to an integer timestamp and to store the offset time as UTC in our database:

```
public function beforeValidate()
{
   $this->time = (int)strtotime($this->time);
   $this->offset = ($this->offset*60 + $this->time);

   return parent::beforeValidate();
}
```

The Events model

Next, we're going to add and update several methods in our `protected/models/Events.php` model. The steps are as follows:

1. First verify that the relations have been properly set up:

   ```
   public function relations()
   {
      return array(
          'user' => array(self::BELONGS_TO, 'Users', 'user_id'),
          'reminders' => array(self::HAS_MANY, 'Reminders', 'event_id'),
      );
   }
   ```

2. Then add a `beforeValidate()` method to automatically adjust the submission and time and to automatically set the user to the currently logged-in user:

   ```
   public function beforeValidate()
   {
      $this->time = (int)strtotime($this->time);

      // Set the user_id to be the current user
      $this->user_id = Yii::app()->user->id;

      return parent::beforeValidate();
   }
   ```

   > `Yii::app()->user` is a reference to a `CWebUser` object that will handle the identity of our user once we are authenticated. To read more about `CWebUser`, check out http://www.yiiframework.com/doc/api/1.1/CWebUser.

3. Next, add the following getter method to our model. This method will allow us to retrieve the requested data from the URL to search against our events database:

   ```
   private function getDate()
   {
       if (isset($_GET['date']))
           return $_GET['date'];

       return gmdate("Y-m-d");
   }
   ```

4. Then, we're going to update our model's `search()` method to enable us to search for all events that occur between a certain time, specifically over the period of a single day. Modify the method signature to look as follows:

   ```
   public function search($between = false)
   ```

5. Then, add the following before the method returns:

   ```
   if ($between)
       $criteria->addBetweenCondition('time', strtotime($this-
   >getDate() . ' 00:00:00'), strtotime($this->getDate() . '
   23:59:59'));
   ```

Searching for events and displaying them

Before we get too involved with our controllers, let's take a look at what our frontend will look like to search for and display events as it will help to explain the model changes to the Events model and will help us identify what we still need to implement. Have a look at the following screenshot:

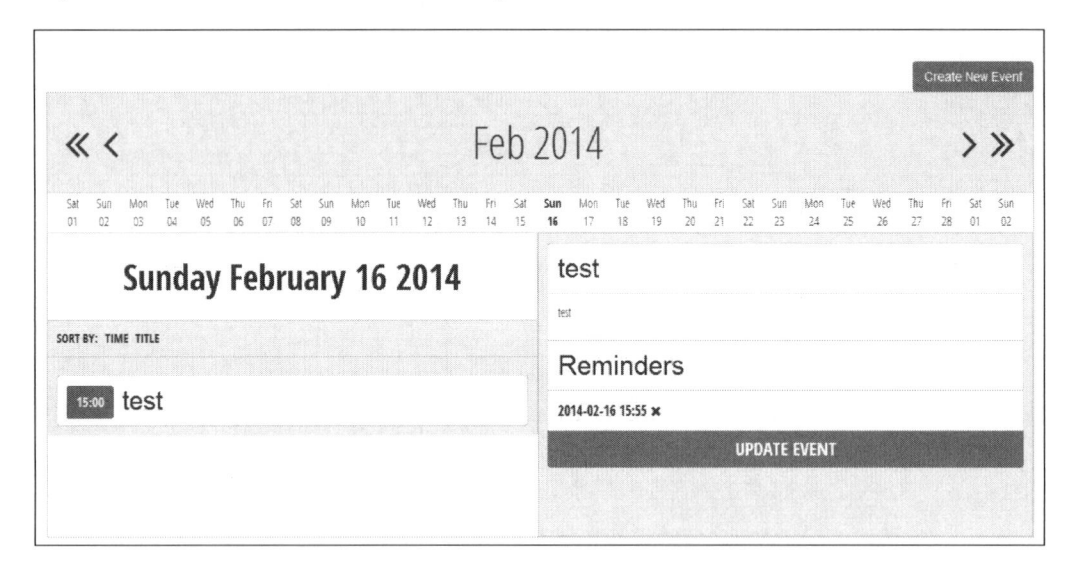

Our frontend view is broken down into several different components. First, we have a button in the top-right corner that should link to a simple CRUD form to create and update events. We also have a month and year picker that shows the current selected year and allows us to advance forwards or backwards in time by one month or one year increments. Directly below that, we have a date picker that shows the currently selected date (or the current date if none is selected) with fifteen days on each side of it.

On the left-hand side, we have the currently selected date displayed in text, followed by a sorter for both time and title of the events displayed below it, which occur on the selected day.

Finally, on the right-hand side, we have an Ajax view, which will appear when an event is clicked on showing the event details as well as all reminders associated with that event with some extra functionality to immediately remove that reminder. Additionally, we'll be providing the user with a link to edit the selected event.

To achieve this level of functionality, we're going to have to create a custom list view, which will extend `CListView`, add a custom URL route, and create several new controller methods. Let's get started.

Custom routing for dates

The first change that we'll need to make is a change to the `urlManager` in our main configuration file. Within the `urlManager['rules']` array, add the following route:

```
'event/date/<date:[\w-]+>' => 'event/index',
```

This custom route will allow us to arbitrarily set a date string in the URL and pass it as a `$_GET` parameter automatically to the `indexAction()` method of our `EventController` class, which we will create shortly.

Creating the controller for events

Let's move on to our `EventController`. This controller will handle all of the actions necessary for working with events in our application. Create a new file in `protected/controllers` called `EventController.php` that has the following class definition:

```
<?php class EventController extends CController{}
```

Perform the following steps:

1. The first method we should create is our `indexAction()`. The `$_GET` parameters passed to this method will determine what events will ultimately be displayed on the page. To do this, we'll take advantage of our event model's `search()` method. When searching, we'll also want to ensure that we only display data for the currently logged-in user:

   ```
   public function actionIndex()
   {
       $model = new Events('search');
       $model->unsetAttributes();

       if (isset($_GET['Events']))
   ```

Scheduled Reminders

```
        $model->attributes = $_GET['Events'];

    $model->user_id = Yii::app()->user->id;

    $this->render('index', array('model' => $model));
}
```

2. Next, we need to create a utility method to load our model by a given primary key. We'll be using this method throughout our model:

```
private function loadModel($id)
{
    if ($id == NULL)
        throw new CHttpException(400, 'Bad Request');

    $model = Events::model()->findByPk($id);

    if ($model == NULL)
        throw new CHttpException(404, 'No model with that ID was found');

    return $model;
}
```

3. Finally, we need to create an AJAX method to display the details of a particular event within our list view:

```
public function actionDetails($id = NULL)
{
    if (Yii::app()->request->isAjaxRequest)
    {
        $model = $this->loadModel($id);

        $this->renderPartial('details', array('model' => $model));
        Yii::app()->end();
    }
     Throw new CHttpException(400, 'Bad Request');
}
```

4. While we are in our `EventController`, it's worthwhile implementing the remaining functionality necessary to both save and delete events. Our `save()` method will simply accept the `$_POST` input from the view file and should look as follows:

```
public function actionSave($id = NULL)
{
    if ($id != NULL)
        $model = $this->loadModel($id);
    else
        $model = new Events;
```

```
    if (isset($_POST['Events']))
    {
        $model->attributes = $_POST['Events'];

        if ($model->save())
            $this->redirect($this->createUrl('/event/save',
array('id' => $model->id)));
    }

    $this->render('save', array('model' => $model));
}
```

5. Finally, there's our `delete()` method, which will facilitate the deletion of events:

```
public function actionDelete($id = NULL)
{
    $model = $this->loadModel($id);

    if ($model->delete())
        $this->redirect($this->createUrl('/event'));

    throw new CHttpException(400, 'Bad Request');
}
```

Creating the reminders controller

The next controller we'll want to implement is our `ReminderController`. Unlike our `EventController`, this controller should only serve AJAX responses and won't require any views.

We'll start by creating a new file at `protected/controllers` called `ReminderController.php` and have the class extend `CController`. Perform the following steps:

1. First, we'll want to make sure that only POST requests are sent to this controller. An easy way to force all requests to the controller to be POST requests is by checking the request type before each action runs. We can implement that check by using the `beforeAction()` method:

```
public function beforeAction($action)
{
    if (!Yii::app()->request->isPostRequest)
        throw new CHttpException(400, 'Bad Request');

    return parent::beforeAction($action);
}
```

Scheduled Reminders

2. Next, we should implement a method to load a particular reminder and another method to verify that we have access to the associated event for a particular reminder, as follows:

```
private function loadEvent($event_id)
{
   $event = Events::model()->findByPk($event_id);
   if ($event == NULL)
      return false;

   if ($event->user_id != Yii::app()->user->id)
      return false;

   return true;
}

private function loadModel($id)
{
   if ($id == NULL)
      throw new CHttpException(400, 'Bad Request');

   $model = Reminders::model()->findByPk($id);

   if ($model == NULL)
      throw new CHttpException(404, 'No model with that ID was found');

   return $model;
}
```

3. We'll then add in the functionality necessary to delete a reminder:

```
public function actionDelete($id = NULL)
{
   $model = $this->loadModel($id);

   if (!$this->loadEvent($model->event_id))
      return false;

   if ($model->delete())
```

```
        return true;

    throw new CHttpException(400, 'Bad Request');
}
```

4. Finally, we'll add in the functionality necessary to save and modify a reminder:

```
public function actionSave($id = NULL)
{
    if ($id != NULL)
        $model = $this->loadModel($id);
    else
        $model = new Reminders;

    if (isset($_POST['Reminders']))
    {
        $model->attributes = $_POST['Reminders'];

        if (!$this->loadEvent($model->event_id))
            return false;

        if ($model->save())
            return true;
        else
            throw new CHttpException(400, print_r($model->getErrors(), true));
    }

    return true;
}
```

Our `save()` method is built to allow reminders to both be created and modified through a single action rather than multiple actions.

Creating the layout

The first view that we should implement is our `main.php` file at `views/layouts/`. Since this file will look identical to the layout we created in the previous two chapters, copy the `views/layouts/main.php` file from the project resources folder into your application.

Creating the main view

Next, we'll implement our list view that will display all of our events. To do this, we'll be extending the `CListView` class. Perform the following steps:

1. First, create the view file `index.php` in `protected/views/events` that will call this custom class, and then add a button to allow the user to create a new event:

   ```
   <?php echo CHtml::link('Create New Event', $this->createUrl('/event/save'), array('class' => 'pull-right btn btn-primary')); ?>
   <div class="clearfix"></div>
   ```

2. Then, add the following to implement the list view. First, we'll need to instantiate a new widget that will contain our custom list view:

   ```
   <?php $this->widget('application.components.EventListView', array(
   ```

3. After that, we'll need to specify `dataProvider` that will populate our model. This is where our previous changes to the event model's `search()` method come into play:

   ```
   'dataProvider'=>$model->search(true),
   ```

4. Next, we'll want to specify the template that our list view will use and also the element tag our list view should be contained in:

   ```
   'template' => '{items}',
   'itemsTagName' => 'ul',
   ```

5. Then, we'll enable sorting with the list view and specify which model attributes can be sorted against:

   ```
   'enableSorting' => true,
   'sortableAttributes' => array(
       'time',
       'title'
   ),
   ```

6. Finally, we'll need to specify `itemView`, which will define what each item in our list will look like:

   ```
   'itemView'=>'_event'
   ));
   ```

At the end of this file, we should also register the CSS that will be used to make our view look pretty in addition to creating the CSS file `/css/calendar.css` so that Yii doesn't throw an error during the next steps. Please refer to the source code of this chapter to retrieve the `calendar.css` file:

```
Yii::app()->clientScript->registerCssFile(Yii::app()->baseUrl . '/css/calendar.css');
```

Creating the item view

The next file that we need to create is our `itemView` file, `protected/views/events/_event.php`, as follows:

```
<li class="event" data-attr-id="<?php echo $data->id; ?>">
    <div class="time"><?php echo gmdate("H:i", $data->time); ?></div>
    <h2 class="title"><?php echo CHtml::encode($data->title); ?></h2>
</li>
```

To save some time later, let's go ahead and implement a view to show the details of a particular event in `protected/views/events/details.php`. We'll add the JavaScript bindings to show this when we create `EventListView`. Grab this file from the project resources folder, and add it into your application.

Creating the event list view

With our views in place, we now need to implement our `EventListView` that will display our calendar picker and our events. The steps are as follows:

1. To do this, create a new file in `protected/components` called `EventListView.php`. This class should extend `CListView`, which we will have to explicitly load to make Yii aware of it. By extending `CListView`, we immediately get access to several useful functions, such as sorting and displaying our events:

   ```
   <?php
   Yii::import('zii.widgets.CListView');
   class EventListView extends CListView {}
   ```

2. Next, we'll need to create another custom getter to retrieve the current date from the URL:

   ```
   public function getDate()
   {
       if (isset($_GET['date']))
           return $_GET['date'];

       return gmdate("Y-m-d");
   }
   ```

Scheduled Reminders

3. Now, we're going to overload the `CListView` `renderItems()` method, which will allow us to display our events as we like. To do this, create the `renderItems()` method, as follows:

   ```
   public function renderItems()
   {
      echo CHtml::openTag('div', array('class' => 'event_container'));
      echo CHtml::closeTag('div');
   }
   ```

4. Within the `events_container` div that we just created, we need to add our month/year picker. These links will determine what the next and previous month and year are by the current date, which it will retrieve from the `getDate()` method we defined earlier:

   ```
   echo CHtml::openTag('div', array('class' => 'month_year_picker'));
      echo CHtml::link(NULL, $this->controller->createUrl('/event', array('date' => gmdate("Y-m-d", strtotime($this->date ." previous year")))), array('class' => 'fa fa-angle-double-left pull-left'));
      echo CHtml::link(NULL, $this->controller->createUrl('/event', array('date' => gmdate("Y-m-d", strtotime($this->date ." previous month")))), array('class' => 'fa fa-angle-left pull-left'));
      echo CHtml::tag('span', array(), date('M Y', strtotime($this->date)));
      echo CHtml::link(NULL, $this->controller->createUrl('/event', array('date' => gmdate("Y-m-d", strtotime($this->date ." next year")))), array('class' => 'fa fa-angle-double-right pull-right'));
      echo CHtml::link(NULL, $this->controller->createUrl('/event', array('date' => gmdate("Y-m-d", strtotime($this->date ." next month")))), array('class' => 'fa fa-angle-right pull-right'));
   echo CHtml::closeTag('div');
   ```

5. Immediately following this closing `div`, we then need to add our date picker that will show 15 days on each side of the currently selected date. We can implement that as follows:

   ```
   echo CHtml::openTag('div', array('class' => 'day_picker'));
      echo CHtml::openTag('ul');
         $this->renderDays(gmdate('Y-m-d', strtotime($this->date . ' -15 days')), $this->date);
         $this->renderDays($this->date, gmdate('Y-m-d', strtotime($this->date . ' +15 days')));
      echo CHtml::closeTag('ul');
   echo CHtml::closeTag('div');
   ```

6. To make our lives easier, we can create a utility method that will display a range of dates for us automatically, called `renderDays()`. This will allow our code to be more readable and easier to debug should we need to. This method should accept two arguments: a start date and an end date:

```
private function renderDays($start, $end)
{
    $start     = new DateTime($start);
    $end       = new DateTime($end);
    $interval  = new DateInterval('P1D');
    $period    = new DatePeriod($start, $interval, $end);

    foreach ($period as $dt)
        $this->renderDay($dt->format('Y-m-d'));
}
```

7. Then, we'll need to create another utility method to display a particular date and provide a link to it:

```
private function renderDay($date)
{
    $class = 'day';
    if ($this->date == $date)
        $class .= ' selected';
    echo CHtml::openTag('li', array('class' => $class));
        echo CHtml::tag('span', array('class' => 'day_string'), gmdate('D', strtotime($date)));
        echo CHtml::link(date('d', strtotime($date)), $this->controller->createUrl('/event', array('date' => gmdate('Y-m-d', strtotime($date)))), array('class' => 'day_date'));
    echo CHtml::closeTag('li');
}
```

The final part of our custom view is a container to display the sorter, the items, and the details for a particular item. We should add the `day_picker` div immediately that we opened earlier. Because we took advantage of `CListView`, we can simply reference the parent class' `renderItems()` method to display all of our items, and the parent class' `renderSorter()` method to display the sorter according to the configuration we passed in our index view:

```
echo CHtml::openTag('div', array('class' => 'outer_container'));
    echo CHtml::openTag('div', array('class' => 'inner_container'));
        echo CHtml::openTag('div', array('class' => 'selected_date'));
            echo CHtml::tag('span', array('class' => 'selected_date_date'), gmdate("l F d Y", strtotime($this->date)));
        echo CHtml::closeTag('div');
```

Scheduled Reminders

```
        $this->renderSorter();
        parent::renderItems();
    echo CHtml::closeTag('div');

    // Details container is populated via Ajax Request
    echo CHtml::tag('div', array('class' => 'details'), NULL);
    echo CHtml::tag('div', array('class' => 'clearfix'), NULL);
    echo CHtml::closeTag('div');
```

Then, let's add some AJAX to display the details of an event when we click on an event and to remove a reminder if the event has any attached to it. We can add this right before we close our `renderItems()` method:

```
Yii::app()->clientScript->registerScript('li_click', '
    $(".items li").click(function() {
        var id = $(this).attr("data-attr-id");
        $.get("/event/details/" + id, function(data) {
            $(".details").replaceWith(data);

            $(".fa-times").click(function() {
                var id = $(this).parent().attr("id");
                var self = $(this).parent();
                $.post("/reminder/delete/id/" + id, function() {
                    $(self).remove();
                })
            });
        });
    });
');
```

Once you've added the CSS from the `calendar.css` file in the associated project source code, our view should be complete. Have a look at the following screenshot:

Creating and saving events

Now that we have a way to display events, we need to actually create them. This view will allow us to both save events as well as dynamically add multiple reminders to an existing event. Begin by creating `protected/views/events/save.php`, as follows:

1. First we're going to create the functionality necessary to modify the core attributes of the event: the title, date, and time:

    ```
    <h3><?php echo $model->isNewRecord ? 'Create New' : 'Update'; ?>
    Event</h3>
    <?php $form=$this->beginWidget('CActiveForm', array(
       'id'=>'project-form',
       'htmlOptions' => array(
          'class' => 'form-horizontal',
          'role' => 'form'
       )
    )); ?>
       <?php echo $form->errorSummary($model); ?>

       <div class="form-group">
          <?php echo $form->labelEx($model,'title', array('class' =>
    'col-sm-2 control-label')); ?>
          <div class="col-sm-10">
             <?php echo $form->textField($model,'title', array('class'
    => 'form-control')); ?>
          </div>
       </div>

       <div class="form-group">
          <?php echo $form->labelEx($model,'data', array('class' =>
    'col-sm-2 control-label')); ?>
          <div class="col-sm-10">
             <?php echo $form->textArea($model,'data', array('class'
    => 'form-control')); ?>
          </div>
       </div>

       <div class="form-group">
          <?php echo $form->labelEx($model,'time', array('class' =>
    'col-sm-2 control-label')); ?>
          <div class="col-sm-10">
             <div class="input-append date">
                <?php echo $form->textField($model, 'time',
    array('value' => $model->isNewRecord ? NULL : gmdate('Y-m-d
    H:i:s', $model->time), 'class' => 'form-control')); ?>
    ```

Scheduled Reminders

```
        </div>
      </div>
   </div>
```

2. Next, we'll want to display all of the reminders attached to our event if the event has been created. Since we've already established a relationship between reminders and events, we can do this simply by iterating through the `$events->reminders` relations, which will be populated with all of the reminders associated with our event:

```
<?php if (!$model->isNewRecord): ?>
    <input type="hidden" id="event_id" value="<?php echo $model->id; ?>" />
    <hr />
    <h3>Reminders</h3>
    <div class="reminders_container">
        <?php foreach ($model->reminders as $reminder): ?>
            <div class="form-group">
                <?php echo CHtml::tag('label', array('class' => 'col-sm-2 control-label'), 'Reminder'); ?>
                <div class="col-sm-9">
                    <?php echo CHtml::tag('input', array(
                        'id' => $reminder->id,
                        'name' => 'Reminders[' . $reminder->id . '][time]',
                        'class' => 'form-control',
                        'value' => gmdate('Y-m-d H:i:s', $reminder->time)
                    ), NULL); ?>
                </div>
                <span class="fa fa-times"></span>
            </div>
        <?php endforeach; ?>
    </div>
<?php endif; ?>
```

3. Within this `if` clause, we'll also want to create a template reminder that we can attach and clone with JavaScript. This will allow us to create as many reminders as we want for our events:

```
<div class="form-group template" style="display:none">
    <?php echo CHtml::tag('label', array('class' => 'col-sm-2 control-label'), 'Reminder'); ?>
    <div class="col-sm-9">
        <?php echo CHtml::tag('input', array(
            'id' => NULL,
            'name' => 'Reminders[0][time]',
```

```
            'class' => 'form-control'
        ), NULL); ?>
    </div>
</div>
```

4. Finally, we need to add some buttons and close our widget:

   ```
   <div class="row buttons">
       <?php echo CHtml::submitButton($model->isNewRecord ? 'Create'
   : 'Save', array('class' => 'btn btn-primary pull-right col-md-
   offset-1')); ?>

       <?php if (!$model->isNewRecord): ?>
           <?php echo CHtml::link('Delete Event', $this->createUrl('/
   event/delete', array('id' => $model->id)), array('class' => 'btn
   btn-danger pull-right col-md-offset-1')); ?>
           <?php echo CHtml::link('Add Reminder', '#', array('class' =>
   'btn btn-success pull-right', 'id' => 'add_reminder')); ?>
       <?php endif; ?>
   </div>
   <?php $this->endWidget(); ?>
   ```

In its present state, our time fields aren't very user friendly as the user has to manually enter a specific date timestamp, such as `2014-02-21 19:50:00`. To make this experience easier on our users, we can download a plugin from GitHub called bootstrap-datetimepicker. Simply clone the repository to the `/js` directory of the application using `git` or download the package directly:

`git clone https://github.com/smalot/bootstrap-datetimepicker`

Then, register the relevant CSS and JavaScript:

```
<?php Yii::app()->clientScript->registerCssFile(Yii::app()->baseUrl .
'/js/bootstrap-datetimepicker/css/bootstrap-datetimepicker.min.css');
?>
<?php Yii::app()->clientScript->registerScriptFile(Yii::app()->baseUrl
. '/js/bootstrap-datetimepicker/js/bootstrap-datetimepicker.js',
CClientScript::POS_END); ?>
```

Finally, we can add the JavaScript bindings necessary to display the date time picker and to dynamically add new reminders. Within the project resources folder, copy the remaining JavaScript code from the `save.php` file at `protected/views/events/` into this file.

Since we've already created all the necessary controller actions to save and display events, we can now create and modify new events, add reminders, and view them in the interface that we built earlier. Check it out!

Creating the controller to manage users

Next, we'll need to implement the necessary methods to create and modify users within our application. Since our `users` table doesn't have any concept of roles yet, we'll manage our users from the command line through `CConsoleCommand`. This method will ensure that only authenticated users (users who have access to our server) can modify the user's information. In a real-world application, this functionality can be moved to a secured `UsersController` in our application.

Creating users

To start with our user management, create a new console command in `protected/commands/UserCommand.php`, and add the following:

```php
<?php class UserCommand extends CConsoleCommand {}
```

The `CConsoleCommand` class is very similar to our controllers. In that, we can define actions that we want to run as well as any parameters that we want added. The first action we should create is an action to create our users. Since we've already set up our Users model to handle the appropriate password hashing, we can simply use the following:

```php
public function actionCreateUser($email, $password)
{
    $model = new Users;
    $model->attributes = array(
        'email' => $email,
        'password' => $password
    );

    if (!$model->validate())
        echo "Missing Required Attribute\n";
    else
    {
        try {
            if ($model->save())
                echo "User Created\n";
            else
                print_r($model->getErrors);
```

```
            return;
        } catch (Exception $e) {
            print_r($e->getMessage());
        }
    }
}
```

We can then create new users from the command line, as follows:

`php protected/yiic.php user createuser --email=test@test.com --password=password123`

If successful, the command will output `User Created`; otherwise, it will return an error.

Deleting users

Deletion of users can also be a callable action that takes a user's e-mail address as an argument:

```
public function actionDeleteUser($email)
{
    $model = Users::model()->findByAttributes(array('email' => $email));
    if ($model == NULL)
    {
        echo "No user with that email was found.\n";
        return 0;
    }

    if ($model->delete())
        echo "User has been deleted.\n";
    else
        echo "User could not be deleted.\n";
}
```

We can then call the action we just created by running the following command from our command line:

`php protected/yiic.php user deleteuser --email=test@test.com`

Changing the user's password

Next, we'll want to provide the functionality to change a user's password. Before we change the user's password, we need to verify the user's identity. Usually, we accomplish this by verifying that they have the password to their account. We can implement this, as follows, within protected/commands/UserCommand.php:

```php
public function actionChangePassword($email, $oldPassword,
$newPassword)
{
    $model = Users::model()->findByAttributes(array('email' =>
$email));

    if ($model == NULL)
    {
        echo "No user with that email was found.\n";
        return 0;
    }

    if (password_verify($oldPassword, $model->password))
    {
        $model->password = password_hash($newPassword, PASSWORD_BCRYPT,
array('cost' => 13));

        if ($model->save())
            echo "Password has been changed.\n";
        else
            echo "Password could not be changed.\n";
    }
    else
        echo "Unable to Verify Old Password.\n";
}
```

Once again, we're taking advantage of PHP's password_* functions, which include the ability to verify a password:

```php
if (password_verify($oldPassword, $model->password))
```

Assuming the user's password is valid, we can then hash the password they provided on the command line and store it with the model:

```php
$model->password = password_hash($newPassword, PASSWORD_BCRYPT,
array('cost' => 13));
```

From the command line, this command can be run as follows:

```
php protected/yiic.php user changepassword --email=test@test.com
--oldpassword=password123 --newpassword=newsecurepassword
```

> While managing users from the command line is simple, it isn't very secure because user's passwords may be stored in plain text in your terminal's command history. In a real-world application, consider managing users from a web interface over a secure connection.

Authenticating with Bcrypt

The last thing that we need to implement for our users is authentication. To do this, we'll expand upon the authentication process we developed in *Chapter 1, A Task-management Application*, and modify it to work with our Bcrypt hashed passwords.

First, copy the following files from the source code of *Chapter 1, A Task-management Application* (or from the source code in this chapter) into our project:

- css/signin.css
- protected/views/layouts/signin.php
- protected/views/site/login.php
- protected/models/LoginForm.php
- protected/controllers/SiteController.php
- protected/components/UserIdentity.php

Since the majority of the work involved in authenticating a user is done, the only changes we need to make to our authentication process is in our UserIdentity class. Begin by opening up protected/components/UserIdentity.php. We'll start by defining the class as follows:

> Yii may have already generated this file for you. If so, delete the contents of it entirely, and follow the instructions as outlined in this section.

```
class UserIdentity extends CUserIdentity {}
```

Scheduled Reminders

Perform the following steps:

1. First, we want to ensure that each user's ID from the database is stored with our `WebUser` property. To do this, create a new private attribute called `$_id`:

   ```
   private $_id;
   ```

2. Then, create a getter to retrieve it:

   ```
   public function getId()
   {
       return $this->_id;
   }
   ```

3. Next, we need to define our `authenticate()` method that will be called from `LoginForm`:

   ```
   public function authenticate() {}
   ```

4. Within this method, we'll need to find the appropriate user model using the e-mail address that was provided to us by the user through `LoginForm`:

   ```
   $record = Users::model()->findByAttributes(array('email'=>$this->username));
   ```

5. With this information, we can then verify that a user with that e-mail address exists:

   ```
   if ($record == NULL)
       $this->errorCode = self::ERROR_UNKNOWN_IDENTITY;
   ```

6. Then, we need to verify that the user's password matches the one we have on record. If it does, we should make sure that no errors are returned to the `LoginForm` and set the `WebUser` ID:

   ```
   else if (password_verify($this->password, $record->password))
   {
       $this->errorCode = self::ERROR_NONE;
       $this->_id       = $record->id;
   }
   ```

7. Then, we should reject anything else that comes through the method:

   ```
   else
       $this->errorCode = self::ERROR_UNKNOWN_IDENTITY;
   ```

8. Finally, return the error code back to the `LoginForm`:

   ```
   return !$this->errorCode;
   ```

> In a real-world application, we will want to expose as little information as possible about a potential login attempt to the user or a potential attacker, which is why we return ERROR_UNKNOWN_IDENTITY. During debugging of your application, you may find it useful to return either ERROR_USERNAME_INVALID or ERROR_PASSWORD_INVALID to help you better understand why a login request failed.

Requiring authentication

Finally, we can force our users to authenticate against our database by adding the following to both `EventController` and `ReminderController`:

```
public function filters()
{
    return array(
        'accessControl',
    );
}

public function accessRules()
{
    return array(
        array('allow',
            'users'=>array('@'),
        ),
        array('deny',   // deny all users
            'users'=>array('*'),
        ),
    );
}
```

Sending e-mail reminders

At this point, users can create new events and reminders for themselves through our web interface; however, they aren't able to receive these reminders yet. To send out these reminders, we'll create a new console command called `RemindersCommand` in `protected/commands/RemindersCommand.php`. When we're done, we'll be able to add this command to either our crontab or to our scheduled tasks and have it automatically process reminders in the background.

Scheduled Reminders

Once the `RemindersCommand` file has been created, create the class definition in addition to an action to send the reminders that takes a time interval as an argument. This interval will define the length of time in minutes that we should run our command for. It will find all of the reminders within that interval's timeframe to process:

```php
class RemindersCommand extends CConsoleCommand
{
    public function actionSendReminders($interval) {}
}
```

Within our action, define the UNIX timestamp that we should begin at as well as the time we should end at for the particular interval we are working with. The end time should be all microseconds before the next interval begins so that we do not send duplicate reminders out:

```php
$time = time();
$start = $time - ($time % $interval * 60);
$end = $start + (($interval *60) - 1));
```

With our time interval defined, we can now create a database search criteria with `CDBCriteria` that we can pass to our reminders `find()` method:

```php
$criteria = new CDbCriteria;
$criteria->addBetweenCondition('offset', $start, $end);
$reminders = Reminders::model()->findAll($criteria);
```

The `find()` method will return all reminders within the time interval that we specified. We can now simply iterate through the `$reminders` array and send an e-mail to the user the reminder belongs to:

```php
foreach ($reminders as $reminder)
{
    // Load the PHPMailer Class
    $mail = new PHPMailer;

    // Tell PHP Mailer to use SMTP with authentication
    $mail->isSMTP();
    $mail->SMTPAuth = true;

    // Specify the Host and Port we should connect to
    $mail->Host = Yii::app()->params['smtp']['host'];
    $mail->Port = Yii::app()->params['smtp']['port'];

    // Specify the username and password we should use
```

```
    // (if required by our SMTP server)
    $mail->Username = Yii::app()->params['smtp']['username'];
    $mail->Password = Yii::app()->params['smtp']['password'];

    // Set the security type of required
    $mail->SMTPSecure = 'tls';

    // Set the from and to addresses
    $mail->from = Yii::app()->params['smtp']['from'];
    $mail->addAddress($reminder->event->user->email);

    // This should be an HTML email
    $mail->isHTML(true);

    // Set the subject and body
    $mail->Subject ='Reminder from Scheduled Reminders';
    $mail->Body = 'This is a reminder that '.$reminder->event->title.' is due on '. gmdate("Y-m-d H:i UTC", $reminder->offset) . '. This event has the following details:<br />' . $reminder->event->data;

    // Then send the email
    if (!$mail->send())
        echo $mail->ErrorInfo . "\n";
    else
        echo ".";
}
```

> If you are using a remote SMTP server and have already populated your `protected/config/params.php` file with your SMTP information, the previous code should work for you. If you're using a local mail server, such as Postfix or another setup, be sure to read the PHPMailer documentation at `https://github.com/PHPMailer/PHPMailer` on how to propery configure PHPMailer.

From the command line, we can now send reminders by running the following command (in the example we are using a 5-minute interval):

php protected/yiic.php reminders sendreminder --interval=5

Once you have created events in your database, you can run the command or put this command on your crontab or scheduled tasks and have your application automatically send reminders to your users.

Summary

We covered quite a bit of information in this chapter! We learned how to integrate our application with a MySQL database, started storing user information securely in our database, and expanded upon our knowledge of console commands. We also covered how to add behaviors and how to add relations to our models. Additionally, we went over including Composer and Composer dependencies into our project to reduce the amount of code that have to import manually.

In the next chapter, we'll be expanding on the knowledge we learned and the tools we developed to build even more complex and integrated web applications. Before continuing on, be sure to take a look at all the classes we referenced in the chapter in the official Yii documentation located at `http://www.yiiframework.com/doc/`.

4
Developing an Issue-tracking Application

In the previous chapters, we worked on very simple and practical applications. As we move forward, our applications will become more complex and intricate. For our next project, we will develop an issue-tracking system that will allow customers to report issues and allow us to manage those users and issues from a single application. In this application, we will also provide support to create and update issues over e-mail. Finally, we'll be expanding upon our user management system to allow per-user roles.

In this chapter, we'll cover the following topics:

- Creating a user management interface
- Adding role-based authorization
- Sending and receiving e-mails from a Yii application
- Integrating third-party libraries and tools into our application

Prerequisites

Before we get started, there are a couple of things that we'll need to have set up and working:

- Since we'll send and receive e-mails from our application, we're going to need a registered and active domain name. If you do not already have a working domain name, you can purchase one from a domain registrar such as www.namecheap.com, www.name.com, or www.gandi.net.

- We'll also need the ability to modify the Domain Name System (DNS) records for this domain. For our application to receive e-mails, we'll need to be able to modify the DNS records for our domain. Most registrars provide a rudimentary DNS management system. If yours does not, you can use a free DNS hosting service, such as www.cloudflare.com or http://www.rackspace.com/cloud/dns.

- Next, you'll need to have a web server with a public facing IP address. This will allow e-mails to be sent to our application. Many cloud **Virtual Private Server** (**VPS**) providers are available to use for low monthly or hourly prices. Such services include www.digitalocean.com, www.linode.com, and http://www.rackspace.com/cloud/servers.

- Rather than create, configure, and maintain our own e-mail server and SMTP relay, we can take advantage of third-party tools and libraries. This will allow us to focus on the development of our application rather than the maintenance of a secondary service. Using this service and its accompanying PHP library, we can take advantage of code that has already been thoroughly tested and vetted, which allows us as developers to get straight to coding. To take advantage of SendGrid, we'll create a free SendGrid developer account, which can be set up at https://www.sendgrid.com/developers. For now, simply set up your account. Later in the chapter, we'll go through the process of setting up our application to receive e-mails from this service.

- In this chapter, we'll once again use the latest version of MySQL (at the time of this writing, MySQL 5.6). Make sure that your MySQL server is set up and running on your server.

- Finally, we'll need to download and install Composer from https://getcomposer.org/.

Once you have acquired everything listed in the preceding steps, create a subdomain on the domain name you are using, and point it to your server. In this chapter, I'll be using chapter4.example.com to refer to this subdomain. After everything is set up and your server is responding to that domain name, we can get started.

Describing the project

Our issue-tracking project can be broken down into the following three main components:

- Users who will create and respond to issues
- Issues that can be updated by the end user or a supporter (a specific type of user that will support our end users)
- A publicly available endpoint for SendGrid to POST to with any emails we may receive

Users

The first component of our application is the user who will be using it. For this application, we will be using the same database structure that we did in *Chapter 3, Scheduled Reminders*, with the addition of a new column called `role_id`, which will allow us to distinguish which position the user has within our application. For this application, we will expand upon our login process to ensure that the user's role is available for us to reference and manipulate within our application.

Roles

Rather than have a single administrator who is capable of managing our system, in this application, we can have multiple users who we can promote or demote to different roles within our application. The role that we associate with our user will allow us to determine what users of that role are permitted to do within our application.

For this application, we will be supporting three basic roles: a customer who will submit issues and updates, a supporter who has the same permissions as a customer in addition to being able to update issues that belong to other customers, and an administrator who has the same permissions as a supporter and can also manage the roles of other users.

To store this information, we'll use a simple roles table in our database setup as follows. We'll then set up a relationship between users and role so that this information is automatically associated with our users.

```
ID INTEGER PRIMARY KEY
name STRING
created INTEGER
updated INTEGER
```

Issues

The second component of our application is the issue that users will create. An issue is an item that can be created either within the application or from outside of it by sending an e-mail to our application. Issues can also be updated from within the application or by an e-mail sent by the customer. Issues will also have a status associated with them that will help our supporters track the current project of a particular issue. The database that we'll be using will look as follows:

```
ID INTEGER PRIMARY KEY
customer_id INTEGER FK
title STRING
```

```
description TEXT
status_id INTEGER FK
created INTEGER
updated INTEGER
```

Statuses

Associated with each issue will be a unique status. These statuses will allow our supporters to track the project of an issue and will allow us to trigger specific events when an issue changes from one status to another. Our table for these records will look identical to our roles table:

```
ID INTEGER PRIMARY KEY
name STRING
created INTEGER
updated INTEGER
```

Updates

Also associated with each issue is an update. Each issue can have one or many updates attached to them, which will allow supporters to see what work has been done to a particular issue and which will serve as a medium for the user to communicate with our supporters. Each update will be associated with both a user and an issue. Our database table for this information will look as follows:

```
ID INTEGER PRIMARY KEY
issue_id INTEGER FK
author_id INTEGER FK
update TEXT
created INTEGER
updated INTEGER
```

Receiving e-mails

The final component of our application will allow customers to create new issues and update existing issues via e-mail. To the end user, this process will feel seamless, yet it will allow our supporters to keep track of the work and updates that are done to a given issue. This custom endpoint will also allow us to seamlessly create new users within our application and associate information with those users as necessary.

Initializing the project

By now, you should be comfortable with creating projects from scratch. To provide us with a common starting ground, a skeleton project has been included with the project resources for this chapter. Included with this skeleton project are the necessary migrations, data files, controllers, and views to get us started. Also included is the login system that we'll use for authentication throughout this chapter.

We'll start by copying the skeleton project included with the chapter resources to our web server and configure it so that it responds to chapter4.example.com as outlined in the beginning of the chapter, and then follow the next steps to make sure everything is set up:

1. Since a skeleton project was provided, begin by adjusting the path to Yii framework in index.php to point to your Yii installation path. At this point, you'll also want to adjust the permissions on the assets and protected/runtime folders.

2. Next, create the MySQL user and database table that our application will use. If you don't want to alter the main configuration file that is provided, the following MySQL commands will create the database and user for you:

   ```
   CREATE USER 'ch4_issue'@'localhost' IDENTIFIED BY 'ch4_issue';
   CREATE DATABASE IF NOT EXISTS `ch4_issue` ;
   GRANT ALL PRIVILEGES ON `ch4\_issue` . * TO 'ch4_issue'@'localhost';
   FLUSH PRIVILEGES;
   ```

3. Next, we'll need to run the initial migrations and then import the sample data that is provided in the protected/data folder. This sample data will allow us to immediately log in to our application and start using it once the application is running. Navigate to the root of the project, and then run the following commands:

   ```
   php protected/yiic.php migrate up --interactive=0
   mysql -u ch4_issue -p ch4_issue < protected/data/combined.sql
   ```

4. We need to update params.php at protected/config/ with our SendGrid information. Your username and password will correspond to your SendGrid username and password. In keeping with our example domain, set the from address to noreply@chapter4.example.com.

5. Finally, we need to install the necessary composer dependencies:

   ```
   composer install
   ```

After performing these steps, you should be able to navigate to `chapter4.example.com` in your browser and see a login page to our application. After logging in to our application using one of the credentials that are provided in the table just after this paragraph, you should see the page following this table load:

Username	Password
customer@example.com	test
supporter@example.com	test
admin@example.com	test

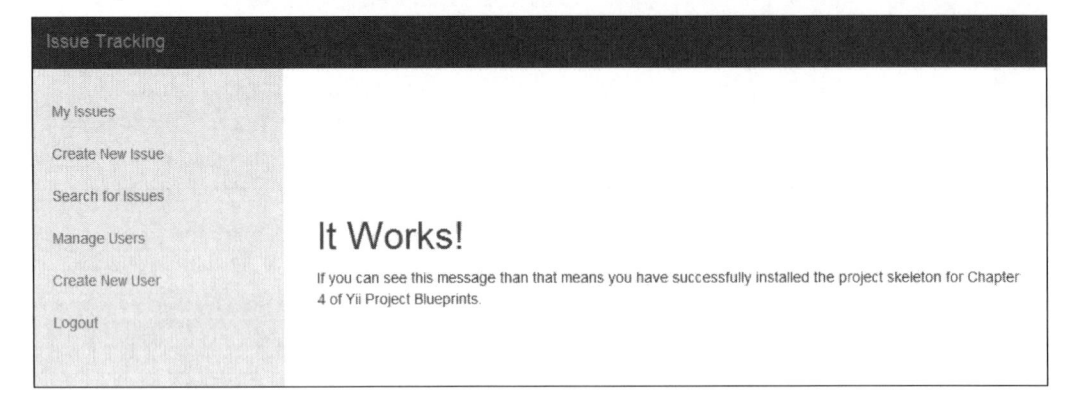

Managing users

Before we can begin working on issues, we first need to make sure that users can be both created and managed from within our application. In *Chapter 3, Scheduled Reminders*, we used a command-line tool to do this. In this chapter, we will create a complete user management tool from a web interface to supplement that tool.

Roles and authentication

Before we get into managing our users, let's take a look at how authentication and roles are handled within our application. Within the `UserController` and `IssueController` provided with the skeleton application is a more complex `accessRules()` method that has a new attribute added to it. Let's take a look at this method within `UserController`:

```
public function accessRules()
{
    return array(
        array('allow',
            'actions' => array('search', 'view'),
```

```
                'users'=>array('@'),
                'expression' => 'Yii::app()->user->role>=2'
            ),
            array('allow',
                'actions' => array('index', 'save', 'delete'),
                'users'=>array('@'),
                'expression' => 'Yii::app()->user->role==3'
            ),
            array('deny',  // deny all users
                'users'=>array('*'),
            ),
        );
    }
```

As you can see, we now have a new attribute called `expression` listed within this method. Internally, Yii will evaluate this expression to a Boolean value. If that expression resolves to true, and the actions and user condition match, then a user is allowed to proceed to the action. In our case, we are checking that `Yii::app()->user->role` has a particular value.

Out of the box, Yii doesn't know what that value should be, so unless we define it, it will be undefined. Since `Yii::app()->user` is a `CWebUser` object, we can add additional information to it when we create the `UserIdentity` component. If we take a look at the `UserIdentity` component supplied with the project, we can see this attribute being added via the `CUserIdentity setState()` method:

```
public function authenticate()
{
    $record = User::model()->findByAttributes(array('email'=>$this->username));

    if ($record == NULL)
        $this->errorCode = self::ERROR_UNKNOWN_IDENTITY;
    else if (password_verify($this->password, $record->password))
    {
        $this->errorCode = self::ERROR_NONE;
        $this->_id              = $record->id;
        $this->setState('email', $record->email);
        $this->setState('role', $record->role_id);
    }
    else
        $this->errorCode = self::ERROR_UNKNOWN_IDENTITY;

    return !$this->errorCode;
}
```

Yii will then store this information within our $_SESSION variable once the user logs in, allowing us to reference it as long as the session is active.

> While using simple Boolean expressions is easy, should we ever want to change which users have access to our system, we would have to refactor our controller methods rather than data in our database. Consider instead creating a model method, such as User::isSupporter() or User::isAdmin(). These methods make it more clear who has access to our actions and will make your application easier to maintain in the future.

Listing users

Now that we know how roles work within our application, let's start building our controller methods for our `UserController`. Open `protected/controllers/UserController.php`, and you can see that we already have definitions for the methods we will be implementing.

To display a list of our users, we'll be using the `User::search()` method within our controller and a `CGridView` widget within our view:

```php
public function actionIndex()
{
    $users = new User('search');
    $users->unsetAttributes();
    
    if (isset($_GET['User']))
        $users->attributes = $_GET['Users'];
    
    $this->render('index', array(
        'model' => $users
    ));
}
```

Within our `index.php` file at `views/user/`, we'll load a `CGridView` instance:

```php
<h3>Manage Users</h3>
<?php $this->widget('zii.widgets.grid.CGridView', array(
    'itemsCssClass' => 'table table-striped',
    'enableSorting' => true,
    'dataProvider'  =>$model->search(),
```

```
    'columns' => array(
        'id',
        'email',
        'name',
       array(
            'class'=>'CButtonColumn',
            'template' => '{view}{update}{delete}',
            'viewButtonOptions' => array(
                'class' => 'fa fa-search'
            ),
            'viewButtonLabel' => false,
            'viewButtonImageUrl' => false,
            'viewButtonUrl' => 'Yii::app()->createUrl("user/view",
 array("id" => "$data->id"))',
            'updateButtonOptions' => array(
                'class' => 'fa fa-pencil'
            ),
            'updateButtonLabel' => false,
            'updateButtonImageUrl' => false,
            'updateButtonUrl' => 'Yii::app()->createUrl("user/save",
 array("id" => "$data->id"))',
            'deleteButtonOptions' => array(
                'class' => 'fa fa-trash-o'
            ),
            'deleteButtonLabel' => false,
            'deleteButtonImageUrl' => false,
            'deleteButtonUrl' => 'Yii::app()->createUrl("user/delete",
 array("id" => "$data->id"))'
        ),
    )
));
```

Within our CGridView instance's columns attribute, we've defined a custom column called CButtonColumn. CButtonColumn allows us to add a series of useful buttons to a CGridView instance, such as a view button, an update button, and a delete button, with all the necessary JavaScript. By taking advantage of this column, we now have quick access to these actions from within our view.

> You can read more about CButtonColumn on its Yii Class Reference page located at http://www.yiiframework.com/doc/api/1.1/CButtonColumn.

Deleting users

Next, we should implement an `actionDelete()` method to work with our delete button. To make things easier, we can add a helpful `loadModel()` method as well to perform all the necessary checks for us. Have a look at the following code:

```
public function actionDelete($id=NULL)
{
   if ($id == Yii::app()->user->id)
      throw new CHttpException(403, 'You cannot delete yourself');

   $user = $this->loadModel($id);

   if ($user->delete())
      $this->redirect($this->createUrl('user/index'));

   throw new CHttpException(400, 'Bad Request');
}

private function loadModel($id=NULL)
{
   if ($id == NULL)
      throw new CHttpException(400, 'Missing ID');

   $model = User::model()->findByPk($id);

   if ($model == NULL)
      throw new CHttpException(404, 'No user with that ID could be found');

   return $model;
}
```

Creating and updating users

Next, we can create our `actionSave()` method that will handle both creating and updating our users. Since our view will be passing us all the information we need, we use a simple `$user->save()` call to save our information. Have a look at the following code:

```
public function actionSave($id=NULL)
{
   if ($id == NULL)
```

```
            $user = new User;
        else
            $user = $this->loadModel($id);

        if (isset($_POST['User']))
        {
            $user->attributes = $_POST['User'];

            try
            {
                if ($user->save())
                {
                    Yii::app()->user->setFlash('success', 'The user has sucessfully been updated');
                    $this->redirect($this->createUrl('user/save', array('id' => $user->id)));
                }
            } catch (Exception $e) {
                $user->addError('email', 'A user with that email address already exists');
            }
        }

        $this->render('save', array(
            'model' => $user
        ));
    }
```

In this action, we've also deliberately thrown a `try/catch` block around our `save` method. We've done this because we've put a unique index constraint on the `email` field of our database. If we attempt to save two users to our database with the same e-mail, Yii will throw an internal error since it doesn't know how to handle the constraint. Within our controller, we can catch this error and simply return a more friendly error to the user in `$form->errorSummary($model)` in our view via the `$user->addError()` method.

Then, copy the `view/user/save.php` file from the project resources folder into your project. Within our view, we can populate a select dropdown of all the roles currently in our database using `CHtml::listData()`. Using this method allows us to add new roles to our database without having to alter a view in the future:

```
CHtml::listData(Role::model()->findAll(), 'id', 'name');
```

Viewing users and associated issues

Finally, we should create a view to display a particular user and all the unresolved issues currently assigned to them. For our `actionView()` method, add the following code:

```php
public function actionView($id=NULL)
{
    $user = $this->loadModel($id);
    $issues = new Issue('search');
    $issues->unsetAttributes();

    if(isset($_GET['Issue']))
        $issues->attributes=$_GET['Issue'];
    $issues->status_id = '<5';

    $issues->customer_id = $user->id;

    $this->render('view', array(
        'user'   => $user,
        'issues' => $issues
    ));
}
```

Then, copy the `view.php` file at `views/user/` from the project resources folder into our project, and open it. At the bottom of this file, you'll see a call to `renderPartial()` to render a view that we haven't created yet:

```php
<?php $this->renderPartial('//issue/issues', array('model' =>
$issues)); ?>
```

> In Yii, the `//` notation before a layout indicates that Yii should search for the view file in the main application `views` folder. You can read more about how Yii loads view files at `http://www.yiiframework.com/doc/api/1.1/CController#getLayoutFile-detail`.

We'll use this view file across our application to ensure that all of our lists look consistent. Before moving on, let's create this issue view. Create a new file in `views/issues/issue.php` and add the following `CGridView` widget:

```php
<?php $this->widget('zii.widgets.grid.CGridView', array(
    'itemsCssClass' => 'table table-striped',
    'enableSorting' => true,
```

```
            'dataProvider'=>$model->search(),
        'columns' => array(
            'id',
            'customer_id' => array(
                'name' => 'Customer',
                'value' => '$data->customer->name'
            ),
            'title',
             'status_id' => array(
                 'name' => 'Status',
                 'value' => '$data->status->name'
             ),
            'updated' => array(
                'name' => 'Last Updated',
                'value' => 'date("F m, Y @ H:i", $data->updated) . " UTC"'
            ),
            array(
                'class'=>'CButtonColumn',
                'template' => '{update}',
                'updateButtonOptions' => array(
                    'class' => 'fa fa-pencil'
                ),
                'updateButtonLabel' => false,
                'updateButtonImageUrl' => false
            ),
        )
));
```

While our view will now render, we don't yet have any issues in our database to display, so results will not be shown. Once we've added issues, we can come back to this view to see all the issues associated with a user.

Implementing the issue-management component

At the core of our application are the issues that users will submit. For this application, we'll assume that users will submit new issues for themselves, and that supporters will be supporting those issues. To ensure that issues are created for just the logged-in user, we have to make a few changes to our Issues model. Open `protected/models/Issues.php`, and let's get started.

The Issues model

Provided at the top of our skeleton model are properties designed to help us later in the model:

```
private $_isNewRecord = false;
public  $_isEmailCreate = false;
```

The first property `$_isNewRecord` is a Boolean value that we'll use within our `afterSave()` method to determine what e-mail will be sent. While `CActiveRecord` provides a property called `$isNewRecord`, Yii changes this value to FALSE before the `afterSave()` method.

The second property `$_isEmailCreate` is also a Boolean value. Since the e-mails we receive won't have a session associated with them, we need to know what user to associate the issue with. Since we'll restrict issues' owners to the currently logged-in user, we need a way to override this behavior for e-mail submissions.

After verifying that these properties are added, we can begin work on the other methods that we need to add to this model:

1. The first method we'll need to implement in our Issue model is a `beforeSave()` method to restrict the customer of an issue. Within this method, we'll want to also set the status of new issues to New, and flag our `$_isNewRecord` property so that we can use it in our `afterSave()` method. Additionally, we'll want to prevent accidental changes to `customer_id` should it somehow be changed on an existing issue:

```
public function beforeSave()
{
   if ($this->isNewRecord)
   {
      // If this is a new issue, set the customer_id to be the
currently logged in user
      if (!$this->_isEmailCreate)
         $this->customer_id = Yii::app()->user->id;

      // And set the status to 'New'
      $this->status_id = 1;

      // Set IsNewRecord so that afterSave can pick this up
      $this->_isNewRecord = true;
   }
   else // Otherwise reset the customer_id back to what it
previously was (prevent it from being changed)
      $this->customer_id = $this->_oldAttributes['customer_id'];

   return parent::beforeSave();
}
```

2. Next, we need to update the `afterSave()` method so that it sends e-mails to the customer. For this model, we'll send an e-mail to the user if an issue has been created for them or if an issue's status has been resolved. To do this, we'll use SendGrid. Before adding this method, verify that your `params.php` file at `protected/config/` has the correct credentials in it:

```php
public function afterSave()
{
    $user = User::model()->findByPk($this->customer_id);
    $sendgrid = new SendGrid(Yii::app()->params['sendgrid']['username'], Yii::app()->params['sendgrid']['password']);
    $email    = new SendGrid\Email();
    $email->setFrom(Yii::app()->params['sendgrid']['from'])
        ->addTo($user->email);

    if ($this->_isNewRecord)
    {
        $email->setSubject("[Issue #$this->id] $this->subject | A New Issue Has Been Created For You")
            ->setText('Issue has been created')
            ->setHtml(Yii::app()->controller->renderPartial('//email/created', array('issue' => $this, 'user' => $user), true));

        // Send the SendGrid email
        $sendgrid->send($email);
    }
    else
    {
        if ($this->status_id == 5 && $this->_oldAttributes['status'] != 5)
        {
            $email->addTo($user->email)
                ->setSubject("[Issue #$this->id] Issue has been resolved")
                ->setText('Issue has been resolved')
                ->setHtml(Yii::app()->controller->renderPartial('//email/resolved', array('issue' => $this, 'user' => $user), true));

            // Send the SendGrid email
            $sendgrid->send($email);
        }
    }

    return parent::afterSave();
}
```

3. The final change we'll need to make to the Issue model is in the `search()` method. Ideally, we'd like our supporters to be able to search for an issue by either the ID of the issue or a keyword in the title or description. To do this, we can simply repurpose the `Issue::search()` method by changing the `$criteria->compare()` call on those two attributes to `$criteria->addSearchCondition()`:

   ```
   $criteria->addSearchCondition('title',$this->title,true, 'OR');
   $criteria->addSearchCondition('description',$this->title,true, 'OR');
   ```

The Issues Update model

Before working on the `IssueController`, we'll also need to make a few changes to our `protected/models/Update.php` model. These changes will allow us to automatically assign the correct owner of an update to the update and help us send an e-mail to the user when an update is added to the issue.

Once again in our model, we have a property that we can use to find out whether this update came from an e-mail or not:

```
public $isEmailUpdate = false;
```

In this model, we're using this attribute to determine whether an e-mail should be sent to the user or not as we shouldn't notify the user of an update that they submitted.

Additionally, we'll need to make two updates to our model methods:

1. The first update we need to make to our model is in the `beforeSave()` method. If the user is logged in, the author of that update should be assigned to that user. Have a look at the following code:

   ```
   public function beforeSave()
   {
       // Allow the author_id to be set, but reset it to the logged in user->id if it isn't set
       if ($this->author_id == NULL)
           $this->author_id = Yii::app()->user->id;

       if ($this->update == '')
           return false;

       return parent::beforeSave();
   }
   ```

2. Then we should update our `afterSave()` method so that the e-mail is sent to the user in the appropriate instances:

```php
public function afterSave()
{
    // If the issue was created by the currently logged in user,
    or this is an email update, don't send an email
    $issue = Issue::model()->findByPk($this->issue_id);
    
    // Don't send an email if the customer provides an update, if
    this came from email, or the status of the issue is resolved
    if ($issue->customer_id == Yii::app()->user->id || $this-
    >isEmailUpdate || $issue->status_id == 5)
        return parent::afterSave();
    
    // If this is a NEW issue, send the user an email with the
    detais
    $user = User::model()->findByPk($issue->customer_id);
    
    // Init the SendGrid object and the Email Object
    $sendgrid = new SendGrid(Yii::app()->params['sendgrid']
    ['username'], Yii::app()->params['sendgrid']['password']);
    $email    = new SendGrid\Email();
    
    $email->setFrom(Yii::app()->params['sendgrid']['from'])
        ->addTo($user->email)
        ->setSubject("[Issue #$issue->id] $this->subject | Issue
    has been updated")
        ->setText('Issue has been updated')
        ->setHtml(Yii::app()->controller->renderPartial('//email/
    updated', array('issue' => $issue, 'update' => $this, 'user' =>
    $user), true));
    
    $sendgrid->send($email);
    
    return parent::afterSave();
}
```

Showing issues that belong to the user

With the updates to our models completed, we can now start working on the `IssueController`. The first method that we should implement is `actionIndex()`, which will show the logged-in users all the unresolved issues currently assigned to them:

```php
public function actionIndex()
{
    $issues = new Issue('search');
    $issues->unsetAttributes();
    
    if(isset($_GET['Issue']))
```

```
        $issues->attributes=$_GET['Issue'];

    // Don't search resolved issues
    $issues->status_id = '<5';

    $issues->customer_id = Yii::app()->user->id;

    $this->render('index', array(
        'issues' => $issues
    ));
}
```

Then in our `index.php` file at `views/issue/`, we can reuse the partial view that we created earlier to display all of these issues:

```
<h3>My Issues</h3>
<?php $this->renderPartial('issues', array('model' => $issues)); ?>
```

Searching for issues

The next method we need to implement is the `actionSearch()` method that will allow us to search for issues either by the issue ID or by a keyword in the title or description. To do this, we'll create a search view that will post to our action with the search parameters. If that `$_GET` parameter is numeric, and we can find an issue with that ID, we'll immediately redirect to it. Otherwise, we'll use the `Issue::search()` method that we modified earlier to search through all the issues in our database. Our controller action will look as follows:

```
public function actionSearch()
{
    $issues = new Issue('search');
    $issues->status_id = '<5';

    if (isset($_GET['issue']))
    {
        if (is_numeric($_GET['issue']))
        {
            $issue = Issue::model()->findByPk($_GET['issue']);
            if ($issue != NULL)
                $this->redirect($this->createUrl('issue/update',
array('id' => $issue->id)));
        }

        $issues->title = $_GET['issue'];
        $issues->description = $_GET['issue'];
```

```
    }
    $this->render('search', array(
        'issues' => $issues
    ));
}
```

Then, our `search.php` file at `views/issue/` will look as follows:

```
<h3>Search for Issues</h3>
<?php $form=$this->beginWidget('CActiveForm', array(
    'id'=>'project-form',
    'method' => 'get',
    'htmlOptions' => array(
        'class' => 'form-horizontal',
        'role' => 'form',
    )
)); ?>
    <p>Search for issues...</p>
    <div class="form-group">
        <?php echo CHtml::textField('issue', isset($_GET['issue']) ? $_GET['issue'] : NULL, array('class' => 'form-control', 'placeholder' => 'Search for Issues by ID, Title, or Description...')); ?>
    </div>
    <div class="row buttons">
        <?php echo CHtml::submitButton('Search', array('class' => 'btn btn-primary pull-right col-md-offset-1')); ?>
    </div>
<?php $this->endWidget(); ?>

<?php if ($issues != NULL): ?>
    <?php $this->renderPartial('issues', array('model' => $issues)); ?>
<?php endif; ?>
```

Creating issues

Next, we'll need to implement an action and view to create new issues. Since new issues won't have updates associated with them, create and update actions will need to be separate. For the `actionCreate()` method, we'll simply populate the values from the `$_POST` parameters:

```
public function actionCreate()
{
    $issue = new Issue;
    if (isset($_POST['Issue']))
```

```
    {
        $issue->attributes = $_POST['Issue'];

        if ($issue->save())
        {
            Yii::app()->user->setFlash('success', "Issue #{$issue->id} has successfully been created");
            $this->redirect($this->createUrl('issue/update', array('id' => $issue->id)));
        }
    }

    $this->render('create', array(
        'model' => $issue
    ));
}
```

Then, copy the create.php file located at views/issue/ from our project resources folder into your project.

Within this controller action is another reference to our CWebUser object. In previous chapters, every time we made a change to a database item from our controllers, we either reloaded the page or redirected to a new page. To make our applications more user friendly, we can set flash messages that will only show up once. To set these messages, we'll use the setFlash() method of our CWebUser object:

```
Yii::app()->user->setFlash($key, $value);
```

Then, from within our views, we can see whether a flash message exists for a particular key using hasFlash():

```
Yii::app()->user->hasFlash($key);
```

Then, display that flash message using getFlash():

```
Yii::app()->user->getFlash($key);
```

Alternatively, if we don't want to look for flash messages in a particular view, we can tell our layout to find all flash messages and display them. Have a look at the following code:

```
foreach (Yii::app()->user->getFlashes() as $key => $message)
    echo '<div class="flash-' . $key . '">' . $message . "</div>";
```

Viewing and updating issues

Now that we can create and find issues, we need to be able to view and update them. For this action, we'll be consolidating both functions into a single action. Because users of different roles will be accessing this action, we need to adjust it so that users of a particular role can only perform certain tasks:

1. First, we should generate a `loadModel()` method:

    ```
    private function loadModel($id=NULL)
    {
       if ($id == NULL)
          throw new CHttpException(400, 'Missing ID');

       $model = Issue::model()->findByPk($id);

       if ($model == NULL)
          throw new CHttpException(404, 'No issue with that ID was found');

       return $model;
    }
    ```

2. Then we'll need to create the `actionUpdate()` function. We'll start by loading the model with that ID and creating a new `Update` object in case an update is sent over `$_POST`:

    ```
    public function actionUpdate($id=NULL)
    {
       // Load the necessary models
       $issue = $this->loadModel($id);
       $update = new Update;
       $update->update = NULL;
       $customer_id = $issue->customer_id;
    ```

3. Then, we should make sure that only administrators, supporters, or the issue owner can view the issue. Have a look at the following code:

    ```
    if (Yii::app()->user->role == 1)
    {
       if (Yii::app()->user->id != $customer_id)
          throw new CHttpException(403, 'You do not have permission to view this issue');
    }
    ```

[123]

4. Then, we should allow administrators and supporters to modify the `Issue` object itself as follows:

```
if (Yii::app()->user->role >= 2)
{
    if (isset($_POST['Issue']))
    {
        $issue->attributes = $_POST['Issue'];
        if ($issue->save())
            Yii::app()->user->setFlash('success', "Issue #{$issue->id} has successfully been updated");
    }
}
```

5. Then, allow any user to submit an update as follows:

```
if (isset($_POST['Update']))
{
    $update->issue_id = $issue->id;
    $update->update = $_POST['Update']['update'];
    if ($update->save())
    {
        Yii::app()->user->setFlash('success', "Issue #{$issue->id} has successfully been updated");
        $this->redirect($this->createUrl('issue/update', array('id' => $issue->id)));
    }
}
```

6. Finally, we should render the view. When rendering the view, we are also going to pass down a `CMarkdownParser` object. Rendering the issue updates in Markdown syntax will allow us to easily have access to many different formatting features, such as line breaks, text styles, and quoting features. Rendering the updates in Markdown will also give us protection against simple XSS attacks, such as JavaScript injection attempts:

```
$this->render('update', array(
    'issue' => $issue,
    'update' => $update,
    'md' => new CMarkdownParser
));
```

> You can learn more about the Markdown syntax and how to use Markdown at http://daringfireball.net/projects/markdown/.

Finally we'll create an update view that will allow us to see the issue and updates from different roles. Copy the `update.php` view located at `view/issue/` from the project resources folder into your project.

E-mail views

Before we can start using our application, we need to create three different e-mail views, one for each type of e-mail that will be sent to the user. These views will contain information about the issue itself and information about whatever change was applied to it. It will also contain special formatting that will enable the user to reply to that e-mail and allow us to understand what parts of the e-mail should be included as an update:

1. The first view that we should create is a created view. This view will have information about a newly created issue. It will also contain a special marker that our application will be able to identify so that only the user's response is included in the update. Create a new file in `views/email/created.php`, and add the following code:

```
-------------- DO NOT EDIT BELOW THIS LINE --------------
<div class="email">
    Hello <?php echo $user->name; ?>,<br /><br />

    This is a notification that a new issue (#<?php echo $issue->id; ?>) has been opened for you. A member of our team will review this shortly.<br /><br />

    As a reminder, here is the description of the issue you provided:<br /><br />

    <strong><?php echo $issue->title; ?></strong>
    <blockquote>
        <?php echo $issue->description; ?>
    </blockquote>

    <br /><br />

    To add additional information to this issue, you may either reply to this email, or login <?php echo CHtml::link('here', $this->createAbsoluteUrl('issue/update', array('id' => $issue->id))); ?>.
    <br /><br />

    Thank you,<br />
    Issue Tracking System
</div>
```

[125]

2. Then create an updated view in `views/email/updated.php`. This e-mail will tell the user that their issue was updated and will contain the update that was applied to the issue. Once again, it will contain a special marker so that if the user replies to our e-mail, we know what content to include in the update and what content to ignore:

```
--------------- DO NOT EDIT BELOW THIS LINE ---------------
<div class="email">
    Hello <?php echo $user->name; ?>,<br /><br />

    This is a notification that a new issue (#<?php echo $issue->id; ?>) has been updated with the following message:<br /><br />

    <blockquote>
        <?php echo $update->update; ?>
    </blockquote>
    <hr />
    As a reminder, here is the description of the issue you provided:<br /><br />
    <strong><?php echo $issue->title; ?></strong>
    <blockquote>
        <?php echo $issue->description; ?>
    </blockquote>
    <br /><br />
    To reply to this issue you may either reply to this email, or login <?php echo CHtml::link('here', $this->createAbsoluteUrl('issue/update', array('id' => $issue->id))); ?>.
    <br /><br />
    Thank you,<br />
    Issue Tracking System
</div>
```

3. Finally, we need to create a view to notify the user that their issue has been resolved. Open `resolved.php` at `views/email/` and add the following:

```
--------------- DO NOT EDIT BELOW THIS LINE ---------------
<div class="email">
    Hello <?php echo $user->name; ?>,<br /><br />

    This is a notification that a new issue (#<?php echo $issue->id; ?>) has been resolved.<br /><br />

    Thank you,<br />
    Issue Tracking System
</div>
```

Testing our application

Since the domain `example.com` is not a valid domain to send e-mails, create for yourself a new user with a valid e-mail address, log in as that user, and create several issues. For each issue you create, a new e-mail will be sent to you notifying you that the issue has been created. Moreover, updating an issue as any supporter or administrator will notify the current supporter of the issue via e-mail with the provided update. Finally, if you have a supporter or an administrator resolve an issue, then you will receive an e-mail to notify you that the issue was resolved.

Once you have verified that all the functionality is working, we can move on to handling and parsing inbound e-mails with SendGrid.

Handling inbound e-mail parsing

While there are many different ways of handling inbound e-mail parsing, one of the easiest ways is to send that e-mail to a third party, who will then parse the contents for us, and send it as a `$_POST` request to an open endpoint in our application. This is exactly what SendGrid will do for us. However, before we can start using SendGrid, we need to make a couple of changes to our DNS server for our domain and to our SendGrid account.

Sending e-mails to SendGrid

To direct our e-mails to SendGrid in order to pass, we first need to make a change to our DNS settings. In keeping with our example domain `chapter4.example.com`, we first need to log in to our DNS host and add a new Mail Exchange (MX) record to our subdomain. Specifically, we need to add an MX record with a priority of `10` to `mx.sendgrid.net`. In most DNS systems, that record would look as follows:

```
chapter4    IN    MX    10    mx.sendgrid.net.
```

Alternatively, if you're using a service like CloudFlare to handle your DNS, your entry may look as follows:

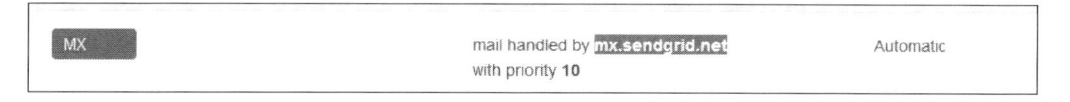

| MX | mail handled by **mx.sendgrid.net** with priority **10** | Automatic |

> Depending upon your DNS provider, DNS settings may take up to 24 to 48 hours to propagate. Before leaving this step, verify that the MX record was added and propagated using either a command-line tool, such as a DIG or a free, online web tool.

Adjusting SendGrid Parse settings

Once you've updated your DNS settings, you then need to update your SendGrid Parse API settings so that SendGrid knows where to send your e-mails. Navigate to `www.sendgrid.com/developer/reply`, and then fill in the parse settings page as follows and submit the record:

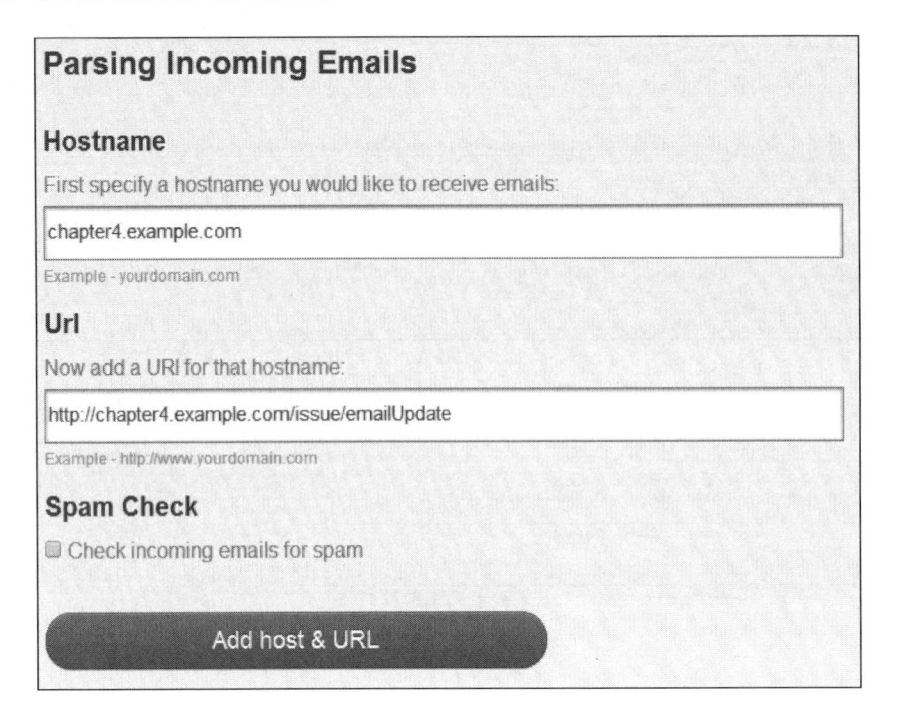

Parsing Incoming Emails

Hostname
First specify a hostname you would like to receive emails:

    chapter4.example.com

Example - yourdomain.com

Url
Now add a URI for that hostname:

    http://chapter4.example.com/issue/emailUpdate

Example - http://www.yourdomain.com

Spam Check
☐ Check incoming emails for spam

[Add host & URL]

Once you've added the record, you should see confirmation at the bottom of the page. Once this has been completed, you can now send e-mails to `*@chapter4.example.com`, and SendGrid will parse it and forward it onto your `actionEmailUpdate()` method of our `IssueController`.

> You can read more about the SendGrid Parse API webhook at `http://sendgrid.com/docs/API_Reference/Webhooks/parse.html`.

Creating and updating issues over e-mail

Now that our DNS settings and SendGrid account are set, we need to add the necessary functionality to both create and update issues over e-mail. Then, the action that we create will also create new users in our database if a new user creates an issue for us:

1. With SendGrid configured, our `actionEmailUpdate()` method will receive a `POST` request from SendGrid anytime someone sends an e-mail to our application.. All the information that we will need to work with will be in a `$_POST` variable once it arrives. However, some of this information may not be readily accessible. For instance, the e-mail address will reach us as `Example User" <test@chapter4.example.com>"` which isn't very useful to us. To make this e-mail more useful, we need to create a utility function that will break this information apart for us in our `IssueController` as follows:

    ```php
    private function _parseEmailAddress($raw)
    {
        $name = "";
        $email = trim($raw, " '\"");

        if (preg_match("/^(.*)<(.*)>.*$/", $raw, $matches))
        {
            array_shift($matches);
            $name = trim($matches[0], " '\"");
            $email = trim($matches[1], " '\"");
        }

        return array(
            "name"  => $name,
            "email" => $email,
            "full"  => $name . " <" . $email . ">"
        );
    }
    ```

2. Then, within our `actionEmailUpdate()` method, we'll begin by retrieving this information:

    ```php
    $from = $this->_parseEmailAddress($_POST['from']);
    $subject = $_POST['subject'];
    ```

3. Then, we'll need to search for the subject of the e-mail for the ID of our issue. In the e-mails we're sending out, the subject has the format `[Issue #<ID>] <info>`. Have a look at the following code:

```
$idString = NULL;
preg_match('/\[Issue #.*?\]/', $subject, $idString);
$id = str_replace(']', '', str_replace('[Issue #', '',
(isset($idString[0]) ? $idString[0] : 0)));
```

4. Then, we need to find a user in our system with that e-mail address. If we are unable to find that user, we need to create a new user with that e-mail address:

```
$user = User::model()->findByAttributes(array('email' =>
$from['email']));

if ($user == NULL)
{
    $user = new User;
    $user->attributes = array(
        'name' => $from['name'],
        'email' => $from['email'],
        'password' => 'changeme9',
        'role_id' => 1
    );

    if (!$user->save())
        return true;
}
```

5. Then, we need to locate an issue with that ID. If an issue with that ID doesn't exist, or the issue doesn't belong to the user we're working with, we should create a new issue rather than updating an existing one:

```
$issue = Issue::model()->findByPk($id);

// If the user or ID are NULL, or that email address doesn't
belong to that customer, Create a new issue
if ($issue == NULL || $id == NULL || $issue->customer_id != $user->id)
{
    // create the issue, save it, then return - no further work
needs to be done.
```

```
    $issue = new Issue;
    $issue->_isEmailCreate = true;

    $issue->attributes = array(
       'title' => $subject,
       'description' => $_POST['text'],
       'customer_id' => $user->id
    );

    $issue->save();
    return true;
}
```

6. Finally, if we have a good user and issue, we should apply the update. At this point, we'll split the contents of our e-mail along our special marker and only include the contents above it in our update. This reduces the amount of data we need to store in our database and keeps our interface looking clean and clear of e-mail clutter:

```
$body = explode('--------------- DO NOT EDIT BELOW THIS LINE ---------------', $_POST['text']);
$body = $body[0];

// Set the update
$update = new Update;
$update->author_id = $user->id;
$update->issue_id = $issue->id;
$update->update = $body;
$update->isEmailUpdate = true;

$update->save();
return true;
```

Now that our application can receive e-mails, reply to one of the e-mails you received earlier. After a short while, you will be able to navigate to that issue and see that your update sent over e-mail was indeed applied. Alternatively, you can send a new e-mail to your application. In a short while, a new issue will be created, and the application will respond to you with an e-mail notifying you that a new issue was created.

Summary

We covered a lot of ground in this chapter! We went over creating and managing users from within our application, sending e-mails about certain events, and how to receive e-mails and incorporate that information into our application. We also added roles to our users and made our application only respond to certain actions of users with a particular role.

Before continuing, think of ways in which you could improve this application, and try to implement them. For example, you could change it so that the access rules expressions are answered by the models rather than hard-coded values. Alternatively, you could add new statuses to the application and send out different e-mails when those statuses change. Think of all the ways you could make this application better to use for the end user.

After adding some new features, go through the Yii documentation located at http://www.yiiframework.com/doc/ to help you better understand some of the methods and properties we used in this chapter.

In the next chapter, we will be expanding upon our knowledge to implement a micro blogging platform similar to Twitter. To our micro-blogging platform, we'll add a registration and password reset system for our end users and allow our end users to manage their own accounts. Once you're ready, turn the page and get ready to dive deeper into Yii!

5
Creating a Microblogging Platform

For our next project, we will be developing a scalable microblogging platform similar to Twitter. This platform will allow users to share content with others, mention other users in their share, and view a timeline of their shares. Additionally, users will be able to register, manage, and change certain account details such as their e-mail address and password. Finally, our platform will enable users to share content with other external social networks such as Twitter.

By the end of this chapter, we'll have a social network that will allow us to share content and manage our accounts, as shown in the following screenshot:

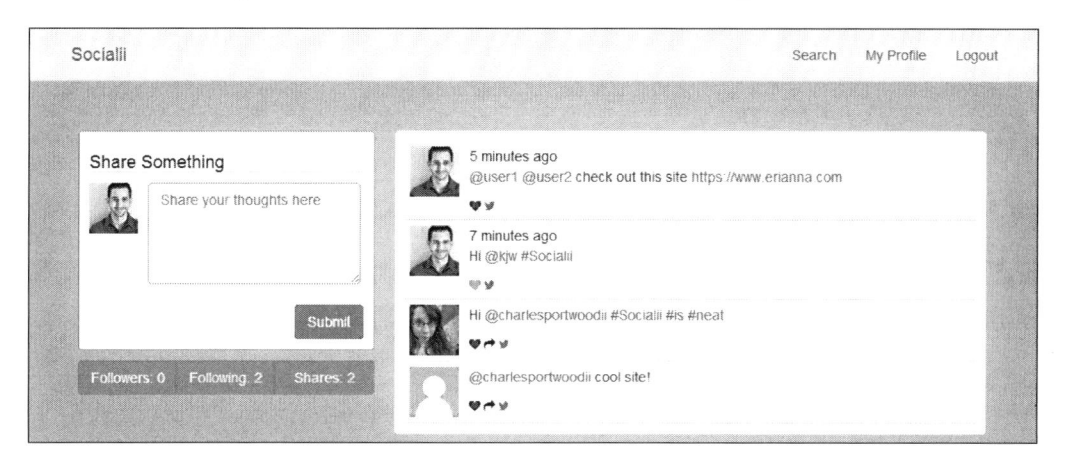

Our users will also have the ability to directly reply to and share individual posts that they make, as shown in the following screenshot:

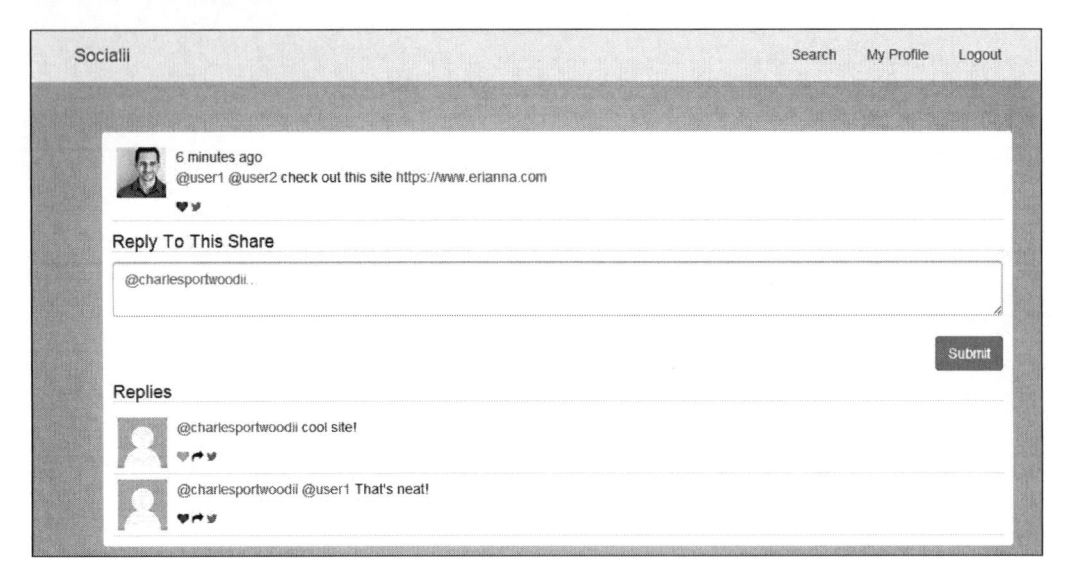

Prerequisites

Before we get started, there are a couple of things that we'll need to set up and have working:

- Since we'll be sending and receiving e-mails from our application, we're going to need a registered and active domain name. If you do not already have a working domain name, you can purchase one from a domain registrar such as https://www.namecheap.com, www.name.com, or www.gandi.net.
- Next, you'll need to have a web server with a public-facing IP address. This will allow e-mails to be sent to our application. Many cloud **Virtual Private Server** (**VPS**) providers are available for use for low monthly or hourly prices. Such services include https://www.digitalocean.com, https://www.linode.com, and www.rackspace.com/cloud/servers.
- In order to send e-mails in our application, we'll once again be utilizing a free SendGrid Developer Account, which can be set up at https://www.sendgrid.com/developers.
- In this chapter, we'll once again be using the latest version of MySQL (at the time of writing this, it is MySQL 5.6). Make sure that your MySQL server is set up and running on your server.

- For this project, we'll once again be managing our dependencies through Composer, which you can download and install from `https://getcomposer.org/`.
- Finally, you'll need a Twitter Developer account, which can be obtained from `https://dev.twitter.com/`. This account will allow us to enable the sharing of our content to Twitter as the logged-in user via Twitter's OAuth API.

Once you have acquired the listed items, create a subdomain on the domain name you are using and point it to your server. In this chapter, I'll be using `chapter5.example.com` to refer to this subdomain. After everything is set up and your server is responding to that domain name, we can get started.

Describing the project

Our microblogging platform can be broken down into two big components:

- Users who will be following other users and creating, sharing, and liking content
- Text-based shares that will be created by the users

Users

The first component of our application is the set of users who will be performing all the tasks in our application. For this application, we're going to be largely reusing the user database and authentication system that we expanded upon in *Chapter 4, Developing an Issue-tracking Application*. In this chapter, we'll be expanding upon the `users` database table, and adding several new relations such as followers and likes.

Followers

In this application, users will be able to follow and be followed by other users. This relationship will allow users to stay up-to-date with other users by showing content that other users have recently created. Moreover, it will allow them to know how many people are following them and see how much of an influence they have over their network. For this application, our `followers` table will just contain the primary keys of users who are either following or being followed by another user. Our database table will look as follows:

```
ID INTEGER PRIMARY KEY
follower_id INTEGER
followee_id INTEGER
created INTEGER
updated INTEGER
```

Likes

In this application, users will also be able to indicate that they like a particular share. Similar to our `followers` table, the `likes` table will only contain the primary keys of the `users` and the `shares` table. Our database table will look as follows:

```
ID INTEGER PRIMARY KEY
user_id INTEGER
share_id INTEGER
created INTEGER
updated INTEGER
```

Shares

The second component of our application will be the shares that users create. For our purposes, we will define a share as a piece of text that can contain unique markers such as the @ sign for mentioning other users, and the # character for tagging a share. Shares can also be in reply to another share, which will allow them to be viewed on the share's view page. Finally, shares can be reshared users who wish to share another user's share with their network. Our database table will look as follows:

```
ID INTEGER PRIMARY KEY
text STRING
author_id INTEGER
reshare_id INTEGER
reply_id INTEGER
created INTEGER
updated INTEGER
```

Initializing the project

By now, you should be comfortable with creating projects from scratch. To provide us with a common starting ground, a skeleton project has been included with the project resources for this chapter. Included with this skeleton project are the necessary migrations, data files, controllers, and views that we need to get started. The login system that we'll be using for authentication throughout this chapter is also included. Copy the skeleton project from the project resources folder to your web server and configure it so that it responds to `chapter5.example.com` as outlined at the beginning of the chapter, and then perform the following steps to make sure everything is set up:

1. Adjust the permissions on the `assets` and `protected/runtime` folders so that they are writable by your web server.

2. Next, create the MySQL user and database table that our application will use. If you don't want to alter the provided main configuration file, the following MySQL commands will create the database and user for you:

   ```
   CREATE USER 'ch5_socialii'@'localhost' IDENTIFIED BY ''ch5_socialii'';
   CREATE DATABASE IF NOT EXISTS `'ch5_socialii'` ;
   GRANT ALL PRIVILEGES ON `'ch5\_socialii'` . * TO ''ch5_socialii''@'localhost';
   FLUSH PRIVILEGES;
   ```

3. Next, we'll need to run the initial migrations and then import the sample data that is provided in the `protected/data` folder. This sample data will allow us to immediately log in to our application and start using it once the application is running. Navigate to the root of the project, and then run the following commands:

   ```
   php protected/yiic.php migrate up --interactive=0
   ```
   ```
   mysql -u ch5_socialii -pch5_socialii ch5_socialii < protected/data/combined.sql
   ```

4. Then, we will need to update `params.php` located at `protected/config/` with our SendGrid information. Your username and password will correspond to your SendGrid username and password. Keeping in line with our example domain, set the `from` address to `socialii@chapter5.example.com`.

5. Finally, we will need to install the necessary Composer dependencies:

   ```
   composer install
   ```

At this point, you should be able to open `http://chapter5.example.com` in your browser and see the following page:

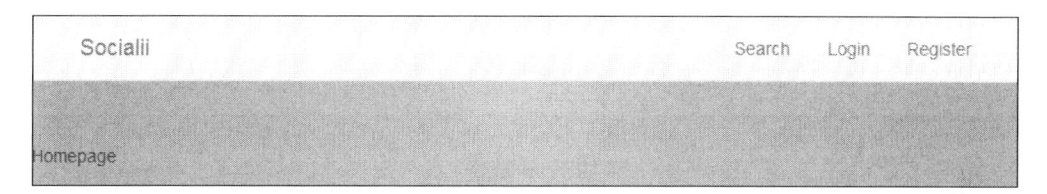

Making a better Yii bootstrap file

One thing you may have noticed was that we didn't have to declare where the Yii framework was located for our site to work. That's because we included Yii framework as a dependency in our `composer.json` file, as follows:

```
"yiisoft/yii": "1.1.14"
```

Creating a Microblogging Platform

There are several benefits to including Yii as a dependency in our project rather than hardcoding it in our bootstrapper, which are as follows:

- Including it in our bootstrapper as a Composer dependency means that we don't have to bother installing Yii framework on our server before we push our code to it
- We can now automate our deployment process, and be certain that the dependencies in our development environment match those of our production environment
- The code used for this project is now separate from other projects that might also use Yii framework
- Finally, this separation allows us to upgrade Yii or use a different fork of Yii without having to worry about how we're going to deploy Yii framework to our server—Composer will simply take care of the installation for us

We've also made a few improvements and changes to our Bootstrap file to make developing and debugging easier for us. Let's take a look at the changes in our index.php file:

1. First, we include our configuration file:

   ```
   $config=require dirname(__FILE__).'/protected/config/main.php';
   defined('DS') or define('DS', DIRECTORY_SEPARATOR);
   ```

2. Next, we're going to set YII_DEBUG and YII_TRACE to variables that are defined in our main.php file at protected/config/. This will allow us to toggle the debug mode and the trace level without having to alter the code in index.php:

   ```
   defined('YII_DEBUG') or define('YII_DEBUG',isset($config['params']['debug']) ? $config['params']['debug'] : false);
   defined('YII_TRACE_LEVEL') or define('YII_TRACE_LEVEL',isset($config['params']['trace']) ? $config['params']['trace'] : 0);
   ```

3. In our main.php file at protected/config/, we can toggle these variables by setting params[debug] and params[trace]:

   ```
   'params' => array(
      'includes' => require __DIR__ . '/params.php',
      'debug' => true,
      'trace' => 3
   )
   ```

4. Then, we're going to load our Composer dependencies. Depending on whether YII_DEBUG is set or not, load yii.php or yiilite.php. For most configurations, and when coupled with APC Cache or Zend OPcache, yiilite.php should improve the performance of your application:

```
require_once(__DIR__ . '/vendor/autoload.php');
require(__DIR__.DS.'vendor'.DS.'yiisoft'.DS.'yii'.DS.'framework'.
DS.(YII_DEBUG ? 'yii.php' : 'yiilite.php'));
```

> If you want to learn more about yiilite, take a look at the official Yii documentation at http://www.yiiframework.com/doc/guide/1.1/en/topics.performance#using-x-9x.

5. Next, we're going to automatically enable logging, and turn error reporting to its maximum value when we're in the debug mode. This will allow us to easily view full stack traces when an error occurs and get detailed log messages about what's going on in our application. This option will help with development and won't be loaded when we are running in a production environment:

```
if (YII_DEBUG && YII_TRACE_LEVEL == 3)
{
   error_reporting(-1);
   ini_set('display_errors', 'true');

   // Enable WebLogRouteLogging
   $config['preload'][] = 'log';
   $config['components']['log']['routes'][0]['enabled'] = true;
}
```

6. For the preceding step to work, we then need to define a logging method that we want to use. In our development environment, it makes sense to use CWebLogRoute so that we can see our log messages in our browser. To enable this route, we'll add the following to the components section of our main.php file located at protected/config/:

```
'log' => array(
   'class' => 'CLogRouter',
      'routes' => array(
      array(
         'class' => 'CWebLogRoute',
         'levels' => 'error, warning, trace, info',
         'enabled' => false
      )
   )
)
```

> Yii provides several different logging methods that you can use in both production and development environments. To learn more about logging, take a look at the official Yii documentation at http://www.yiiframework.com/doc/guide/1.1/en/topics.logging.

7. Finally, we're going to bootstrap our application:

   ```
   Yii::createWebApplication($config)->run();
   ```

Enabling users to manage their information

In the previous chapters, our users haven't been able to do much besides interacting with content. In this chapter, we'll be expanding upon the base User model so that they can register with our application, securely activate their accounts, reset their passwords if they forget them, and change their e-mail address.

Upgrading our UserIdentity class

Before implementing the previously mentioned functionality, we need to make sure that we can address our users appropriately without having to ask our database for some basic information about the currently logged-in user. To do this, we're going to add some information to our UserIdentity.php file located at protected/components/ as shown next in the highlighted sections of our authenticate() method. Additionally, we're going to enhance this class so that if YII_DEBUG is enabled, we can get more information about what is going on if authentication fails:

```
public function authenticate()
{
    $record = User::model()->findByAttributes(array('email'=>$this->username));

    if ($record == NULL)
        $this->errorCode = YII_DEBUG ? this->errorCode=self::ERROR_USERNAME_INVALID : self::ERROR_UNKNOWN_IDENTITY;
    else if (password_verify($this->password, $record->password))
    {
        $this->errorCode = self::ERROR_NONE;
        $this->_id       = $record->id;
```

```
        $this->setState('email', $record->email);
        $this->setState('role', $record->role_id);
        $this->setState('username', $record->username);
        $this->setState('name', $record->name);
    }
    else
        $this->errorCode = YII_DEBUG ? self::ERROR_PASSWORD_INVALID :
self::ERROR_UNKNOWN_IDENTITY;

    return !$this->errorCode;
}
```

Defining user relations

Next, we'll want to make sure that our relations are set up so that we can tell which data is associated with our users. This includes shares, followers, and followees. Within our `protected/models/User.php` file, make sure the following is set to our `relations()` method:

```
return array(
    'followees' => array(self::HAS_MANY, 'Follower', 'followee_id'),
    'followers' => array(self::HAS_MANY, 'Follower', 'follower_id'),
    'shares' => array(self::HAS_MANY, 'Share', 'author_id'),
    'role' => array(self::BELONGS_TO, 'Role', 'role_id'),
);
```

We're also going to add a new relational type to our `relations()` method so that we can quickly retrieve the number of shares, followers, and followees a user has. This relation type is called STAT, and behaves the same as a HAS_MANY relation, except that it performs a count at the database level and returns a number rather than returning an array of objects:

```
'followeesCount' => array(self::STAT, 'Follower', 'followee_id'),
'followersCount' => array(self::STAT, 'Follower', 'follower_id'),
'sharesCount' => array(self::STAT, 'Share', 'author_id')
```

By using the STAT relation, we can reduce the strain on our database when we want to know how many followers a user has. In a small database with a few users, a HAS_MANY relationship isn't very significant; however, when dealing with thousands of users, repeatedly running a HAS_MANY query will result in a large number of results to be returned, which can result in our application running out of memory and crashing.

Determining whether a user is following another user

The last change we need to make to our model for our relations is to add a quick method that will allow us to determine whether the currently logged-in user is following another user. We'll use this information later on to adjust what's displayed in our views. Add the following method to your User.php file located at protected/models/:

```
public static function isFollowing($id=NULL)
{
    if ($id == NULL || Yii::app()->user->isGuest)
        return false;

    $following = Follower::model()->findByAttributes(array('follower_id' => Yii::app()->user->id, 'followee_id' => $id));

    return $following != NULL;
}
```

Implementing a secure registration process

One of the more difficult parts of creating a secure web application is ensuring that the users who register on our site are really the users they claim to be. Often, this is accomplished by sending an e-mail to the user with a unique single-use token. If the user is able to visit our site with that secure token, we can assume that they are real users, and that they have access to the e-mail address. By employing this method of validation, we can ensure that the users who register on our site are who they claim to be, and that they choose to engage with our application.

While we could handle the majority of this functionality directly within our controller and bloat our User model with unnecessary methods, our tool of choice for this task will be CFormModel. In this book, we've only utilized CFormModel for our LoginForm model, which we've been using for logging users in. Before moving forward, let's take a deeper look into what CFormModel is and explore how we can use it.

CFormModel is very similar to CActiveRecord, in that it extends CModel and inherits many of the methods that CActiveRecord has, such as attributeLabels, attributes, and rules. The primary difference between CFormModel and CActiveRecord is that CFormModel is used to collect information from an HTML form, and the data submitted to CFormModel is acted upon rather than stored and manipulated in a database. By taking advantage of the methods inherited from CModel, we can cleanly and easily use CFormModel to validate input and reduce the amount of code clutter in our controllers and models.

> To learn more about CFormModel, check out the official Yii documentation at http://www.yiiframework.com/doc/api/1.1/CFormModel.

To get started, create a new file in protected/models/RegistrationForm.php and add the following to it:

```
<?php class RegistrationForm extends CFormModel {}
```

The next steps are as follows:

1. The first item we'll be placing in this class is our attributes. These model attributes are publicly exposed, and can be set from our controllers:

    ```
    public $email;
    public $name;
    public $password;
    public $username;
    ```

2. Next, we'll define our attribute labels for these attributes:

    ```
    public function attributeLabels()
    {
        return array(
            'email' => 'Your Email Address',
            'name' => 'Your Full Name',
            'password' => 'Your Password',
            'username' => 'Your Username'
        );
    }
    ```

3. Then, we'll want to set up our validation rules. For new users, we want to verify that all attributes are set, the e-mail address is a valid one, the password is at least 8 characters long, and the username the user's trying to register with is not already taken:

    ```
    public function rules()
    {
        return array(
            array('email, username, name, password', 'required'),
            array('password', 'length', 'min'=>8),
            array('email', 'email'),
            array('username', 'validateUsername') ,
            array('email', 'verifyEmailIsUnique')
        );
    }
    ```

4. Since Yii doesn't provide a native validator for usernames, we will then need to define our own `validateUsername()` method, which will do a simple existence check against our database:

```
public function validateUsername($attributes, $params)
{
    $user = User::model()->findByAttributes(array('username' => $this->username));

    if ($user === NULL)
        return true;
    else
    {
        $this->addError('username', 'That username has already been registered');
        return false;
    }
}
```

5. We'll also want to define a validator to ensure that our e-mail address is not already taken:

```
public function verifyEmailIsUnique($attributes, $params)
{
    $user = User::model()->findByAttributes(array('email' => $this->email));

    if ($user === NULL)
        return true;
    else
    {
        $this->addError('email', 'That email address has already been registered');
        return false;
    }
}
```

> Notice that when validation fails, we're not only returning false but also adding an error to our model. We're doing this for three reasons: to enhance the user experience and ensure that the user knows what went wrong, to ensure that the `validate()` method of CModel fails when an error is thrown (it will return true unless `$this->addError()` is called), and to ensure that we can run these validators independently of the form.

6. Out of preference, the last method we'll be creating is a `save()` method, which will perform the validation, send a verification e-mail to the user, and insert the new record into our database. To achieve this, start by creating a new method called `save()`:

   ```
   public function save()
   ```

   Then, within the method, first perform the validation:

   ```
   if (!$this->validate())
   return false;
   ```

   Then, create a new `User` object:

   ```
   $user = new User;
   $user->attributes = array(
      'email' => $this->email,
      'name' => $this->name,
      'password' => $this->password,
      'username' => str_replace(' ', '',$this->username),
      'activated' => 0
   );
   ```

   Then, attempt to save the user and send that user an e-mail address with the activation details:

   ```
   if ($user->save())
   {
      // Send an email to the user
      $sendgrid = new SendGrid(Yii::app()->params['includes']['sendgrid']['username'], Yii::app()->params['includes']['sendgrid']['password']);
      $email    = new SendGrid\Email();

      $email->setFrom(Yii::app()->params['includes']['sendgrid']['from'])
         ->addTo($user->email)
         ->setSubject("Activate Your Socialii Account")
         ->setText('Activate Your Socialii Account')
         ->setHtml(Yii::app()->controller->renderPartial('//email/activate', array('user' => $user), true));

      // Send the email
      $sendgrid->send($email);

      // Return true if we get to this point
      return true;
   }
   ```

7. Next, we'll want to update our User models so that the activation key is set when the user is first created. To generate the activation key, we'll be using a library that was included in our `composer.json` file that securely generates strings:

```php
public function beforeSave()
{
   if ($this->isNewRecord)
   {
      $this->generateActivationKey();
      $this->role_id = 1;
   }

   return parent::beforeSave();
}

public function generateActivationKey()
{
   $factory = new CryptLib\Random\Factory;
   $this->activation_key = $factory->getHighStrengthGenerator()->generateString(16);
   return $this->activation_key;
}
```

8. Now, we can add a register action to our `UserController.php` file located at `protected/controllers/` that will allow the user to register with our site. Since majority of the work has already been done in our form, all we have to do is collect the data from the `$_POST` request, apply it to the model, and call the `save()` method on the model. To provide a better user experience, we can also attempt to automatically log the user in using their new credentials:

```php
public function actionRegister()
{
   // Authenticated users shouldn't be able to register
   if (!Yii::app()->user->isGuest)
      $this->redirect($this->createUrl('timeline/index'));

   $form = new RegistrationForm;
   if (isset($_POST['RegistrationForm']))
   {
      $form->attributes = $_POST['RegistrationForm'];

      // Attempt to save the user's information
      if ($form->save())
      {
```

```
                // Try to automagically log the user in, if we fail
    though just redirect them to the login page
            $model = new LoginForm;
            $model->attributes = array(
                'username' => $form->email,
                'password' => $form->password
            );

            if ($model->login())
            {
                // Set a flash message associated to the new
    Yii::app()->user
                Yii::app()->user->setFlash('sucess', 'You successfully
    registred an account!');

                // Then redirect to their timeline
                $this->redirect($this->createUrl('timeline/index'));
            }
            else
                $this->redirect($this->createUrl('site/login'));
        }
    }

    $this->render('register', array('user' => $form));
}
```

9. Then, from the project resources folder, copy the following view files into your project: `protected/views/user/register.php`, `protected/views/email/activate.php`, and `protected/views/site/index.php`. Now, either from the `site/index` or `user/register` route, you can register a new account in your site.

10. Finally, create a new method in your `UserController.php` file located at `protected/controllers/` called `actionActivate()` that will actually activate our user. To do so, we're simply going to verify that the ID parameter sent to us in the route matches with what we have on file for the user:

```
public function actionActivate($id=NULL)
{
    if ($id == NULL)
        throw new CHttpException(400, 'Activation ID is missing');

    $user = User::model()->findByAttributes(array('activation_key'
=> $id));

    if ($user == NULL)
```

```
        throw new CHttpException(400, 'The activation ID you
    supplied is invalid');

        // Don't allow activations of users who have a password reset
    request OR have a change email request in
        // Email Change Requests and Password Reset Requests require an
    activated account
        if ($user->activated == -1 || $user->activated == -2)
            throw new CHttpException(400, 'There was an error fulfilling
    your request');

        $user->activated = 1;
        $user->password = NULL;              // Don't reset the password
        $user->activation_key = NULL;        // Prevent reuse of their
    activation key

        if ($user->save())
        {
            $this->render('activate');
            Yii::app()->end();
        }

        throw new CHttpException(500, 'An error occurring activating
    your account. Please try again later');
    }
```

We can also reuse the form we just created on our home page to allow users to log in or register a new account from there. Since we've already copied the view over, we simply need to adjust the `SiteController` `actionIndex()` method:

```
    public function actionIndex()
    {
        if (!Yii::app()->user->isGuest)
            $this->redirect($this->createUrl('timeline/index'));

        $this->layout = 'main';
        $this->render('index', array('loginform' => new LoginForm, 'user'
    => new RegistrationForm));
    }
```

Handling forgotten passwords

As previously shown, using `CFormModel` to handle input from an HTML form makes it very easy to validate submitted information and act upon it while keeping our models and controllers very clear. We can once again use `CFormModel` to handle forgotten password requests from a user.

To handle forgotten passwords, we're going to request that the user provides us with the e-mail address they used to register their account. Next, we'll verify that we have an e-mail address on file, and then send the user an e-mail with a single use token that will allow them to securely reset their password. To start, create a new file called `ForgotForm.php` in `protected/models` and add the following to it:

```php
<?php class ForgotForm extends CFormModel {}
```

The next steps are as follows:

1. Begin by declaring the public attributes of our form:

    ```php
    public $email;
    public function attributeLabels()
    {
        return array(
            'email' => 'Your Email Address'
        );
    }
    ```

2. We're also going to declare a private property for our User model that we'll be reusing throughout this model:

    ```php
    private $_user;
    ```

3. Next, we'll declare our validation rules and custom validator:

    ```php
    public function rules()
    {
        return array(
            array('email', 'required'),
            array('email', 'email'),
            array('email', 'checkUser'),
        );
    }

    public function checkUser($attribute,$params)
    {
    ```

```
    $this->_user = User::model()->findByAttributes(array('email' =>
$this->email));

    if ($this->_user == NULL)
    {
        $this->addError('email', 'There is no user in our system
with that email address.');
        return false;
    }

    return true;
}
```

4. Then, we will declare our `save()` method that will send the user the e-mail and indicate that they have asked for their password to be reset:

```
public function save()
{
    if (!$this->validate())
        return false;

    // Set the activation details
    $this->_user->generateActivationKey();
    $this->_user->activated = -1;

    if ($this->_user->save())
    {
        $sendgrid = new SendGrid(Yii::app()->params['includes']
['sendgrid']['username'], Yii::app()->params['includes']
['sendgrid']['password']);
        $email    = new SendGrid\Email();

        $email->setFrom(Yii::app()->params['includes']['sendgrid']
['from'])
            ->addTo($this->_user->email)
            ->setSubject('Reset Your Socialii Password')
            ->setText('Reset Your Socialii Password')
            ->setHtml(Yii::app()->controller->renderPartial('//email/
forgot', array('user' => $this->_user), true));

        // Send the email
        $sendgrid->send($email);

        return true;
    }
    else
```

```
            $this->addError('email', 'Unable to send reset link. This is
    likely a temporary error. Please try again in a few minutes.');

            return false;
        }
```

5. Then, create an action in `protected/controllers/UserController.php` to handle the form submission:

    ```
    public function actionForgot()
    {
        $form = new ForgotForm;

        if (isset($_POST['ForgotForm']))
        {
            $form->attributes = $_POST['ForgotForm'];

            if ($form->save())
            {
                $this->render('forgot_success');
                Yii::app()->end();
            }
        }

        $this->render('forgot', array('forgotform' => $form));
    }
    ```

6. Finally, copy `protected/views/user/forgot.php`, `protected/views/user/forgot_success.php` and `protected/views/email/forgot.php` from the project resources folder into your application.

Resetting a forgotten password

Once the user has the single-use token we sent them, we can then allow the user to securely change their password to whatever they want. Start by creating a new file in `protected/models` called `PasswordResetform.php` with the following:

```
<?php class PasswordResetForm extends CFormModel {}
```

The next steps are as follows:

1. Begin by declaring the public attributes for this form:

    ```
    public $password;
    public $pasword_repeat;
    public $user;
    ```

2. Then, add the validation rules. The user's new password should have the same requirements as when the user registered. Since we're requesting the password twice, we'll want to compare the two passwords using the compare validator. This validator validates the first attribute against the `attribute_repeat` attribute:

```
public function rules()
{
   return array(
      array('password', 'length', 'min' => 8),
      array('password, password_repeat, user', 'required'),
      array('password', 'compare', 'compareAttribute' => 'password_repeat'),
   );
}
```

3. Then, add the `save()` method to reset the user's password:

```
public function save()
{
   if (!$this->validate())
      return false;

   $this->user->password = $this->password;

   // Verify that this activation key can't be used again
   $this->user->activated = 1;
   $this->user->activation_key = NULL;

   if ($this->user->save())
      return true;

   return false;
}
```

4. Then, create our controller action:

```
public function actionResetPassword($id = NULL)
{
   if ($id == NULL)
      throw new CHttpException(400, 'Missing Password Reset ID');

   $user = User::model()->findByAttributes(array('activation_key' => $id));

   if ($user == NULL)
```

```
            throw new CHttpException(400, 'The password reset id you
    supplied is invalid');

        $form = new PasswordResetForm;

        if (isset($_POST['PasswordResetForm']))
        {
            $form->attributes = array(
                'user' => $user,
                'password' => $_POST['PasswordResetForm']['password'],
                'password_repeat' => $_POST['PasswordResetForm']
    ['password_repeat']
            );

            if ($form->save())
            {
                $this->render('resetpasswordsuccess');
                Yii::app()->end();
            }
        }

        $this->render('resetpassword', array(
            'passwordresetform' => $form,
            'id' => $id
        ));
    }
```

5. Finally, copy `protected/views/user/resetpassword.php` and `protected/views/user/resetpassword_success.php` from the project resources folder into your application.

Enabling users to manage their details

At this point, we can now log in, register an account, and reset our passwords if we forgot them. Now, let's work on allowing users to manage their own details. This includes allowing them to change their password, e-mail address, and the other pieces of information that we collect during the registration process. The steps are as follows:

1. We'll start by once again creating a new `CFormModel` in `protected/models` called `ProfileForm.php`:

   ```
   <?php class ProfileForm extends CFormModel {}
   ```

Creating a Microblogging Platform

2. Then, we'll add our attributes and labels:

```
public $email;
public $password;
public $name;
public $newpassword = NULL;
public $newpassword_repeat = NULL;
private $_user;
public function attributeLabels()
  {
     return array(
        'email'              => 'Your New Email Address',
        'password'           => 'Your Current Password',
        'name'               => 'Your Name',
        'newpassword'        => 'Your NEW password',
        'newpassword_repeat' => 'Your NEW password (again)'
     );
  }
```

3. We'll then add our basic validation rules:

```
public function rules()
{
   return array(
      array('email, name, password', 'required'),
      array('newpassword', 'length', 'min' => 8),
      array('email', 'email'),
      array('password', 'verifyPassword'),
      array('newpassword', 'compare', 'compareAttribute' => 'newpassword_repeat')
   );
}
```

4. Before allowing the user to change any of their information (including their password and e-mail address), we're going to require them to enter their current password. This will validate that they have control over the account:

```
public function verifyPassword($attribute,$params)
{
   // Only allow change requests from the currently logged inuser
   $this->_user = User::model()->findByPk(Yii::app()->user->id);

   // User doesn't exist. Something bad has happened
   if ($this->_user == NULL)
      return false;

   // NULL the new password if it isn't set
```

[154]

```
    if ($this->newpassword == '' || $this->newpassword == NULL)
        $this->newpassword == NULL;

    // Validate the password
    if (!password_verify($this->password, $this->_user->password))
    {
        $this->addError('password', 'The password you entered is invalid');
        return false;
    }
    return true;
}
```

5. We'll then add our `save()` method that will update the user's information:
   ```
   public function save()
   {
       if (!$this->validate())
           return false;

       // Set the user attributes
       $this->_user->attributes = array(
           // If the email submitted is different than the current email, change the new_email field
           'new_email' => $this->email == $this->_user->email ? NULL : $this->email,

           // Set the new password if validation passes
           'password' => $this->newpassword == NULL ? NULL : $this->newpassword,
           'name' => $this->name
       );

       // Save the user's information
       if ($this->_user->save())
       {
           // If the user's password has changed, send the user an email so that they can be aware of it
           if ($this->newpassword != NULL && $this->password != $this->newpassword)
               $this->sendPasswordChangeNotification();

           // If the user entered a NEW email address, and we haven't already sent them a change email notification
           // Send them a change email notification
   ```

```
        if ($this->email != $this->_user->_oldAttributes['email'] &&
$this->_user->activated != -2)
            $this->sendEmailChangeNotification();

        return true;
    }

    return false;
}
```

6. In the `save()` method, we declared two new methods: `sendPasswordChangeNotification()` and `sendEmailChangeNotification()`. These two methods will send e-mails to the user when the event occurs:

   ```
   private function sendPasswordChangeNotification()
   {
       $sendgrid = new SendGrid(Yii::app()->params['includes']
   ['sendgrid']['username'], Yii::app()->params['includes']
   ['sendgrid']['password']);
       $email    = new SendGrid\Email();

       $email->setFrom(Yii::app()->params['includes']['sendgrid']
   ['from'])
           ->addTo($this->_user->email)
           ->setSubject("Your Socialii Password Has Been Changed")
           ->setText('Your Socialii Password Has Been Changed')
           ->setHtml(Yii::app()->controller->renderPartial('//email/
   passwordchange', array('user' => $this->_user), true));

       // Send the email
       return $sendgrid->send($email);
   }
   ```

7. The second method, `sendEmailChangeNotification()` sends an e-mail to the user when the user's e-mail address changes. This allows us to verify their new e-mail address before we start using it in our application:

   ```
   private function sendEmailChangeNotification()
   {
       // Change the user's activation status for the verification
   link
       $this->_user->activated = -2;
       $this->_user->activation_key = $this->_user-
   >generateActivationKey();

       // Save the user's information
       if ($this->_user->save())
   ```

```
    {
        $sendgrid = new SendGrid(Yii::app()->params['includes']
['sendgrid']['username'], Yii::app()->params['includes']
['sendgrid']['password']);
        $email    = new SendGrid\Email();

        $email->setFrom(Yii::app()->params['includes']['sendgrid']
['from'])
            ->addTo($this->_user->new_email)
            ->setSubject("Verify Your New Email Address")
            ->setText('Verify Your New Email Address')
            ->setHtml(Yii::app()->controller->renderPartial('//email/
verify', array('user' => $this->_user), true));

        // Send the email
        return $sendgrid->send($email);
    }

    return false;
}
```

8. Then, within our `UserController`, we'll define our `actionIndex()` method that will collect this information:

```
public function actionIndex()
{
    $user = User::model()->findByPk(Yii::app()->user->id);
    $form = new ProfileForm;
    if (isset($_POST['ProfileForm']))
    {
        $form->attributes = $_POST['ProfileForm'];
        $form->newpassword_repeat = $_POST['ProfileForm']
['newpassword_repeat'];

        if ($form->save())
            Yii::app()->user->setFlash('success', 'Your information
has been successfully changed');
        else
            Yii::app()->user->setFlash('danger', 'There was an error
updating your information');
    }

    $this->render('index', array(
        'user' => $user,
        'profileform' => $form
    ));
}
```

9. Finally, we need to copy `protected/views/user/index.php`, `protected/view/email/passwordchange.php` and `protected/views/email/verify.php` from our project resources folder into our project.

Verifying a new e-mail address

Now, our users can change their own information without having to go through us. Before we close `UserController`, there are a couple of more methods that we need to implement.

One secure way of changing a user's e-mail address is to store the new e-mail address in a temporary table or column in our database and then send to that e-mail address a verification e-mail (this is what we implemented in our `ProfileForm` class). This allows us to indicate that we're aware that the user wants to change their password, but we require them to prove that they have access to the new e-mail address. The e-mail that we sent them contains a secure activation token and a link to the `actionVerify()` method, which will verify that the token belongs to the user, and then move the new e-mail address to the main e-mail address field in our database. We can implement the `actionVerify()` method as follows:

```php
public function actionVerify($id=NULL)
{
   if ($id == NULL)
      throw new CHttpException(400, 'Activation ID is missing');

   $user = User::model()->findByAttributes(array('activation_key' => $id));

   if ($user == NULL)
      throw new CHttpException(400, 'The verification ID you supplied is invalid');

   $user->attributes = array(
      'email' => $user->new_email,
      'new_email' => NULL,
      'activated' => 1,
      'activation_key' => NULL
   );

   // Save the information
   if ($user->save())
   {
      $this->render('verify');
```

```
        Yii::app()->end();
    }

    throw new CHttpException(500, 'There was an error processing your
request. Please try again later');
}
```

The last actions we'll implement for this controller will allow a user to follow and unfollow another user. We'll use these actions in our views later in the chapter. For now, implement the actions as follows:

```
public function actionFollow($id=NULL)
{
    if ($id == NULL)
        throw new CHttpException(400, 'You must specify the user you
wish to follow');

    if ($id == Yii::app()->user->id)
        throw new CHttpException(400, 'You cannot follow yourself');

    $follower = new Follower;
    $follower->attributes = array(
        'follower_id' => Yii::app()->user->id,
        'followee_id' => $id
    );

    if ($follower->save())
        Yii::app()->user->setFlash('success', 'You are now  following '
. User::model()->findByPk($id)->name);

    // Redirect back to where they were before
    $this->redirect(Yii::app()->request->urlReferrer);
}

public function actionUnFollow($id=NULL)
{
    if ($id == NULL)
    throw new CHttpException(400, 'You must specify the user you wish
to unfollow');

    if ($id == Yii::app()->user->id)
        throw new CHttpException(400, 'You cannot unfollow yourself');

    $follower = Follower::model()->findByAttributes(array('follower_id'
=> Yii::app()->user->id, 'followee_id' => $id));
```

```
      if ($follower != NULL)
      {
         if ($follower->delete())
            Yii::app()->user->setFlash('success', 'You are no longer
following ' . User::model()->findByPk($id)->name);
      }

      // Redirect back to where they were before
      $this->redirect(Yii::app()->request->urlReferrer);
   }
```

Before closing this controller, verify that the `accessRules()` method is set up correctly:

```
   public function accessRules()
   {
      return array(
      array('allow',
          'actions' => array('register', 'forgot', 'verify', 'activate',
'resetpassword'),
          'users' => array('*')
          ),
          array('allow',
              'actions' => array('index', 'follow', 'unfollow'),
              'users'=>array('@'),
          ),
          array('deny',  // deny all users
              'users'=>array('*'),
          ),
       );
   }
```

Viewing a timeline of shares

The easiest way to display new content is to simply list it so that the newest items are shown first. On our timeline page, we want to provide the user with the ability to share something, view information about the user they are viewing (such as the number of shares, followers, and followees), and view things that the user has recently shared. To do this, we're going to take advantage of `CListView` loaded asynchronously from our main timeline view. This will allow us to reuse this view later on by simply making a `GET` request to an endpoint that we'll create later. In our `TimelineController.php` file located at `protected/controllers/`, implement the `actionIndex()` method:

```
   public function actionIndex($id = NULL)
   {
```

```php
    // If the ID is not set, set this to the currently logged in user.
    if ($id == NULL)
    {
       if (Yii::app()->user->isGuest)
          $this->redirect($this->createUrl('site/login'));

       $id = Yii::app()->user->username;
    }

    // Get the user's information
    $user = User::model()->findByAttributes(array('username' => $id));
    if ($user == NULL)
       throw new CHttpException(400, 'Unable to find a user with that ID');

    $this->render('index', array(
       'user' => $user,
       'share' => new Share,
       'id' => $user->id
    ));
 }
```

All that we're doing in this action is retrieving the user ID (in this case, the username of the user) from the route and then passing some information down to our view. From the project resources folder, copy the index.php file located at protected/views/timeline/ into your project. Let's take a look at some of the more interesting parts of this file.

The first thing to notice in this file is that we're simply using CActiveForm to display the new share container. Moreover, at the bottom of this file, we've implemented some JavaScript to do some rudimentary form validation checking, to clear the text field upon asynchronous submission, to adjust the number of shares we have, and finally, to prepend the new share to the top of our shares list.

The second thing to notice is that we've implemented conditional follow and unfollow button links to allow our users to simply click on a link to follow or unfollow a particular user:

```php
<?php if (Yii::app()->user->isGuest): ?>
   <?php echo CHtml::link('Login to follow ' . $user->name, $this->createUrl('site/login'), array('class' => 'btn btn-primary')); ?>
      <br /><br />
   <?php else: ?>
      <?php if (!User::isFollowing($id)): ?>
```

Creating a Microblogging Platform

```php
            <?php echo CHtml::link('Follow This User', $this-
>createUrl('user/follow/', array('id' => $id)), array('class' => 'btn
btn-success')); ?>
        <?php else: ?>
            <?php echo CHtml::link('Stop Following This User', $this-
>createUrl('user/unfollow/', array('id' => $id)), array('class' =>
'btn btn-danger')); ?>
    <?php endif; ?>
<?php endif; ?>
```

The last thing to notice in this file is our use of the count relations we set up earlier in our User model:

```php
<a type="button" class="btn btn-primary" disabled>Followers: <?php
echo $user->followeesCount; ?></a>
<a type="button" class="btn btn-primary" disabled>Following: <?php
echo $user->followersCount; ?></a>
<a type="button" class="btn btn-primary" disabled>Shares: <span
class="share-count"><?php echo $user->sharesCount; ?></span></a>
```

Finally, we're loading our shares for this user by registering an asynchronous callback to fetch the appropriate shares, regardless of which user we are viewing the share for:

```php
<?php Yii::app()->clientScript->registerScript('loadshares', '$.get("'
. $this->createUrl('share/getshares', array('id' => $id)) . '"',
function(data) { $(".shares").html(data); }); '); ?>
```

Retrieving shares

Now, let's implement our action that will display our shares. This action will have slightly different behaviors depending on whether we're viewing our timeline or a timeline of another user. Within our `ShareController.php` file located at `protected/controllers/`, implement `actionGetShares`, as follows:

```php
public function actionGetShares($id=NULL) {}
```

The next steps are as follows:

1. Since this is an asynchronous callback, we don't want to render anything from our layout:

    ```php
    $this->layout = false;
    ```

2. Next, we're going to either throw an error if a user wasn't provided and we're not logged in, or set the user to ourselves if we are logged in and an ID was given to us:

    ```php
    if ($id == NULL)
    ```

```
    {
        if (Yii::app()->user->isGuest)
            throw new CHttpException(400, 'Cannot retrieve shares for
that user');

        $id = Yii::app()->user->id;
    }
```

3. Then we're going to implement CListView, which will retrieve data from our GET parameters:

   ```
   $myFollowers = array();

   // CListView for showing shares
   $shares = new Share('search');
   $shares->unsetAttributes();

   if(isset($_GET['Share']))
       $shares->attributes=$_GET['Share'];
   ```

4. When viewing another user's timeline, we only care about the shares that they have shared with the world. However, when we're viewing our timeline, we want to view both our shares and the shares of the user we are following. We can implement the controller portion of this as follows:

   ```
       // If this is NOT the current user, then only show stuff that
   belongs to this user
       if ($id != Yii::app()->user->id)
           $shares->author_id = $id;
       else
       {
           // Alter the criteria to do a search of everyone the current
   user is following
           $myFollowers[] = Yii::app()->user->id;

           $followers = Follower::model()->findAllByAttributes(array('f
   ollower_id' => Yii::app()->user->id));
           if ($followers != NULL)
           {
               foreach ($followers as $follower)
                   $myFollowers[] = $follower->followee_id;
           }
       }

       $this->render('getshares', array('shares' => $shares,
   'myFollowers' => $myFollowers));
   }
   ```

5. Then, we'll need to implement our getshares.php view file at protected/views/shares/ as CListView. Notice that we're passing down $myFollowers as a custom parameter to our Share model's search() method:

```php
<?php $this->widget('zii.widgets.CListView', array(
    'dataProvider'=>$shares->search($myFollowers),
    'itemView'=>'share',
    'emptyText' => '<div class="center">This user hasn\'t shared anything yet!</div>',
    'template' => '{items}{pager}',
    'afterAjaxUpdate' => 'js:function() { init(); }
',
    'pager' => array(
        'header' => ' ',
        'selectedPageCssClass' => 'active',
        'htmlOptions' => array('class' => 'pagination')
    )
));

Yii::app()->clientScript->registerScript('init', '
function init() {
    $(".fa-heart").click(function() {
        var id = $(this).parent().parent().parent().attr("data-attr-id");
        var self = this;
        $.post("' . $this->createUrl('share/like') . '/" + id, function(data) {
                $(self).toggleClass("liked");
        });
    });

    $(".fa-mail-forward").click(function() {
        var id = $(this).parent().parent().parent().attr("data-attr-id");
        var self = this;
        $.post("' . $this->createUrl('share/re-share') . '/" + id, function(data) {
                $(self).toggleClass("liked");
        });
    });
}

init();
');
```

6. Then, within our model, we're going to adjust our `search()` method so that it conditionally loads the appropriate data:

```php
public function search($items = array())
{
    $criteria=new CDbCriteria;

    $criteria->compare('id',$this->id);
    $criteria->compare('text',$this->text,true);
    $criteria->compare('reply_id',$this->reply_id);
    $criteria->compare('created',$this->created);

    if (empty($items))
        $criteria->compare('author_id',$this->author_id);
    else
        $criteria->addInCondition('author_id', $items);

    $criteria->order = 'created DESC';
    return new CActiveDataProvider($this, array(
        'criteria' => $criteria,
    ));
}
```

7. Finally, we can implement our individual share view by copying `protected/views/share/share.php` from our project resources folder into our project.

Within this file, we're going to implement some custom logic so that hashtags (#) and @ mentions are displayed as links. This will allow us to store unformatted text in our database, which in turns means we could adjust the way our views work without having to modify our data. We're also going to render our text in Markdown to allow our users to add links or other custom formatting, but prevent them from attempting XSS injection:

```php
<?php
$data->text = preg_replace("/#([A-Za-z0-9\/\.]*)/", "<a target=\"_new\" href=\"" . Yii::app()->controller->createAbsoluteUrl('timeline/search') ."?q=$1\">#$1</a>", $data->text);
$data->text = preg_replace("/@([A-Za-z0-9\/\.]*)/", "<a href=\"" . Yii::app()->controller->createAbsoluteUrl('timeline/index')."/$1\">@$1</a>", $data->text);
$md = new CMarkdownParser;
echo $md->safeTransform($data->text);
```

Sharing new content

At this point, if we had shares in our database, we'd be able to see them. So let's work on sharing new content! From within our controller, the action to handle sharing is simply going to be loading a new Share model and populating it. Have a look at the following code:

```
public function actionCreate()
{
   $share = new Share;

   if (isset($_POST['Share']))
   {
      $share->attributes = array(
         'text' => $_POST['Share']['text'],
         'reply_id' => isset($_POST['Share']['reply_id']) ? $_POST['Share']['reply_id'] : NULL,
         'author_id' => Yii::app()->user->id
      );

      // Share the content
      if ($share->save())
      {
         $this->renderPartial('share', array('data' => $share));
         Yii::app()->end();
      }
   }

   throw new CHttpException(500, 'There was an error sharing your content');
}
```

Though, the real power behind sharing content happens in the `beforeSave()` method of our Share model. From here, we handle all the mentioning that may occur within our model, and send an e-mail to everyone who was mentioning in the share. The code is as follows:

```
public function afterSave()
{
   preg_match_all('/@([A-Za-z0-9\/\.]*)/', $this->text, $matches);
   $mentions = implode(',', $matches[1]);

   if (!empty($matches[1]))
   {
      $criteria = new CDbCriteria;
```

```
        $criteria->addInCondition('username', $matches[1]);
        $users = User::model()->findAll($criteria);

        foreach ($users as $user)
        {
            $sendgrid = new SendGrid(Yii::app()->params['includes']
['sendgrid']['username'], Yii::app()->params['includes']['sendgrid']
['password']);
            $email    = new SendGrid\Email();

            $email->setFrom(Yii::app()->params['includes']['sendgrid']
['from'])
                ->addTo($user->email)
                ->setSubject("You've Been @mentioned!")
                ->setText("You've Been @mentioned!")
                ->setHtml(Yii::app()->controller->renderPartial('//email/
mention', array('share' => $this, 'user' => $user), true));

            // Send the email
            $sendgrid->send($email);
        }
    }

    return parent::afterSave();
}
```

Resharing

Since everything in our model is already implemented, we can easily implement resharing now as a new controller action within `protected/controllers/ShareController.php`. Resharing allows a user to share something another user shared, while still giving that user credit for the original share. In our controller, what we're going to do is load the share we want to reshare with our network, change the author to us, and then indicate that this is a reshare of another share.

First, let's create a `loadModel()` utility method:

```
private function loadModel($id=NULL)
{
    if ($id == NULL)
        throw new CHttpException(400, 'Missing Share ID');

    return Share::model()->findByPk($id);
}
```

Then, we'll implement the resharing ability as described in the *Describing the project* section:

```
public function actionReshare($id=NULL)
{
    // Load the share model
    $share = $this->loadModel($id);

    // You can't reshare your own stuff
    if ($share->author_id == Yii::app()->user->id)
    return false;

    // You can't reshare stuff you've already reshared
    $reshare = Share::model()->findByAttributes(array(
        'author_id' => Yii::app()->user->id,
        'reshare_id' => $id
    ));

    if ($reshare !== NULL)
    return false;

    // Create a new Share as a reshare
    $model = new Share;

    // Assign the shared attributes
    $model->attributes = $share->attributes;

    // Set the reshare other to the current user
    $model->author_id = Yii::app()->user->id;

    // Propogate the reshare if this isn't original
    if ($model->reshare_id == 0 || $model->reshare_id == NULL)
    $model->reshare_id = $share->id;

    // Then save the reshare, return the response. Yii will set a 200
or 500 response code automagically if false
    return $model->save();
}
```

Liking and unliking shares

Next, we'll implement the actions and methods necessary for a user to like and unlike a given share. The only restriction on likes should be that a user can't like a share more than once.

We can implement the action for liking in `ShareController` as follows:

```
public function actionLike($id=NULL)
{
    $share = $this->loadModel($id);
    if ($share->isLiked())
        return $share->unlike();

    return $share->like();
}
```

Then, within our Share model, we'll implement the method necessary to check whether an action has already been liked by a user or not:

```
public function isLiked()
{
    $like = Like::model()->findByAttributes(array(
        'user_id' => Yii::app()->user->id,
        'share_id' => $this->id
    ));

    return $like != NULL;
}
```

Then, we will implement the `like()` method:

```
public function like()
{
    $like = Like::model()->findByAttributes(array(
        'user_id' => Yii::app()->user->id,
        'share_id' => $this->id
    ));

    // Share is already liked, return true
    if ($like != NULL)
        return true;

    $like = new Like;
    $like->attributes = array(
        'share_id' => $this->id,
        'user_id' => Yii::app()->user->id
    );

    // Save the like
    return $like->save();
}
```

Creating a Microblogging Platform

Finally, we will implement the `unlike()` method:

```
public function unlike()
{
    $like = Like::model()->findByAttributes(array(
        'user_id' => Yii::app()->user->id,
        'share_id' => $this->id
    ));

    // Item is not already liked, return true
    if ($like == NULL)
        return true;

    // Delete the Like
    return $like->delete();
}
```

Viewing shares

At this point, we can do everything with a share except dive into one and view all the replies to a share. Let's implement the `actionView()` method so that our users can view a particular share. In `ShareController`, we'll implement this as follows:

```
public function actionView($id=NULL)
{
    $share = $this->loadModel($id);

    if ($share == NULL)
        throw new CHttpException(400, 'No share with that ID was found');

    $this->render('view', array(
        'share' => $share,
        'replies' => Share::model()->findAllByAttributes(array('reply_id' => $id), array('order' => 'created DESC')),
        'reply' => new Share
    ));
}
```

Then, we will copy `protected/views/share/view.php` from our project resources folder into the project. Within our view, we can now share something and click on the eye icon on the share in order to view it in more detail.

Searching for shares

One of the most important parts of any application is the ability to search for and discover new content. For this application, we'll be implementing a search method that will allow users to search for content and users. To do this, we'll check whether the query string in our search method contains the @ character. If it does, we'll perform a second search for that user and display information about that user in our view. We'll implement that method as follows:

1. We'll start by implementing `actionSearch()` as follows:

    ```
    public function actionSearch() {}
    ```

2. We'll then retrieve the query string from our `$_GET` parameters and define the scope for our models:

    ```
    $query = isset($_GET['q']) ? $_GET['q'] : NULL;
    $users = $shares = NULL;
    ```

3. Then, as long as there is a query to run against, we'll create two `CDbCriteria` objects; one for users and the other for shares:

    ```
    if ($query != NULL)
    {
        $userCriteria = new CDbCriteria;
        $searchCriteria = new CDbCriteria;
    }
    ```

4. Within this `if` bracket, we'll first check whether there were any mentions in our query string, by using `preg_match_all`:

    ```
    preg_match_all('/@([A-Za-z0-9\/\.]*)/', $query, $matches);
    $mentions = implode(',', $matches[1]);
    ```

5. If there are any results, we'll build a query to find all the users who were mentioned in the query, and then, we'll remove that criteria from our query string:

    ```
    if (!empty($matches[1]))
    {
        $userCriteria->addInCondition('username', $matches[1]);
        $users = User::model()->findAll($userCriteria);
        foreach ($matches[1] as $u)
            $query = str_replace('@'.$u,'',$query);
    }
    ```

6. Then, we'll perform a LIKE query search against the text field of our Share model:
   ```
   $searchCriteria->addSearchCondition('text', $query);
   $searchCriteria->limit = 30;
   $shares = Share::model()->findAll($searchCriteria);
   ```

7. Then, we'll render our view:
   ```
   $this->render('search', array(
       'users' => $users,
       'shares' => $shares
   ));
   ```

8. Finally, we'll need to copy our view file from `protected/views/timeline/search.php` into our project folder.

Sharing on Twitter with HybridAuth

Since our application doesn't have a large following yet, it's important to enable our users to share content that they generate on our site to other places. A great way to spread the word about a particular site or service is to take advantage of Twitter. One way to integrate with Twitter is by utilizing their OAuth API. This will allow us to authenticate as a given user and post content on their behalf, at just a click of a button.

To do this, we'll be taking advantage of **HybridAuth**. HybridAuth is an open source library that allows developers to integrate with multiple third-party social networks, and enables developers to make their application more social. For our purposes, we're going to utilize HybridAuth to impersonate a given user (with their permission, of course) and submit content on their behalf upon their request.

> If you want to learn more about HybridAuth, check out the official documentation at http://hybridauth.sourceforge.net/.

Setting up a Twitter application

Before we start using HybridAuth though, we first need to set up a Twitter application and obtain our OAuth credentials. These credentials will allow our application to communicate securely with Twitter, and enable us to sign in and post as our users. The steps are as follows:

> What is OAuth? OAuth is an open standard for authentication, and provides client applications such as the one we are building in this application, secure delegated access to server resources on behalf of that owner, in this case, Twitter. By using OAuth, we can communicate securely with a server without having to transmit our user's credentials to our application. In our application, we'll be using HybridAuth to take care of most of the leg work when dealing with Twitter's OAuth endpoint. Check out `http://oauth.net/about/` for more information about what OAuth is and how it works.

1. To begin, open up your web browser, navigate to `https://apps.twitter.com/`, and sign in using your Twitter credentials.
2. Once authenticated, click on the **Create New App** button in the top-right corner of the page body.
3. On this page, fill out the fields as shown in the next screenshot. Adjust the website URL and **Callback URL** to match what you are using in your application. Note that the endpoint you provide to Twitter must be publicly accessible.

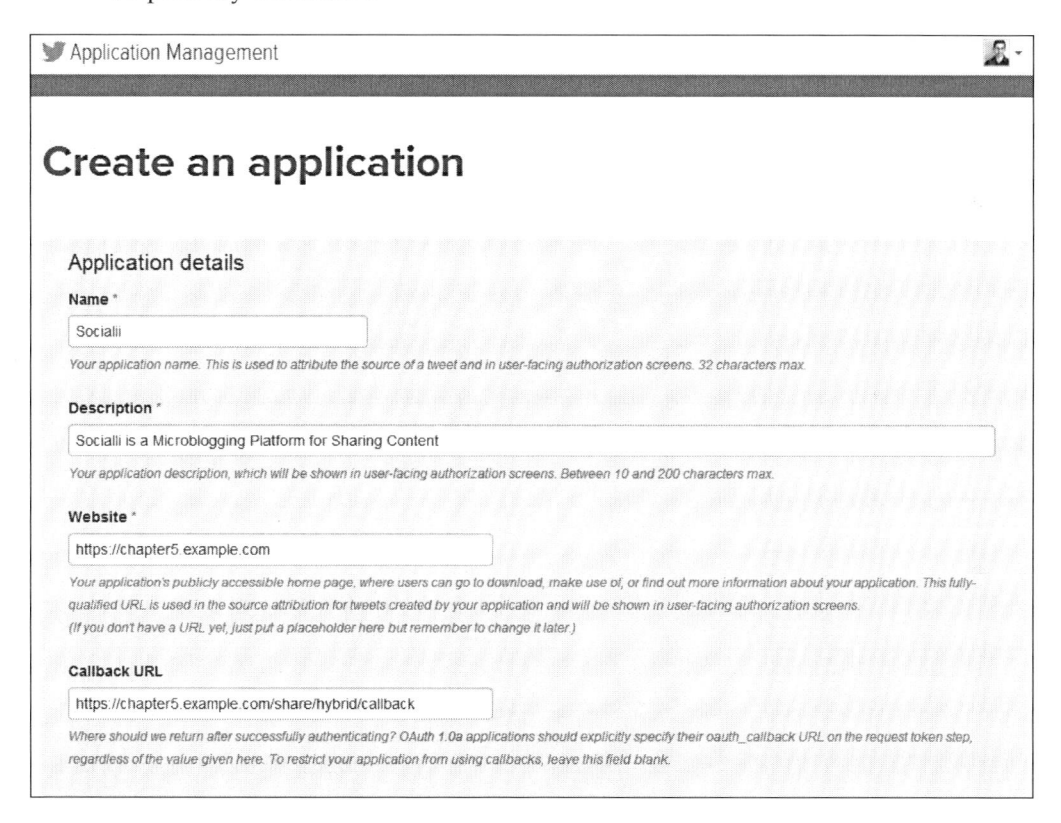

Create an application

Application details

Name *

Socialli

Your application name. This is used to attribute the source of a tweet and in user-facing authorization screens. 32 characters max.

Description *

Socialli is a Microblogging Platform for Sharing Content

Your application description, which will be shown in user-facing authorization screens. Between 10 and 200 characters max.

Website *

https://chapter5.example.com

Your application's publicly accessible home page, where users can go to download, make use of, or find out more information about your application. This fully-qualified URL is used in the source attribution for tweets created by your application and will be shown in user-facing authorization screens.
(If you don't have a URL yet, just put a placeholder here but remember to change it later.)

Callback URL

https://chapter5.example.com/share/hybrid/callback

Where should we return after successfully authenticating? OAuth 1.0a applications should explicitly specify their oauth_callback URL on the request token step, regardless of the value given here. To restrict your application from using callbacks, leave this field blank.

4. On the next page, click on the **Settings** tab, check the **Allow this application to be used to sign into Twitter** checkbox, and click on the **Update Settings** button at the bottom of the page.

5. Then, click on the **Permissions** tab and change the access level to **Read and Write** and save the form.

Configuring HybridAuth

With our Twitter application configured, we now need to install and configure HybridAuth. Fortunately, HybridAuth is available as a Composer dependency, so we can include its source code into our project by adding the following to the require section of our `composer.json` file:

```
"hybridauth/hybridauth": "2.2.0.*@dev"
```

The next steps are as follows:

1. Run the `composer update` command from your command line:

   ```
   composer update
   ```

2. You should see something similar to the following output:

   ```
   Loading composer repositories with package information
   Updating dependencies (including require-dev)
     - Installing hybridauth/hybridauth (2.2.0.x-dev 5774600)
       Cloning 57746000e5b2f96469b229b366e56eb70ab7bf20

   Writing lock file
   Generating autoload files
   ```

3. Next, we'll configure HybridAuth so that it knows what information to use. Open up `protected/config/params.php`, and add the following after our SendGrid information:

   ```
   'hybridauth' => array(
       'baseUrl' => '',
       'base_url' => '',
       'providers' => array(
           'Twitter' => array(
               'enabled' => true,
               'keys' => array(
                   'key' => '<twiter_key>',
   ```

```
                    'secret' => '<twitter_secret>'
                )
            )
        )
    )
```

4. Then, retrieve your Twitter API key and Twitter Secret key from the **API Keys** tab of our Twitter application, as shown in the next screenshot, and replace `<twitter_key>` and `<twitter_secret>` with them in your configuration file:

> Your Twitter OAuth Key and Secret are confidential pieces of information and should be kept out of your DCVS provider. If you ever suspect that your OAuth credentials have been compromised, you should immediately regenerate your API keys. This will prevent potential attacks from gaining the ability to sign on and tweet as your users.

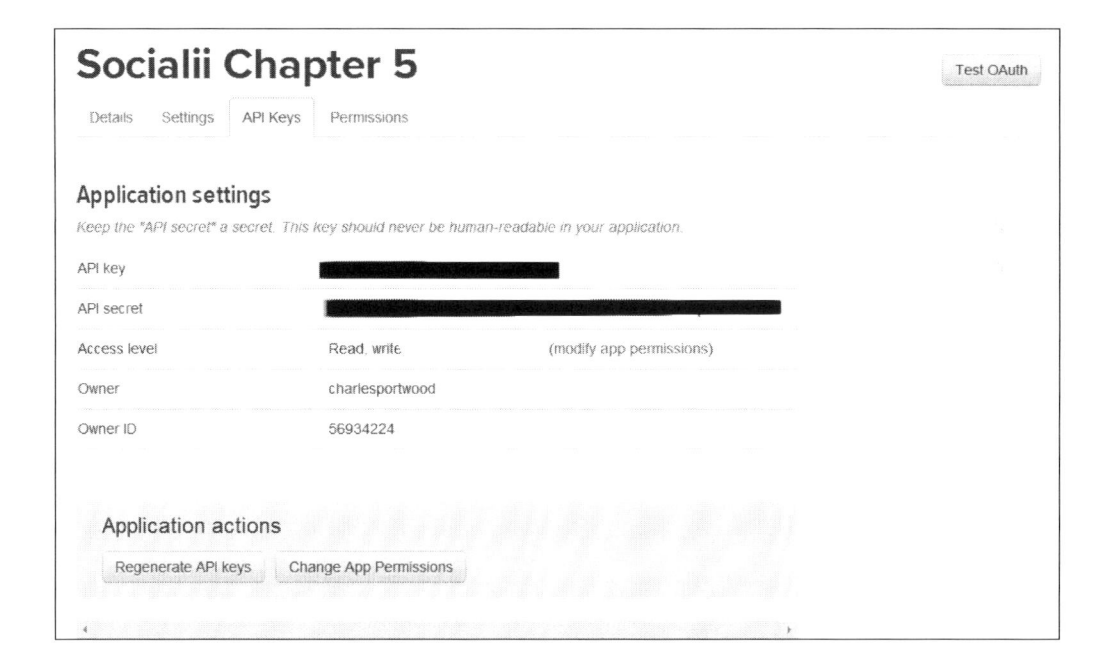

Socialii Chapter 5

Details   Settings   **API Keys**   Permissions

Application settings

Keep the "API secret" a secret. This key should never be human-readable in your application.

API key	████████████████
API secret	████████████████████████
Access level	Read, write (modify app permissions)
Owner	charlesportwood
Owner ID	56934224

Application actions

[Regenerate API keys] [Change App Permissions]

> HybridAuth can be configured with several different options. Be sure to look at a few of the examples if you're interested in implementing social sharing for other providers at http://hybridauth.sourceforge.net/userguide/Configuration.html.

Implementing HybridAuth social sign-on and sharing

Now that our application has Twitter's OAuth credentials, we can implement the social sign-on and sharing features:

1. Begin by adjusting our `accessRules()` method to only allow authenticated users to share content on Twitter:

    ```
    array('allow',
        'actions' => array('create', 'reshare', 'like', 'delete',
    'hybrid'),
        'users' => array('@')
    ),
    ```

2. Then, implement the `actionHybrid()` method:

    ```
    public function actionHybrid($id=NULL) {}
    ```

3. We'll start this action by looking for some specific HybridAuth `$_GET` parameters, and calling `Hybrid_Endpoint::process()` if either of the two are detected:

    ```
    if (isset($_GET['hauth_start']) || isset($_GET['hauth_done']))
        Hybrid_Endpoint::process();
    ```

4. We'll then wrap the next section in a `try/catch` block to catch any errors that HybridAuth may throw if it encounters an error:

    ```
    try {
    } catch (Exception $e) {
        $this->redirect($this->createUrl('timeline/index'));
    }
    ```

5. Within our `try/catch` block, we'll then load our configuration we set in our `params.php` file, and set the base URL for HybridAuth to use internally within our application. This base URL should correspond to the location from where HybridAuth will be called:

    ```
    $config = Yii::app()->params['includes']['hybridauth'];
    $config['baseUrl'] = $config['base_url'] = $this-
    >createAbsoluteUrl('share/hybrid');
    ```

6. We'll initialize HybridAuth with our configuration:

    ```
    $hybridauth = new Hybrid_Auth($config, array());
    ```

7. Then, we'll create a HybridAuth adapter for us to talk to Twitter:

    ```
    $adapter = $hybridauth->authenticate('Twitter');
    ```

8. Next, we should check whether the `adapter` is connected to Twitter:

   ```
   if ($adapter->isUserConnected()) {}
   ```

9. Within this `if` block, we should load the share we want to share on Twitter:

   ```
   $share = $this->loadModel($id);
   ```

10. Then, share our content on Twitter:

    ```
    $response = $adapter->setUserStatus($share->text . ' | #Socialii '
    . $this->createAbsoluteUrl('share/view', array('id' => $id)));
    Yii::app()->user->setFlash('success', 'Your status has been shared
    to Twitter');
    $this->redirect(Yii::app()->user->returnUrl);
    ```

Now, if you share something on our site, then click on the Twitter icon for that share; you'll be redirected to Twitter to sign in, as shown in the following screenshot:

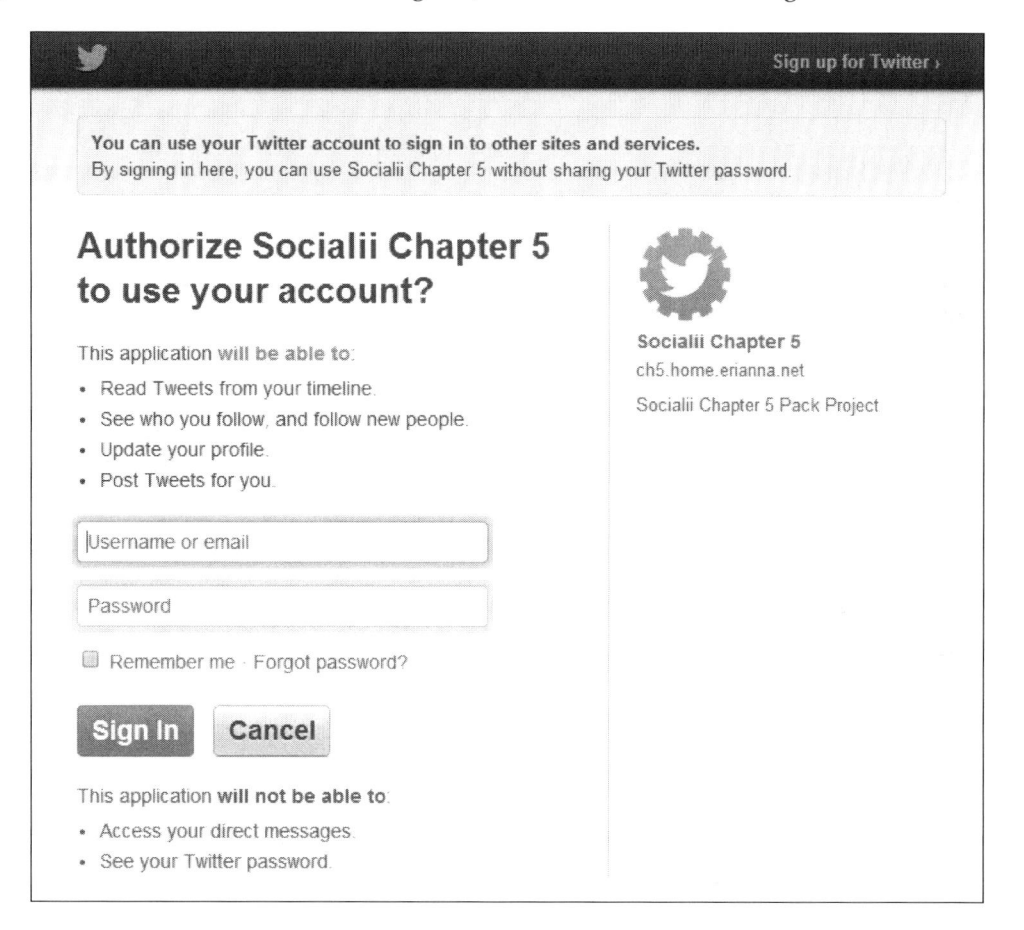

Creating a Microblogging Platform

After signing in, you'll need to authorize our application to update our Twitter profile, as shown in the following screenshot:

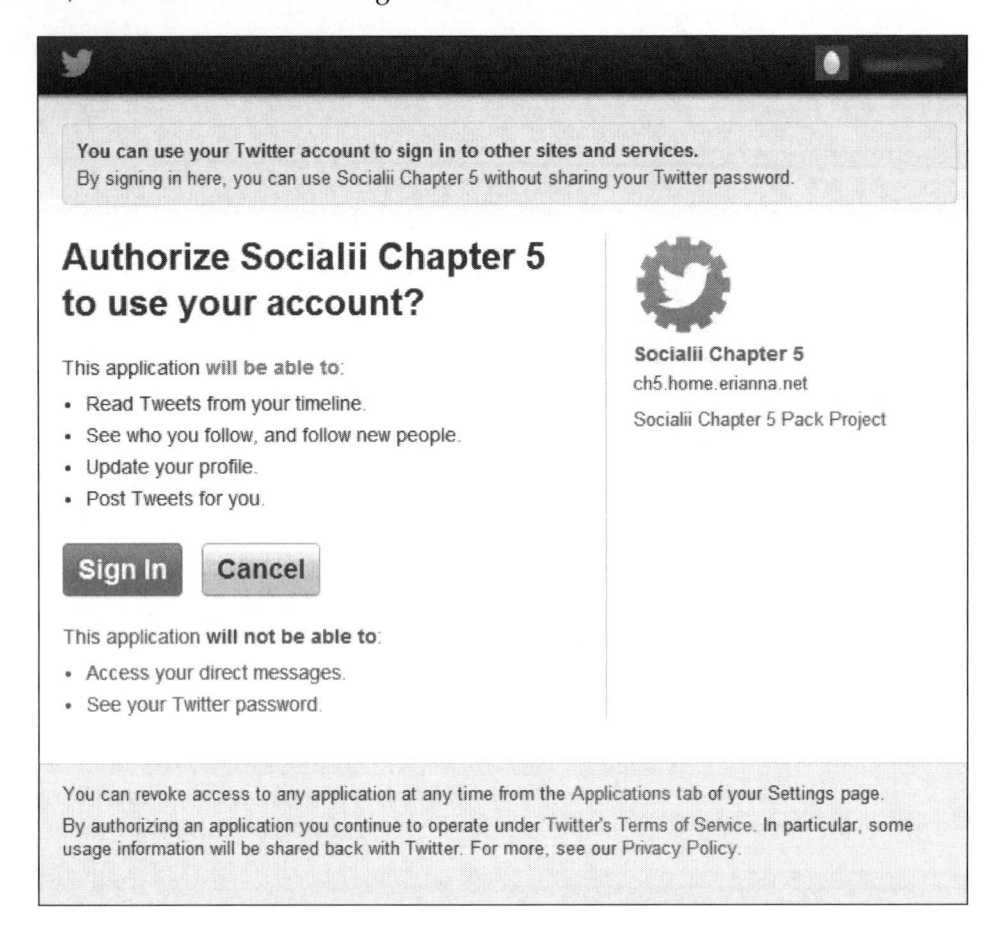

Authorize Socialii Chapter 5 to use your account?

This application will be able to:

- Read Tweets from your timeline.
- See who you follow, and follow new people.
- Update your profile.
- Post Tweets for you.

Socialii Chapter 5
ch5.home.erianna.net
Socialii Chapter 5 Pack Project

This application **will not be able to**:

- Access your direct messages.
- See your Twitter password.

You can revoke access to any application at any time from the Applications tab of your Settings page.

By authorizing an application you continue to operate under Twitter's Terms of Service. In particular, some usage information will be shared back with Twitter. For more, see our Privacy Policy.

Then, our content will be shared on Twitter on our behalf, as shown in the next screenshot. Moreover, if we click on the Twitter button again within our application, our content will be automatically shared on Twitter for us, without us having to reauthenticate against Twitter.

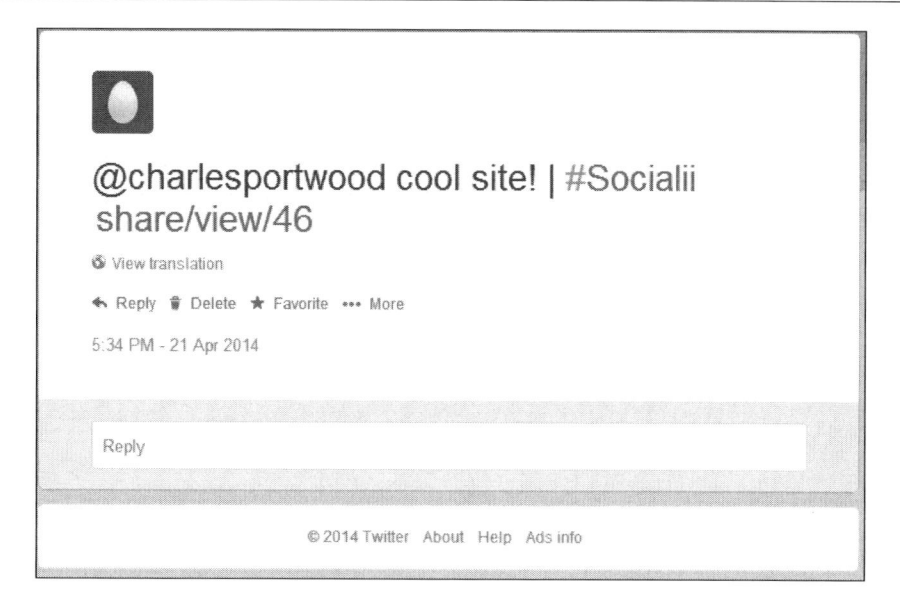

> @charlesportwood cool site! | #Socialii share/view/46
>
> View translation
>
> Reply Delete Favorite More
>
> 5:34 PM - 21 Apr 2014
>
> Reply
>
> © 2014 Twitter About Help Ads info

Summary

Wow, we covered quite a bit in this chapter! We expanded upon our user authentication and management to include secure activation and password resets if a user forgets their password, and enabled our users to securely and safely change both their own e-mail address and password with proper verification and notifications. Moreover, we implemented all of these actions using `CFormModel`, which enabled us to cleanly isolate the logic for handling these actions in forms rather than in our controllers. Finally, we implemented an asynchronous `CListViews` and utilized HybridAuth to share on Twitter using our OAuth credentials.

The user components that we developed in this chapter can easily be used and adapted for almost any application that will require user authentication and management. In the next chapter, we'll be utilizing these components to build a full-scale content management system that will allow us to upload content and photos and also allow us to share this content with others. The CMS that we'll be building will also be SEO-optimized and will include dynamic content slugs and a sitemap feature that can be submitted to the search engines. Before proceeding to the next chapter, be sure to review the Yii Class Reference at `http://www.yiiframework.com/doc/api/` and review all the classes that we used in this chapter. Then, when you're ready, head over to the next chapter where you'll build a CMS!

6
Building a Content Management System

For our next project, we will develop a scalable, multiuser content management system that will allow our users to create and update blog posts and enable them to comment on these blog posts. In addition to reutilizing many of the features we've developed for previous applications, this system will be optimized for optimal placement in search engines. Moreover, this system will feature a social sign-on feature that will allow users to register and log in from a third-party social network provider. We'll also explore the use of themes within our application, which will enable us to change the presentation layer of our application with minimal effort.

When we're finished, our CMS will look as follows:

Prerequisites

Before we get started, there are a couple of things that we'll need to have set up and working:

- Once again, we'll need to have a web server with a public-facing IP address. This will allow e-mails to be sent to our application. Many cloud Virtual Private Server (VPS) providers are available to use for low month or hourly prices. Such services include `https://www.digitalocean.com`, `www.linode.com`, and `www.rackspace.com/cloud/servers`.

- In order to send e-mails in our application, we'll once again utilize a free SendGrid Developer Account, which can be set up at `https://www.sendgrid.com/developers`.

- In this chapter, we'll once again use the latest version of MySQL (at the time of this writing, MySQL 5.6). Make sure that your MySQL server is set up and running on your server.

> Do you want to try something more challenging? After completing this project, try to figure out what changes you need to make to this application to make it work with Postgres rather than MySQL.

- For this project, we'll once again manage our dependencies through Composer, which you can download and install from `https://getcomposer.org/`.

- We'll also be using **Disqus**, a third-party commenting system that we will integrate with to display comments on our site. For this project, you'll need to register an account with `https://www.disqus.com`.

- Finally, you'll need a Twitter Developer account, obtained from `https://dev.twitter.com/`. This account will allow us to enable the social sign-on feature of our application through Twitter's OAuth API.

Once you have acquired the listed prerequisites, create a subdomain on the domain name you are using and point it to your server. In this chapter, I'll use `chapter6.example.com` to refer to this subdomain. After everything is set up and your server is responding to that domain name, we can get started.

Describing the project

Our CMS can be broken down into several different components:

- Users who will be responsible for viewing and managing the content
- Content to be managed
- Categories for our content to be placed into
- Metadata to help us further define our content and users
- Search engine optimizations

Users

The first component of our application is the users who will perform all the tasks in our application. For this application, we're going to largely reuse the `user` database and authentication system we expanded upon in *Chapter 5, Creating a Microblogging Platform*. In this chapter, we'll enhance this functionality by allowing social authentication. Our CMS will allow users to register new accounts from the data provided by Twitter; after they have registered, the CMS will allow them to sign-in to our application by signing in to Twitter.

To enable us to know if a user is a socially authenticated user, we have to make several changes to both our database and our authentication scheme. First, we're going to need a way to indicate whether a user is a socially authenticated user. Rather than hardcoding a `isAuthenticatedViaTwitter` column in our database, we'll create a new database table called `user_metadata`, which will be a simple table that contains the user's ID, a unique key, and a value. This will allow us to store additional information about our users without having to explicitly change our user's database table every time we want to make a change:

```
ID INTEGER PRIMARY KEY
user_id INTEGER
key STRING
value STRING
created INTEGER
updated INTEGER
```

We'll also need to modify our `UserIdentity` class to allow socially authenticated users to sign in. To do this, we'll be expanding upon this class to create a `RemoteUserIdentity` class that will work off the OAuth codes that Twitter (or any other third-party source that works with HybridAuth) provides to us rather than authenticating against a username and password.

Content

At the core of our CMS is our content that we'll manage. For this project, we'll manage simple blog posts that can have additional metadata associated with them. Each post will have a title, a body, an author, a category, a unique URI or slug, and an indication whether it has been published or not. Our database structure for this table will look as follows:

```
ID INTEGER PRIMARY KEY
title STRING
body TEXT
published INTEGER
author_id INTEGER
category_id INTEGER
slug STRING
created INTEGER
updated INTEGER
```

Each post will also have one or many metadata columns that will further describe the posts we'll be creating. We can use this table (we'll call it content_metadata) to have our system store information about each post automatically for us, or add information to our posts ourselves, thereby eliminating the need to constantly migrate our database every time we want to add a new attribute to our content:

```
ID INTEGER PRIMARY KEY
content_id INTEGER
key STRING
value STRING
created INTEGER
updated INTEGER
```

Categories

Each post will be associated with a category in our system. These categories will help us further refine our posts. As with our content, each category will have its own slug. Before either a post or a category is saved, we'll need to verify that the slug is not already in use. Our table structure will look as follows:

```
ID INTEGER PRIMARY KEY
name STRING
description TEXT
slug STRING
created INTEGER
updated INTEGER
```

Search engine optimizations

The last core component of our application is optimization for search engines so that our content can be indexed quickly. SEO is important because it increases our discoverability and availability both on search engines and on other marketing materials. In our application, there are a couple of things we'll perform to improve our SEO:

- The first SEO enhancement we'll add is a `sitemap.xml` file, which we can submit to popular search engines to index. Rather than crawl our content, search engines can very quickly index our `sitemap.xml` file, which means that our content will show up in search engines faster.

- The second enhancement we'll be adding is the slugs that we discussed earlier. Slugs allow us to indicate what a particular post is about directly from a URL. So rather than have a URL that looks like `http://chapter6.example.com/content/post/id/5`, we can have URL's that look like: `http://chapter6.example.com/my-awesome-article`. These types of URLs allow search engines and our users to know what our content is about without even looking at the content itself, such as when a user is browsing through their bookmarks or browsing a search engine.

Initializing the project

To provide us with a common starting ground, a skeleton project has been included with the project resources for this chapter. Included with this skeleton project are the necessary migrations, data files, controllers, and views to get us started with developing. Also included in this skeleton project are the user authentication classes we worked on in *Chapter 5, Creating a Microblogging Platform*. Copy this skeleton project to your web server, configure it so that it responds to `chapter6.example.com` as outlined at the beginning of the chapter, and then perform the following steps to make sure everything is set up:

1. Adjust the permissions on the `assets` and `protected/runtime` folders so that they are writable by your web server.

2. In this chapter, we'll once again use the latest version of MySQL (at the time of writing MySQL 5.6). Make sure that your MySQL server is set up and running on your server. Then, create a username, password, and database for our project to use, and update your `protected/config/main.php` file accordingly. For simplicity, you can use `ch6_cms` for each value.

3. Install our Composer dependencies:

    ```
    Composer install
    ```

4. Run the `migrate` command and install our mock data:

   ```
   php protected/yiic.php migrate up --interactive=0
   psql ch6_cms -f protected/data/postgres.sql
   ```

5. Finally, add your SendGrid credentials to your `protected/config/params.php` file:

   ```
   'sendgrid' => array(
   'username' => '<username>',
       'password' => '<password>',
       'from' => 'noreply@ch6.home.erianna.net'
   )
   ```

If everything is loaded correctly, you should see a 404 page similar to the following:

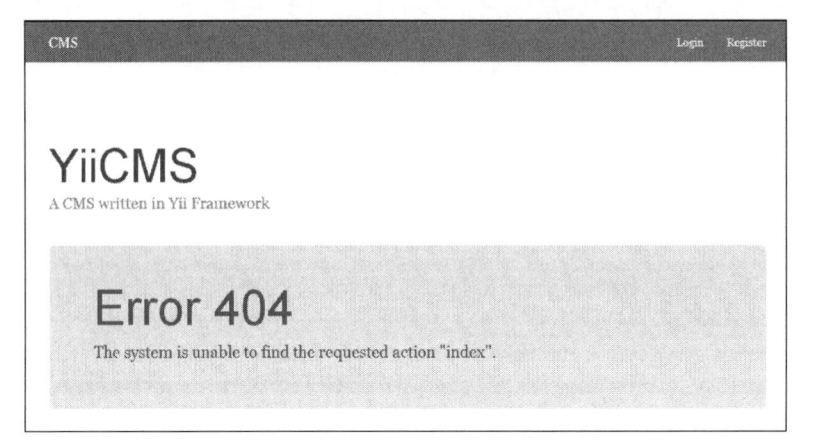

Exploring the skeleton project

There are actually a lot of different things going on in the background to make this work even if this is just a 404 error. Before we start doing any development, let's take a look at a few of the classes that have been provided in our skeleton project in the `protected/components` folder.

Extending models from a common class

The first class that has been provided to us is an ActiveRecord extension called `CMSActiveRecord` that all of our models will stem from. This class allows us to reduce the amount of code that we have to write in each class. For now, we'll simply add `CTimestampBehavior` and the `afterFind()` method we've used in previous chapters to store the old attributes for the time the need arises to compare the changed attributes with the new attributes:

```
class CMSActiveRecordCMSActiveRecord extends CActiveRecord
{
   public $_oldAttributes = array();

   public function behaviors()
   {
      return array(
         'CTimestampBehavior' => array(
            'class'            => 'zii.behaviors.CTimestampBehavior',
            'createAttribute'  => 'created',
            'updateAttribute'  => 'updated',
            'setUpdateOnCreate' => true
         )
      );
   }

   public function afterFind()
   {
      if ($this !== NULL)
         $this->_oldAttributes = $this->attributes;
      return parent::afterFind();
   }
}
```

Creating a custom validator for slugs

Since both Content and Category classes have slugs, we'll need to add a custom validator to each class that will enable us to ensure that the slug is not already in use by either a post or a category. To do this, we have another class called CMSSlugActiveRecord that extends CMSActiveRecord with a validateSlug() method that we'll implement as follows:

```
class CMSSLugActiveRecord extends CMSActiveRecord
{
   public function validateSlug($attributes, $params)
   {
      // Fetch any records that have that slug
      $content = Content::model()->findByAttributes(array('slug' => $this->slug));
      $category = Category::model()->findByAttributes(array('slug' => $this->slug));

      $class = strtolower(get_class($this));

      if ($content == NULL && $category == NULL)
```

```
            return true;
        else if (($content == NULL && $category != NULL) || ($content !=
NULL && $category == NULL))
        {
            $this->addError('slug', 'That slug is already in use');
            return false;
        }
        else
        {
            if ($this->id == $$class->id)
                return true;
        }

            $this->addError('slug', 'That slug is already in use');
            return false;
    }
}
```

This implementation simply checks the database for any item that has that slug. If nothing is found, or if the current item is the item that is being modified, then the validator will return true. Otherwise, it will add an error to the `slug` attribute and return false. Both our Content model and Category model will extend from this class.

View management with themes

One of the largest challenges of working with larger applications is changing their appearance without locking functionality into our views. One way to further separate our business logic from our presentation logic is to use themes. Using themes in Yii, we can dynamically change the presentation layer of our application simply by utilizing the `Yii::app()->setTheme('themename)` method. Once this method is called, Yii will look for view files in `themes/themename/views` rather than `protected/views`. Throughout the rest of the chapter, we'll be adding views to a custom theme called `main`, which is located in the `themes` folder. To set this theme globally, we'll be creating a custom class called `CMSController`, which all of our controllers will extend from. For now, our theme name will be hardcoded within our application. This value could easily be retrieved from a database though, allowing us to dynamically change themes from a cached or database value rather than changing it in our controller. Have a look at the following lines of code:

```
class CMSController extends CController
{
    public function beforeAction($action)
    {
        Yii::app()->setTheme('main');
```

```
        return parent::beforeAction($action);
    }
}
```

> Alternatively, you can use the `theme` attribute from within the `protected/config/main.php` file as outlined in the official documentation http://www.yiiframework.com/doc/guide/1.1/en/topics.theming. While manipulating the theme there is simple, it requires our end user to have knowledge of how to manipulate PHP arrays. If you intend on allowing your end users to manipulate the theme of their site, it is recommended that you do so programmatically via `Yii::app()->setTheme` from a cached or database value. Be sure to check out the documentation for more information about using themes.

Truly dynamic routing

In our previous applications, we had long, boring URLs that had lots of IDs and parameters in them. These URLs provided a terrible user experience and prevented search engines and users from knowing what the content was about at a glance, which in turn would hurt our SEO rankings on many search engines. To get around this, we're going to heavily modify our `UrlManager` class to allow truly dynamic routing, which means that, every time we create or update a post or a category, our URL rules will be updated.

Telling Yii to use our custom UrlManager

Before we can start working on our controllers, we need to create a custom `UrlManager` to handle routing of our content so that we can access our content by its slug. The steps are as follows:

1. The first change we need to make to allow for this routing is to update the `components` section of our `protected/config/main.php` file. This will tell Yii what class to use for the `UrlManager` component:

    ```
    'urlManager' => array(
            'class'          => 'application.components.CMSUrlManager',
            'urlFormat'      => 'path',
            'showScriptName' => false
    )
    ```

2. Next, within our `protected/components` folder, we need to create `CMSUrlManager.php`:

    ```
    class CMSUrlManager extends CUrlManager {}
    ```

3. `CUrlManager` works by populating a rules array. When Yii is bootstrapped, it will trigger the `processRules()` method to determine which route should be executed. We can overload this method to inject our own rules, which will ensure that the action that we want to be executed is executed.

4. To get started, let's first define a set of default routes that we want loaded. The routes defined in the following code snippet will allow for pagination on our search and home page, enable a static path for our `sitemap.xml` file, and provide a route for HybridAuth to use for social authentication:

```
public $defaultRules    = array(
    '/sitemap.xml'             => '/content/sitemap',
    '/search/<page:\d+>'       => '/content/search',
    '/search'                  => '/content/search',
    '/blog/<page:\d+>'         => '/content/index',
    '/blog'                    => '/content/index',
    '/'                        => '/content/index',
    '/hybrid/<provider:\w+>'   => '/hybrid/index',
);
```

5. Then, we'll implement our `processRules()` method:

```
protected function processRules() {}
```

6. `CUrlManager` already has a public property that we can interface to modify the rules, so we'll inject our own rules into this. The `rules` property is the same property that can be accessed from within our config file. Since `processRules()` gets called on every page load, we'll also utilize caching so that our rules don't have to be generated every time. We'll start by trying to load any of our pregenerated rules from our cache, depending upon whether we are in debug mode or not:

```
$this->rules = !YII_DEBUG ? Yii::app()->cache->get('Routes') : array();
```

If the rules we get back are already set up, we'll simple return them; otherwise, we'll generate the rules, put them into our cache, and then append our basic URL rules that we've used throughout the previous chapters:

```
if ($this->rules == false || empty($this->rules))
{
    $this->rules = array();
    $this->rules = $this->generateClientRules();
    $this->rules = CMap::mergearray($this->addRssRules(), $this->rules);

    Yii::app()->cache->set('Routes', $this->rules);
```

```
}

$this->rules['<controller:\w+>/<action:\w+>/<id:\w+>'] =
'<controller>/<action>';
$this->rules['<controller:\w+>/<action:\w+>'] =
'<controller>/<action>';

return parent::processRules();
```

7. For abstraction purposes, within our `processRules()` method, we've utilized two methods we'll need to create: `generateClientRules`, which will generate the rules for content and categories, and `addRSSRules`, which will generate the RSS routes for each category.

   The first method, `generateClientRules()`, simply loads our default rules that we defined earlier with the rules generated from our content and categories, which are populated by the `generateRules()` method:

   ```
   private function generateClientRules()
   {
       $rules = CMap::mergeArray($this->defaultRules, $this->rules);
       return CMap::mergeArray($this->generateRules(), $rules);
   }

   private function generateRules()
   {
       return CMap::mergeArray($this->generateContentRules(), $this->generateCategoryRules());
   }
   ```

8. The `generateRules()` method, that we just defined, actually calls the methods that build our routes. Each route is a key-value pair that will take the following form:

   ```
   array(
       '<slug>' => '<controller>/<action>/id/<id>'
   )
   ```

   Content rules will consist of an entry that is published. Have a look at the following code:

   ```
   private function generateContentRules()
   {
       $rules = array();
       $criteria = new CDbCriteria;
       $criteria->addCondition('published = 1');

       $content = Content::model()->findAll($criteria);
   ```

[191]

Building a Content Management System

```
   foreach ($content as $el)
   {
      if ($el->slug == NULL)
         continue;

      $pageRule = $el->slug.'/<page:\d+>';
      $rule = $el->slug;

      if ($el->slug == '/')
         $pageRule = $rule = '';

      $pageRule = $el->slug . '/<page:\d+>';
   $rule = $el->slug;

   $rules[$pageRule] = "content/view/id/{$el->id}";
   $rules[$rule] = "content/view/id/{$el->id}";
   }

   return $rules;
}
```

9. Our category rules will consist of all categories in our database. Have a look at the following code:

```
private function generateCategoryRules()
{
   $rules = array();
   $categories = Category::model()->findAll();
   foreach ($categories as $el)
   {
      if ($el->slug == NULL)
         continue;

      $pageRule = $el->slug.'/<page:\d+>';
      $rule = $el->slug;

      if ($el->slug == '/')
         $pageRule = $rule = '';

      $pageRule = $el->slug . '/<page:\d+>';
   $rule = $el->slug;

   $rules[$pageRule] = "category/index/id/{$el->id}";
   $rules[$rule] = "category/index/id/{$el->id}";
   }

   return $rules;
}
```

10. Finally, we'll add our RSS rules that will allow RSS readers to read all content for the entire site or for a particular category, as follows:

```
private function addRSSRules()
{
    $categories = Category::model()->findAll();
    foreach ($categories as $category)
        $routes[$category->slug.'.rss'] = "category/rss/id/
{$category->id}";

    $routes['blog.rss'] = '/category/rss';
    return $routes;
}
```

> CUrlManager has many different components. If you have questions, be sure to reference the Yii Class Reference for this class at http://www.yiiframework.com/doc/api/1.1/CUrlManager.

Displaying and managing content

Now that Yii knows how to route our content, we can begin work on displaying and managing it. Begin by creating a new controller called ContentController in protected/controllers that extends CMSController. Have a look at the following line of code:

```
class ContentController extends CMSController {}
```

To start with, we'll define our accessRules() method and the default layout that we're going to use. Here's how:

```
public $layout = 'default';

public function filters()
{
    return array(
        'accessControl',
    );
}

public function accessRules()
{
    return array(
        array('allow',
```

```
            'actions' => array('index', 'view', 'search'),
            'users' => array('*')
        ),
        array('allow',
            'actions' => array('admin', 'save', 'delete'),
            'users'=>array('@'),
            'expression' => 'Yii::app()->user->role==2'
        ),
        array('deny',  // deny all users
            'users'=>array('*'),
        ),
    );
}
```

Rendering the sitemap

The first method we'll be implementing is our sitemap action. In our `ContentController`, create a new method called `actionSitemap()`:

```
public function actionSitemap() {}
```

The steps to be performed are as follows:

1. Since sitemaps come in XML formatting, we'll start by disabling `WebLogRoute` defined in our `protected/config/main.php` file. This will ensure that our XML validates when search engines attempt to index it:

   ```
   Yii::app()->log->routes[0]->enabled = false;
   ```

2. We'll then send the appropriate XML headers, disable the rendering of the layout, and flush any content that may have been queued to be sent to the browser:

   ```
   ob_end_clean();
   header('Content-type: text/xml; charset=utf-8');
   $this->layout = false;
   ```

3. Then, we'll load all the published entries and categories and send them to our sitemap view:

   ```
   $content = Content::model()->findAllByAttributes(array('published' => 1));
   $categories = Category::model()->findAll();

   $this->renderPartial('sitemap', array(
       'content'     => $content,
   ```

```
        'categories'   => $categories,
        'url'          => 'http://'.Yii::app()->request->serverName .
Yii::app()->baseUrl
));
```

4. Finally, we have two options to render this view. We can either make it a part of our theme in `themes/main/views/content/sitemap.php`, or we can place it in `protected/views/content/sitemap.php`. Since a sitemap's structure is unlikely to change, let's put it in the `protected/views` folder:

```
<?php echo '<?xml version="1.0" encoding="UTF-8"?>'; ?>
<urlset xmlns="http://www.sitemaps.org/schemas/sitemap/0.9">
    <?php foreach ($content as $v): ?>
        <url>
            <loc><?php echo $url .'/'. htmlspecialchars(str_replace('/', '', $v['slug']), ENT_QUOTES, "utf-8"); ?></loc>
            <lastmod><?php echo date('c', strtotime($v['updated']));?></lastmod>
            <changefreq>weekly</changefreq>
            <priority>1</priority>
        </url>
    <?php endforeach; ?>
    <?php foreach ($categories as $v): ?>
        <url>
            <loc><?php echo $url .'/'. htmlspecialchars(str_replace('/', '', $v['slug']), ENT_QUOTES, "utf-8"); ?></loc>
            <lastmod><?php echo date('c', strtotime($v['updated']));?></lastmod>
            <changefreq>weekly</changefreq>
            <priority>0.7</priority>
        </url>
    <?php endforeach; ?>
</urlset>
```

> Even though we've told Yii to look for view files within a theme, it's still going to look in the `protected/views` folder if it cannot find the view file within the `themes` folder. This feature allows us to separate views that shouldn't change (such as sitemaps and RSS feeds) from views that will actually be presented to a user.

You can now load `http://chapter6.example.com/sitemap.xml` in your browser to see the sitemap. Before you make your site live, be sure to submit this file to search engines for them to index.

Building a Content Management System

Displaying a list view of content

Next, we'll implement the actions necessary to display all of our content and a particular post. We'll start by providing a paginated view of our posts. Since `CListView` and the Content model's `search()` method already provide this functionality, we can utilize those classes to generate and display this data:

1. To begin with, open `protected/models/Content.php` and modify the return value of the `search()` method as follows. This will ensure that Yii's pagination uses the correct variable in our `CListView`, and tells Yii how many results to load per page.

   ```
   return new CActiveDataProvider($this, array(
   'criteria'     =>$criteria,
   'pagination'   => array(
   'pageSize'     => 5,
   'pageVar'      =>'page'
   )
   ));
   ```

2. Next, implement the `actionIndex()` method with the `$page` parameter. We've already told our `UrlManager` how to handle this, which means that we'll get pretty URI's for pagination (for example, /blog, /blog/2, /blog/3, and so on):

   ```
   public function actionIndex($page=1)
   {
      // Model Search without $_GET params
      $model = new Content('search');
      $model->unsetAttributes();
      $model->published = 1;

      $this->render('//content/all', array(
         'dataprovider' => $model->search()
      ));
   }
   ```

3. Then we'll create a view in `themes/main/views/content/all.php`; this will display the data within our `dataProvider`:

   ```
   <?php $this->widget('zii.widgets.CListView', array(
      'dataProvider'=>$dataprovider,
      'itemView'=>'//content/list',
      'summaryText' => '',
      'pager' => array(
         'htmlOptions' => array(
            'class' => 'pager'
         ),
         'header' => '',
   ```

```
            'firstPageCssClass'=>'hide',
            'lastPageCssClass'=>'hide',
            'maxButtonCount' => 0
        )
));
```

4. Finally, copy `themes/main/views/content/all.php` from the project resources folder so that our views can render.

Since our database has already been populated with some sample data, you can start playing around with the results right away, as shown in the following screenshot:

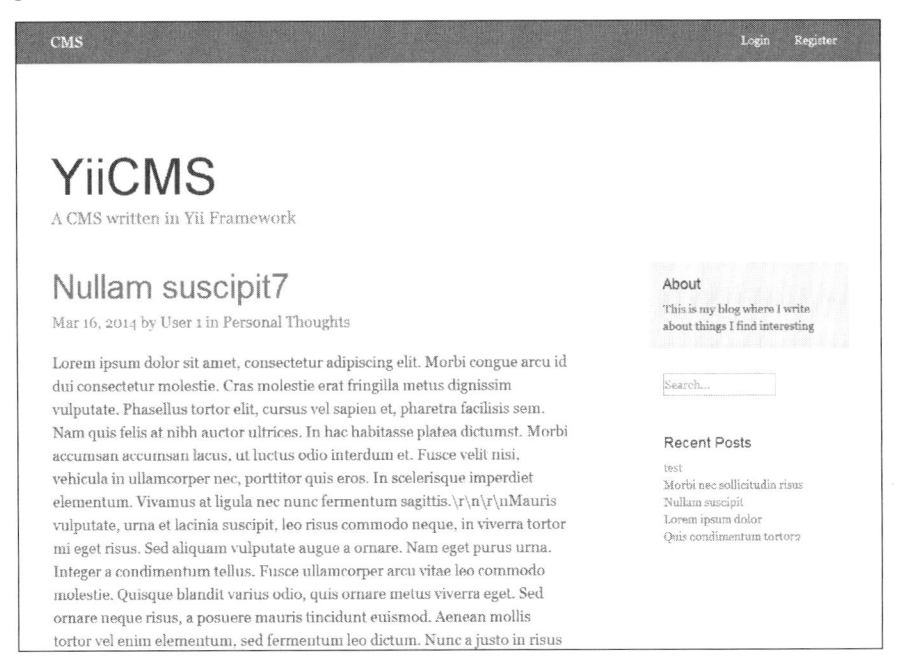

Displaying content by ID

Since our routing rules are already set up, displaying our content is extremely simple. All that we have to do is search for a published model with the ID passed to the view action and render it:

```
public function actionView($id=NULL)
{
    // Retrieve the data
    $content = Content::model()->findByPk($id);
    // beforeViewAction should catch this
    if ($content == NULL || !$content->published)
        throw new CHttpException(404, 'The article you specified does not exist.');
```

```php
    $this->render('view', array(
        'id'   => $id,
        'post' => $content
    ));
}
```

After copying themes/main/views/content/view.php from the project resources folder into your project, you'll be able to click into a particular post from the home page. In its present form, this action has introduced an interesting side effect that could negatively impact our SEO rankings on search engines—the same entry can now be accessed from two URI's. For example, http://chapter6.example.com/content/view/id/1 and http://chapter6.example.com/quis-condimentum-tortor now bring up the same post. Fortunately, correcting this bug is fairly easy. Since the goal of our slugs is to provide more descriptive URIs, we'll simply block access to the view if a user tries to access it from the non-slugged URI.

We'll do this by creating a new method called beforeViewAction() that takes the entry ID as a parameter and gets called right after the actionView() method is called. This private method will simply check the URI from CHttpRequest to determine how actionView was accessed and return a 404 if it's not through our beautiful slugs:

```php
private function beforeViewAction($id=NULL)
{
    // If we do not have an ID, consider it to be null, and throw a 404 error
    if ($id == NULL)
        throw new CHttpException(404,'The specified post cannot be found.');

    // Retrieve the HTTP Request
    $r = new CHttpRequest();

    // Retrieve what the actual URI
    $requestUri = str_replace($r->baseUrl, '', $r->requestUri);

    // Retrieve the route
    $route = '/' . $this->getRoute() . '/' . $id;
    $requestUri = preg_replace('/\?(.*)/','',$requestUri);

    // If the route and the uri are the same, then a direct access attempt was made, and we need to block access to the controller
    if ($requestUri == $route)
        throw new CHttpException(404, 'The requested post cannot be found.');
```

```
       return str_replace($r->baseUrl, '', $r->requestUri);
}
```

Then, right after our `actionView` starts, we can simultaneously set the correct return URL and block access to the content if it wasn't accessed through the slug as follows:

```
Yii::app()->user->setReturnUrl($this->beforeViewAction($id));
```

Adding comments to our CMS with Disqus

Presently, our content is only informative in nature—we have no way for our users to communicate with us what they thought about our entry. To encourage engagement, we can add a commenting system to our CMS to further engage with our readers. Rather than writing our own commenting system, we can leverage comment through Disqus, a free, third-party commenting system. Even through Disqus, comments are implemented in JavaScript and we can create a custom widget wrapper for it to display comments on our site. The steps are as follows:

1. To begin with, log in to the Disqus account you created at the beginning of this chapter as outlined in the prerequisites section. Then, navigate to `http://disqus.com/admin/create/` and fill out the form fields as prompted and as shown in the following screenshot:

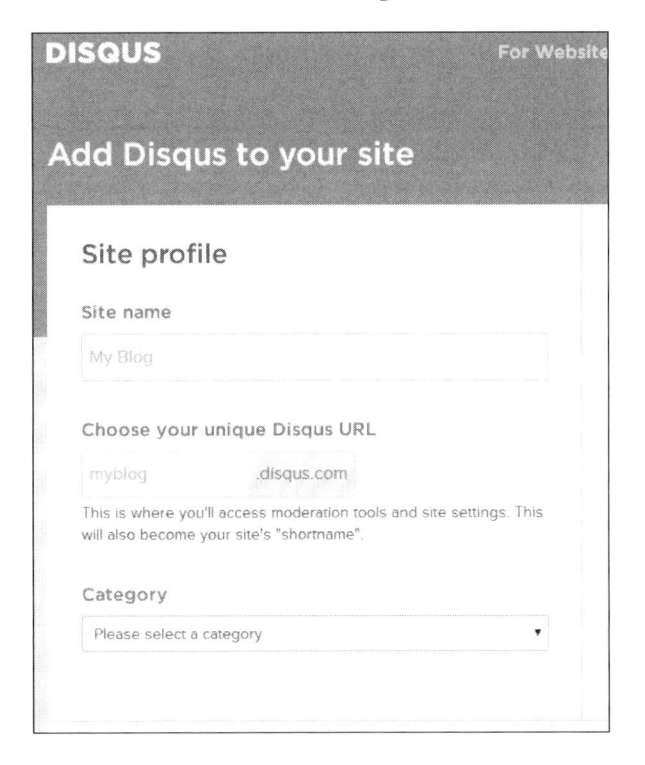

Building a Content Management System

2. Then, add a `disqus` section to your `protected/config/params.php` file with your site `shortname`:

   ```
   'disqus' => array(
       'shortname' => 'ch6disqusexample',
   )
   ```

3. Next, create a new widget in `protected/components` called `DisqusWidget.php`. This widget will be loaded within our view and will be populated by our Content model:

   ```
   class DisqusWidget extends CWidget {}
   ```

4. Begin by specifying the public properties that our view will be able to inject into as follows:

   ```
   public $shortname = NULL;

   public $identifier = NULL;

   public $url = NULL;

   public $title = NULL;
   ```

5. Then, overload the `init()` method to load the Disqus JavaScript callback and to populate the JavaScript variables with those populated to the widget as follows:

   ```
   public function init()
   {
       parent::init();
       if ($this->shortname == NULL)
           throw new CHttpException(500, 'Disqus shortname is required');

       echo "<div id='disqus_thread'></div>";
       Yii::app()->clientScript->registerScript('disqus', "
           var disqus_shortname = '{$this->shortname}';
           var disqus_identifier = '{$this->identifier}';
           var disqus_url = '{$this->url}';
           var disqus_title = '{$this->title}';

           /* * * DON'T EDIT BELOW THIS LINE * * */
           (function() {
               var dsq = document.createElement('script'); dsq.type = 'text/javascript'; dsq.async = true;
               dsq.src = '//' + disqus_shortname + '.disqus.com/embed.js';
   ```

```
            (document.getElementsByTagName('head')[0] || document.
getElementsByTagName('body')[0]).appendChild(dsq);
        })();
    ");
}
```

6. Finally, within our `themes/main/views/content/view.php` file, load the widget as follows:

```
<?php $this->widget('DisqusWidget', array(
        'shortname'  => Yii::app()->params['includes']['disqus']
['shortname'],
        'url'        => $this->createAbsoluteUrl('/'.$post->slug),
        'title'      => $post->title,
        'identifier' => $post->id
    )); ?>
```

Now, when you load any given post, Disqus comments will also be loaded with that post. Go ahead and give it a try!

> The greatest benefit of using Disqus as a service provider is that it enables us to focus solely on the integration of a product rather than raw implementation. By not having to reinvent the wheel each time we need a service, we can save a lot of time and money. When relying on a third party, however, be cognizant of the fact that the service provider may not exist the next day. While unlikely, a large service provider can go out of business overnight, so be prepared to have a plan in place to replace or substitute any third-party service you integrate into your application.

Searching for content

Next, we'll implement a search method so that our users can search for posts. To do this, we'll implement an instance of `CActiveDataProvider` and pass that data to our `themes/main/views/content/all.php` view to be rendered and paginated:

```
public function actionSearch()
{
    $param = Yii::app()->request->getParam('q');

    $criteria = new CDbCriteria;

    $criteria->addSearchCondition('title',$param,'OR');
    $criteria->addSearchCondition('body',$param,'OR');

    $dataprovider = new CActiveDataProvider('Content', array(
        'criteria'=>$criteria,
        'pagination' => array(
            'pageSize' => 5,
            'pageVar'=>'page'
        )
    ));

    $this->render('//content/all', array(
       'dataprovider' => $dataprovider
    ));
}
```

Since our view file already exists, we can now search for content in our CMS.

> In previous chapters, we would have simply queried the $_POST array for our search parameter. A more Yii way of retrieving these variables is to use the Yii::app()->request->getParam() method from the CHttpRequest class. Be warned, however, that this method operates on both $_GET and $_POST parameters. If the same parameter is sent via both HTTP methods (you should avoid doing this when possible), only the $_GET method will be returned. Be sure to read the CHttpRequest Class Reference page for more information at http://www.yiiframework.com/doc/api/1.1/CHttpRequest.

Managing content

Next, we'll implement a basic set of management tools that will allow us to create, update, and delete entries:

1. We'll start by defining our loadModel() method and the actionDelete() method:

   ```
   private function loadModel($id=NULL)
   {
      if ($id == NULL)
         throw new CHttpException(404, 'No category with that ID exists');

      $model = Content::model()->findByPk($id);

      if ($model == NULL)
         throw new CHttpException(404, 'No category with that ID exists');

      return $model;
   }

   public function actionDelete($id)
   {
      $this->loadModel($id)->delete();

      $this->redirect($this->createUrl('content/admin'));
   }
   ```

2. Next, we can implement our admin view, which will allow us to view all the content in our system and to create new entries. Be sure to copy the themes/main/views/content/admin.php file from the project resources folder into your project before using this view:

```php
public function actionAdmin()
{
    $model = new Content('search');

    $model->unsetAttributes();

    if (isset($_GET['Content']))
        $model->attributes = $_GET;

    $this->render('admin', array(
        'model' => $model
    ));
}
```

3. Finally, we'll implement a save view to create and update entries. Saving content will simply pass it through our content model's validation rules. The only override we'll be adding is ensuring that the author is assigned to the user editing the entry. Before using this view, be sure to copy the themes/main/views/content/save.php file from the project resources folder into your project:

```php
public function actionSave($id=NULL)
{
    if ($id == NULL)
        $model = new Content;
    else
        $model = $this->loadModel($id);

    if (isset($_POST['Content']))
    {
        $model->attributes = $_POST['Content'];

        $model->author_id = Yii::app()->user->id;

        if ($model->save())
        {
            Yii::app()->user->setFlash('info', 'The articles was saved');
            $this->redirect($this->createUrl('content/admin'));
        }
    }

    $this->render('save', array(
```

```
            'model' => $model
    ));
}
```

At this point, you can now log in to the system using the credentials provided in the following table and start managing entries:

Username	Password
user1@example.com	test
user2@example.com	test

Viewing and managing categories

Now, let's move to viewing and managing categories. As outlined previously, each category will be accessible via a dedicated route and will only display content within that category. We'll start by defining our default access rules and layout name in `protected/controllers/CategoryController.php`:

```
public $layout = 'default';

public function filters()
{
    return array(
        'accessControl',
    );
}

public function accessRules()
{
    return array(
        array('allow',
            'actions' => array('index', 'view', 'rss'),
            'users' => array('*')
        ),
        array('allow',
            'actions' => array('admin', 'save', 'delete'),
            'users'=>array('@'),
            'expression' => 'Yii::app()->user->role==2'
        ),
        array('deny',  // deny all users
            'users'=>array('*'),
        ),
    );
}
```

Viewing entries in a category

Displaying entries in each category will be nearly identical to displaying all entries, so we can implement our index action as follows. Note that the parameters passed to this method are simply passed from the routes we generated earlier.

```
public function actionIndex($id=1, $page=1)
{
    $category = $this->loadModel($id);

    // Model Search without $_GET params
    $model = new Content('search');
    $model->unsetAttributes();

    $model->attributes = array(
        'published' => 1,
        'category_id' => $id
    );

    $_GET['page'] = $page;

    $this->render('//content/all', array(
        'dataprovider' => $model->search()
    ));
}
```

Viewing an RSS feed for categories

An alternative way of viewing entries in a particular category is through an RSS feed. RSS feeds are a very popular medium that allows your users to subscribe to your content and be regularly notified of updates without having to visit each site individually. Our action to display our category entries in an RSS feed look as follows:

```
public function actionRss($id=NULL)
{
    Yii::app()->log->routes[0]->enabled = false;

    ob_end_clean();
    header('Content-type: text/xml; charset=utf-8');

    $this->layout = false;

    $criteria = new CDbCriteria;

    if ($id != NULL)
```

```
        $criteria->addCondition("category_id = " . $id);

    $criteria->order = 'created DESC';
    $data = Content::model()->findAll($criteria);

    $this->renderPartial('rss', array(
        'data'  => $data,
        'url'   => 'http://'.Yii::app()->request->serverName .
Yii::app()->baseUrl
    ));
}
```

Then, add the following to your `protected/views/category/rss.php` file:

```
<?php echo '<?xml version="1.0" encoding="UTF-8" ?>'; ?>
<rss version="2.0" xmlns:atom="http://www.w3.org/2005/Atom">
    <channel>
        <atom:link href="<?php echo $url.Yii::app()->request->requestUri; ?>" rel="self" type="application/rss+xml" />
        <title><?php echo Yii::app()->name; ?></title>
        <link><?php echo $url; ?></link>
        <description><?php echo Yii::app()->name; ?> Blog</description>
        <language>en-us</language>
        <pubDate><?php echo date('D, d M Y H:i:s T'); ?></pubDate>
        <lastBuildDate><?php echo date('D, d M Y H:i:s T'); ?></lastBuildDate>
        <docs>http://blogs.law.harvard.edu/tech/rss</docs>

        <?php foreach ($data as $k=>$v): ?>
          <item>
            <title><?php echo htmlspecialchars(str_replace('/', '', $v['title']), ENT_QUOTES, "utf-8"); ?></title>
            <link><?php echo $url.'/'.htmlspecialchars(str_replace('/', '', $v['slug']), ENT_QUOTES, "utf-8"); ?></link>
            <description>
                <?php
                    $md = new CMarkdownParser;
                    echo htmlspecialchars(strip_tags($md->transform($v['body'])), ENT_QUOTES, "utf-8");
                ?>
            </description>
            <category><?php echo htmlspecialchars(Category::model()->findByPk($v['category_id'])->name, ENT_QUOTES, "utf-8"); ?></category>
```

```
            <author><?php echo User::model()->findByPk($v['author_
id'])->email; ?> (<?php echo User::model()->findByPk($v['author_id'])-
>username; ?>)</author>
            <pubDate><?php echo date('D, d M Y H:i:s T',
strtotime($v['created'])); ?></pubDate>
            <guid><?php echo $url.'/'.htmlspecialchars(str_
replace('/', '', $v['slug']), ENT_QUOTES, "utf-8"); ?></guid>
        </item>
    <?php endforeach; ?>
    </channel>
</rss>
```

Now, if you navigate to 3, you can view an RSS feed of all uncategorized entries. Each category will have its own RSS feed, allowing users to subscribe to the content they are interested in rather than all the content on your site.

Managing categories

Next, we need to implement management of our categories:

1. We'll start with our `loadModel()` and `actionDelete()` methods:

    ```
    public function actionDelete($id)
    {
       $this->loadModel($id)->delete();

       $this->redirect($this->createUrl('content/admin'));
    }

    public function loadModel($id=NULL)
    {
       if ($id == NULL)
          throw new CHttpException(404, 'No category with that ID
    exists');

       $model = Category::model()->findByPk($id);

       if ($model == NULL)
          throw new CHttpException(404, 'No category with that ID
    exists');

       return $model;
    }
    ```

2. Then, we'll implement the admin action. Be sure to copy the `themes/main/views/category/admin.php` file from the project resources folder. Have a look at the following code:

```
public function actionAdmin()
{
   $model = new Category('search');
   $model->unsetAttributes();

   if (isset($_GET['Category']))
      $model->attributes = $_GET;

   $this->render('admin', array(
      'model' => $model
   ));
}
```

3. Finally, we'll implement the `save()` method. Be sure to copy the `themes/main/views/category/save.php` file from the project resources folder. Have a look at the following code:

```
public function actionSave($id=NULL)
{
   if ($id == NULL)
      $model = new Category;
   else
      $model = $this->loadModel($id);

   if (isset($_POST['Category']))
   {
      $model->attributes = $_POST['Category'];

      if ($model->save())
      {
         Yii::app()->user->setFlash('info', 'The category was saved');
         $this->redirect($this->createUrl('category/admin'));
      }
   }

   $this->render('save', array(
      'model' => $model
   ));
}
```

We've now finished the core of our content management system. The structure that we've built for our CMS, while being extremely simple, provides a lot of flexibility for us to expand upon with very minimal effort.

Social authentication with HybridAuth

In the previous chapter, *Chapter 5, Creating a Microblogging Platform*, we used HybridAuth to sign in as a user to, and share content with, Twitter. In this chapter, we use HybridAuth to register accounts in our CMS and to sign in to our CMS without having to enter a username and password. To achieve this, we'll create three new forms, a new `UserIdentity` class, and a control that will enable us to take advantage of all the providers that HybridAuth has to offer.

Before we get started with any coding, however, we need to first create a new Twitter application similar to the one we created in *Chapter 5, Creating a Microblogging Platform*. This will allow us to focus on development rather than configuration once we start writing code. Once your Twitter application has been created and permissions have been set, add a `hybridauth` section to your `protected/config/params.php` file, containing your OAuth secret token and key:

```
'hybridauth' => array(
    'providers' => array(
        'Twitter' => array(
            'enabled' => true,
            'keys' => array(
                'key' => '<key>',
                'secret' => '<secret>
            )
        )
    )
)
```

> When we're done, you'll be able to add any of the supported HybridAuth providers listed in the HybridAuth documentation at http://hybridauth.sourceforge.net/userguide.html.

Validating remote identities

For our application, we need to register users from a social network, authenticate users from a social network to users in our database, and link existing users to a social identity. We're also going to authenticate users into our system. To achieve this, we're going to create three separate forms, `RemoteRegistrationForm`, `RemoteLinkAccountForm`, and `RemoteIdentityForm`, which will serve as our `LoginForm` for remote users. We'll also create a `RemoteUserIdentity` class that we'll use to authenticate users into our system. Let's get started.

Remote registrations

The first class we'll need to create is `RemoteRegistrationForm`. This form will allow us to register users using information from their social identity. The steps are as follows:

1. To get started, create a new class in `protected/models` called `RemoteRegistrationForm.php` with the following definition. To keep things simple, we're going to be reusing much of the functionality already available from our `RegistrationForm` class. Have a look at the following line of code:

   ```
   class RemoteRegistrationForm extends RegistrationForm {}
   ```

2. We'll then specify two additional attributes, the HybridAuth adapter that we'll provide from the controller we'll create later on and the provider name that we're authenticating with. We'll also set up validators for these attributes to ensure that they are set. Notice that we're using the `mergeArray()` method from the `CMap` class to take advantage of the validation rules that are already in place:

   ```
   public $adapter;

   public $provider;

   public function rules()
   {
       return CMap::mergeArray(parent::rules(), array(
           array('adapter, provider', 'required')
       ));
   }
   ```

3. Finally, we'll overload our `save()` method so that the provider name and OAuth token are written to our database. We'll take advantage of this metadata when we create our `RemoteIdentityForm` class:

   ```
   public function save()
   {
       // If the parent form saved and validated
       if (parent::save())
       {
           // Then bind the identity to this user permanently
           $meta = new UserMetadata;
           $meta->attributes = array(
               'user_id' => $this->_user->id,
   ```

```
                'key' => $this->provider.'Provider',
                'value' => (string)$this->adapter->identifier
            );

            // Save the associative object
            return $meta->save();
        }

        return false;
    }
```

Linking a social identity to an existing account

To assist in linking a social identity to an existing account in our system, we're going to create a new class called `RemoteLinkAccountForm`. This form will prompt an already logged-in user for their password to verify their identity and then bind the OAuth token provided by HybridAuth to that user, so that they can log in using their social identity in the future. The steps are as follows:

1. To get started, create a new class in `protected/models` called `RemoteLinkAccountForm.php` with the following definition:

   `class RemoteLinkAccountForm extends CFormModel {}`

2. We'll then define the public attributes we'll want to collect and create a validator for them. We'll also define a private attribute to store the user information of the user we want to link our social identity to. Have a look at the following lines of code:

   ```
   public $password;

   public $adapter;

   public $provider;

   private $_user;

   public function rules()
   {
       return array(
           array('password, adapter, provider', 'required'),
           array('password', 'validateUserPassword')
       );
   }
   ```

3. For security reasons, we only want the authenticated user to be able to link a social identity to their account. To verify that we are dealing with the account owner, we'll prompt the user for their password. To validate their password, we'll create a custom validator called `validateUserPassword`. Have a look at the following lines of code:

```
public function validateUserPassword($attributes, $params)
{
    $this->_user = User::model()->findByPk(Yii::app()->user->id);

    if ($this->_user == NULL)
    {
        $this->addError('password', 'Unable to identify user.');
        return false;
    }

    $result = password_verify($this->password, $this->_user->password);

    if ($result == false)
    {
        $this->addError('password', 'The password you entered is invalid.');
        return false;
    }

    return true;
}
```

4. Finally, we create a `save()` method that will save the social identity information to our `user_metdata` table provided that the user is able to verify their identity:

```
public function save()
{
    if (!$this->validate())
        return false;

    $meta = new UserMetadata;
    $meta->attributes = array(
        'user_id' => $this->_user->id,
        'key' => $this->provider.'Provider',
        'value' => (string)$this->adapter->identifier
    );

    // Save the associative object
    return $meta->save();
}
```

Authenticating with a social identity

To authenticate with a social identity, we'll need to create a form similar to our `LoginForm`; however, instead of taking a username and password as inputs, it will take the provider name and the HybridAuth adapter we're working with. The steps are as follows:

1. Begin by creating a new form in `protected/models` called `RemoteIdentityForm.php`:

   ```
   class RemoteIdentityForm extends CFormModel {}
   ```

2. As stated previously, we'll collect the provider name and the HybridAuth adapter instead of a username and password, so let's declare those properties. We'll also declare properties to store our user's information if they exist and the `RemoteUserIdentity` class, which we'll ultimately authenticate with:

   ```
   public $adapter;

   public $provider;

   private $_identity;

   public $_user;
   ```

3. We'll then define our validation rules and create a custom validator that will retrieve the appropriate user from within our system. This will prevent unauthorized users from authenticating into our CMS without being able to first authenticate with the social network that the user's account is linked to:

   ```
   public function rules()
   {
       return array(
           array('adapter, provider', 'required'),
           array('adapter', 'validateIdentity')
       );
   }

   public function validateIdentity($attributes, $params)
   {
       // Search the database for a user with that information
       $metadata = UserMetadata::model()->findByAttributes(array(
           'key' => $this->provider.'Provider',
           'value' => (string)$this->adapter->identifier
       ));

       // Return an error if we didn't find them
       if ($metadata == NULL)
       {
   ```

```
            $this->addError('adapter', 'Unable to determine local user
for identity');
            return false;
        }

        // Otherwise load that user
        $this->_user = User::model()->findByPk($metadata->user_id);
        if ($this->_user == NULL)
        {
            $this->addError('adapter', 'Unable to determine local user
for identity');
            return false;
        }

        // And return true
        return true;
    }
```

4. Then we'll create an `authenticate()` method that will behave in the same manner as the `authenticate()` method of our `LoginForm`; however, it will use the `RemoteUserIdentity` class as opposed to the `UserIdentity` class. Have a look at the following code:

```
public function authenticate()
{
    if (!$this->validate())
        return false;

    // Load the RemoteUserIdentity model, and return if we
successfully could authenticate against it
    $this->_identity = new RemoteUserIdentity($this->adapter,
$this->provider, $this->_user);
    return $this->_identity->authenticate();
}
```

5. Finally, we'll create a `login()` method that will actually log our user in to our CMS:

```
public function login()
{
    if (!$this->authenticate())
        return false;

    if($this->_identity->errorCode===RemoteUserIdentity::ERROR_
NONE)
    {
        $duration = 3600*24*30;
```

```
            Yii::app()->user->allowAutoLogin = true;
            Yii::app()->user->login($this->_identity,$duration);
            return true;
    }
    else
        return false;
}
```

Creating a Yii CWebUser object from a remote identity

The last class we'll need to create before linking everything together is a `RemoteUserIdentity` class. This class will retrieve all the information from our forms; if validated, it will log the user in to our CMS in the same way that our `UserIdentity` class does. The steps are as follows:

1. To get started, create a new class in `protected/components` called `RemoteUserIdentity.php`.

    ```
    class RemoteUserIdentity extends CUserIdentity {}
    ```

2. Then, define the attributes that we'll be collecting from our constructor as follows:

    ```
    public $adapter;

    public $provider;

    public $_user;

    public function __construct($adapter, $provider, $user)
    {
        $this->adapter  = $adapter;
        $this->provider = $provider;
        $this->_user    = $user;
    }
    ```

3. We should also define a way to retrieve the user's ID as stored in our system. We'll follow the pattern laid out in our `UserIdentity` class to keep things consistent:

    ```
    private $_id;

    public function getId()
    {
        return $this->_id;
    }
    ```

4. Finally, we'll create an `authenticate()` method that will set our `CWebUser` states. As we need to check that the data is available to us, the information provided to us should already be validated:

```
public function authenticate($force=false)
{
    // Set the error code first
    this->errorCode = self::ERROR_UNKNOWN_IDENTITY;

    // Check that the user isn't NULL, or that they're not in a locked state
    if ($this->_user == NULL)
        $this->errorCode = Yii_DEBUG ? self::ERROR_USERNAME_INVALID : self::ERROR_UNKNOWN_IDENTITY;

    // The user has already been provided to us, so immediately log the user in using that information
    $this->errorCode = self::ERROR_NONE;

    $this->_id       = $this->_user->id;
    $this->setState('email', $this->_user->email);
    $this->setState('role', $this->_user->role_id);

    return !$this->errorCode;
}
```

Putting it all together

With all of the necessary components in place, we can now create our controller that will handle the authentication component with HybridAuth. The steps are as follows:

1. To begin with, create a new controller in `protected/controllers` called `HybridController.php`:

   ```
   class HybridController extends CMSController {}
   ```

2. Next, we'll create three properties to hold the HybridAuth adapter, the provider name, and the user profile that we'll get back from Twitter:

   ```
   protected $_provider;

   private $_adapter = NULL;

   private $_userProfile = NULL;
   ```

We'll also create custom getter and setter methods to set the adapter as follows:

```php
public function setAdapter($adapter)
{
    return $this->_adapter = $adapter;
}

public function getAdapter()
{
    return $this->_adapter;
}
```

3. Then we'll add in a block to retrieve the user's profile information from the social network they are signing in from:

```php
public function getUserProfile()
{
    if ($this->_userProfile == NULL)
        $this->_userProfile = $this->getAdapter()->getUserProfile();

    return $this->_userProfile;
}
```

4. Then, to get and set the provider's name that will be provided from the URI, the following code needs to be used:

```php
public function setProvider($provider=NULL)
{
    // Prevent the provider from being NULL
    if ($provider == NULL)
        throw new CException("You haven't supplied a provider");

    // Set the property
    $this->_provider = $provider;

    return $this->_provider;
}

public function getProvider()
{
    return $this->_provider;
}
```

5. By referencing the HybridAuth documentation (http://hybridauth.sourceforge.net/userguide/Configuration.html), we can determine what variables HybridAuth will require to initialize correctly. Rather than hardcoding all of this information in our configuration file, we can dynamically populate it from within our controller. This method will ensure that our base URLs will always be set correctly, and that logging information will be sent to the correct place. It has the additional benefit of only logging when we enable YII_DEBUG, which means we only have to make one change to our configuration file when debugging rather than multiple changes. Have a look at the following code:

```
public function getConfig()
{
    return array(
        'baseUrl' => Yii::app()->getBaseUrl(true),
        'base_url' => Yii::app()->getBaseUrl(true) . '/hybrid/callback', // URL for Hybrid_Auth callback
        'debug_mode' => YII_DEBUG,
        'debug_file' => Yii::getPathOfAlias('application.runtime.hybridauth').'.log',
        'providers' => Yii::app()->params['includes']['hybridauth']['providers']
    );
}
```

6. Next, we'll define our actionIndex(). This action will serve both as the initialization URL for HybridAuth and our callback URL for our social networks to authenticate against. Within this action, we'll set the provider and start the HybridAuth process:

```
public function actionIndex($provider=NULL)
{
    // Set the provider
    $this->setProvider($provider);

    if (isset($_GET['hauth_start']) || isset($_GET['hauth_done']))
        Hybrid_Endpoint::process();

    try {
        $this->hybridAuth();
    } catch (Exception $e) {
        throw new CHttpException(400, $e->getMessage());
    }
}
```

Building a Content Management System

> *Internally, HybridAuth will throw an exception whenever it encounters an error while dealing with the remote network. To prevent our application from exposing too much information, we can simply inform the user that an error occurred.*

7. Then, we'll define the `hybridauth()` method we started to use earlier. We'll start by initializing the HybridAuth object and setting the adapter if it is not already set:

    ```
    private function hybridAuth()
    {
        // Preload some configuration options
        if (strtolower($this->getProvider()) == 'openid')
        {
            if (!isset($_GET['openid-identity']))
                throw new CException("You chose OpenID but didn't provide an OpenID identifier");
            else
                $params = array("openid_identifier" => $_GET['openid-identity']);
        }
        else
            $params = array();

        $hybridauth = new Hybrid_Auth($this->getConfig());

        if (!$this->adapter)
            $this->setAdapter($hybridauth->authenticate($this->getProvider(),$params));
    }
    ```

    > *We've declared a custom getter and setter for our adapter so that we only load it once during our flow. This will prevent us from hitting the rate limits of the Twitter API during a single request.*

8. At this point, HybridAuth is going to perform several different redirects to authenticate our user against their system. When the request is returned to us, we'll be able to verify that a user is connected to our adapter. If one isn't, it's safe to throw an exception. Have a look at the following code:

    ```
    if ($this->adapter->isUserConnected())
    {
    ```

[220]

```
        // We'll add our actions here...
    }
    else
        throw new CHttpException(403, 'Failed to establish remote
identity');
```

9. Within our `if` statement, we'll try to authenticate the user using our `RemoteIdentityForm` class that we created earlier. We'll display a flash message and redirect the user to the home page if we're able to. If we're not able to authenticate the user, we'll either display the `LinkAccountForm` class if the user is authenticated in our system but not socially, or the `RemoteRegistrationForm` class so that the user can register a new account in our CMS:

```
if ($this->authenticate())
{
    Yii::app()->user->setFlash('success', 'You have been
successfully logged in!');

    $this->redirect(Yii::app()->getBaseUrl(true));
}
else
{
    if (!Yii::app()->user->isGuest)
        $this->renderLinkForm();
    else
        $this->renderRegisterForm();
}
```

10. Our `authenticate()` method will simply return the result of the `RemoteIdentityForm login()` method:

```
private function authenticate()
{
    $form = new RemoteIdentityForm;
    $form->attributes = array(
        'adapter'  => $this->getUserProfile(),
        'provider' => $this->getProvider()
    );

    return $form->login();
}
```

11. If a user is already authenticated in our CMS but hasn't been authenticated with this provider, we'll assume that they want to link their social network identity to their login information; thus, we'll present `RemoteLinkAccountForm` and prompt them for their password. Then, be sure to copy over `themes/main/views/users/linkaccount.php` from the project resources folder into your project:

    ```
    private function renderLinkForm()
    {
        $form = new RemoteLinkAccountForm;

        if (Yii::app()->request->getParam('RemoteLinkAccountForm'))
        {
            // Populate the model
            $form->Attributes = Yii::app()->request->getParam('RemoteLinkAccountForm');
            $form->provider  = $this->getProvider();
            $form->adapter   = $this->getUserProfile();

            if ($form->save())
            {
                if ($this->authenticate())
                {
                    Yii::app()->user->setFlash('success', 'You have been successfully logged in');
                    $this->redirect($this->createAbsoluteUrl('content/index'));
                }
            }
        }

        // Reuse the register form
        $this->render('//user/linkaccount', array('model' => $form));
    }
    ```

12. Finally, if a user is not logged in to our CMS, we'll display our `RemoteRegisterForm` and reutilize the view from `themes/main/views/user/register.php`:

    ```
    private function renderRegisterForm()
    {
        $form = new RemoteRegistrationForm;

        if (Yii::app()->request->getParam('RemoteRegistrationForm'))
        {
            // Populate the model
    ```

```
            $form->attributes = Yii::app()->request-
    >getParam('RemoteRegistrationForm');
            $form->provider   = $this->getProvider();
            $form->adapter    = $this->getUserProfile();

            if ($form->save())
            {
                if ($this->authenticate())
                {
                    Yii::app()->user->setFlash('success', 'You have
    been successfully logged in');
                    $this->redirect($this->createUrl('content/
    index'));
                }
            }
        }

        // Reuse the register form
        $this->render('//user/register', array('user' => $form));
    }
```

Now that we have everything in place, we can test our social authentication. For our first test, log out of our CMS, navigate to `http://chapter6.example.com/site/login`, and click on the **sign in with Twitter** link at the bottom. Click on the link, and enter your Twitter credentials. Upon being redirected, you should see a registration form where you can enter your information for a new account, as shown in the following screenshot:

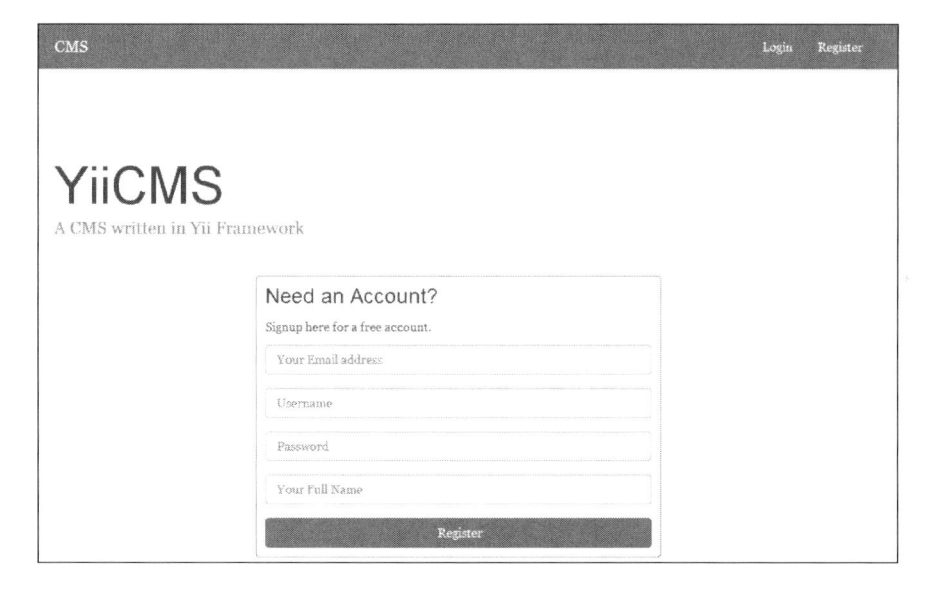

![Screenshot of YiiCMS registration form with "Need an Account?" heading, fields for Email address, Username, Password, Full Name, and a Register button]

Enter your new user's information and then click on **Register**. If successful, you'll be logged in to the CMS as the user you just created, and the activation e-mail we created in the previous chapter will be sent to that e-mail address. Now, if you log out of the CMS and log in using the **Login with Twitter** link, you'll be automatically logged in to the CMS without having to enter your username and password.

After verifying that registering with a social identity works, log out of the CMS and then log in as `user1@example.com` using the credentials previously provided. Log out of Twitter and then navigate to `http://chapter6.example.com/hybrid/twitter`. After signing in to Twitter with a different account from the one you previous signed in with, you'll be prompted to enter your current password as shown in the following screenshot:

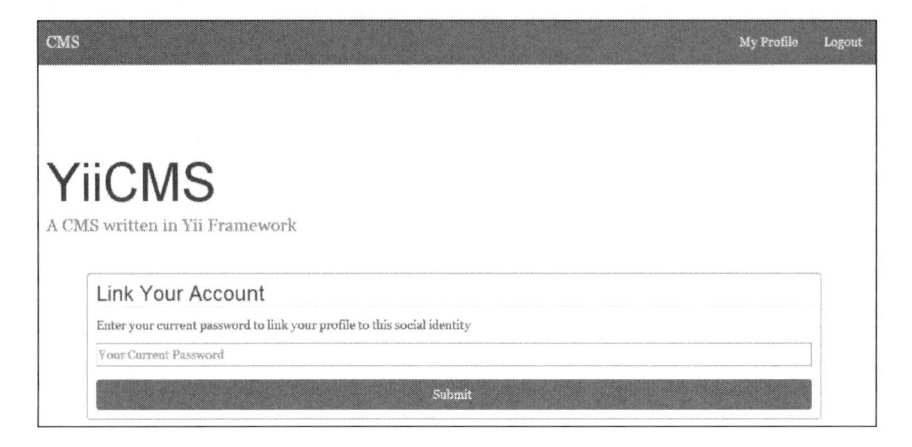

After entering your password, your social identity will be linked to your account, and you'll be able to login via Twitter rather than having to enter your username and password.

Exploring other HybridAuth providers

Due to the way we implemented our controller, we can easily and seamlessly add additional providers to the `hybridauth` section of our `protected/config/params.php` file without having to modify any other code in our system. Be sure to check out the HybridAuth user guide located at `http://hybridauth.sourceforge.net/userguide.html#index` for more information on how to integrate with other third-party providers, such as Google+ and Facebook, and give it a try!

Summary

Wow, we really did implement a lot in this chapter. In this chapter, we created a very robust and reusable content management system that featured both content and categories. We also dug deeper into Yii framework by manipulating our `CUrlManager` class to generate completely dynamic and clean URIs. We also covered the use of Yii's built-in theming to dynamically change the frontend appearance of our site by simply changing a configuration value. Finally, we learned how to integrate with third-party social networks to provide a social sign-on functionality that seamlessly integrates without our application.

In the next chapter, we'll be reusing much of the code built in this chapter to further separate the management functionality of our application from the presentation logic. We'll also dig deeper into Yii framework by learning how to create modules. Before continuing to the next chapter, be sure to go over the Yii Class Reference at `http://www.yiiframework.com/doc/api/` and review all the classes that we used in this chapter. Then, when you're ready, head over to the next chapter, and let's build a custom dashboard module for our CMS!

7
Creating a Management Module for the CMS

For our next project, we will be expanding upon the content management system we built in *Chapter 6*, *Building a Content Management System*, by migrating the management functionality into a module. Moving this functionality into a module will decouple administrative behaviors from the presentation layer of our application. This change will also enable us to develop and deploy administrative changes without having to make changes to our main application.

Our finished project will look as follows:

Prerequisites

Since we'll expanding upon the work we did in *Chapter 6, Building a Content Management System*, the only prerequisite for this chapter is the completed source code from the previous chapter. You can either build the project yourself, or you can use the completed source code available in the project resources folder from the previous chapter.

What are modules?

In Yii, modules are self-contained packages that operate independently of a Yii application but must reside within an existing application or module. Modules can additionally have as much or as little integration with our core application as we desire. In many aspects, modules are identical to Yii applications in that they have controllers, models, views, configurations, and components. This functionality allows us to deploy and manage code independently of our main application. It also provides us with greater usability if we choose to reuse our module across multiple projects. For our application, we'll be using our modules solely to separate the management of our application from the presentation layer and to independently deploy our application without having to make changes to our main application code.

> More information about Yii modules can be found in the official Yii guide located at `http://www.yiiframework.com/doc/guide/1.1/en/basics.module`.

Describing the project

Our dashboard module can be broken down into several components:

- Initializing and configuring the dashboard module
- Enabling custom routing for our module
- Moving the management functionality out of our application and into the module
- Adding file upload capabilities
- Module deployment

Initializing the module

The first component of this project will consist of creating and configuring our module so that it integrates with our primary application. We'll accomplish this by making several changes to our main configuration file as well as creating the basic structure for the module that we'll be using. We'll also go over managing our module assets independently of our main application.

Routing with a module

In the Yii framework, the default routes are defined by the name of the module combined with the default routes that are specified within `CUrlManager`. Unfortunately, Yii does not natively provide the functionality to define our own custom routes for a module without modifying the routes specified in `CUrlManager`. To get around this restriction, we'll be modifying our `CMSURLManager`, which we defined in *Chapter 6, Building a Content Management System*, in order to allow us to store and configure routes independently of our main application. When completed, we'll have a `routes.php` file in the `protected/modules/<module>/config/` file; this will contain all the custom routes for our module and will integrate with our main application without altering the application's behavior.

Moving the management functionality into the module

The third component of this project will entail moving the management functionality from our controls to the module's controllers. This will additionally involve moving the presentation layers out of the theme we created in the previous chapter and into the module itself. For additional security and user experience, we'll also be modifying how our module handles errors for both unauthenticated and unauthorized users.

Adding file upload capabilities

To make our content management system more versatile, we'll also be adding a file upload capability that will allow us to upload files from our content page and store them in our database. We'll also implement the functionality necessary to view these files in a file manager and additionally, to delete them.

Deploying modules

Finally, we'll go over the different deployment options that we can use to easily deploy our module independently of our main application. Using a combination of both Git and Composer, we can deploy our module in a way that makes the most sense for the type of project we are using.

Initializing the project

For this project, we'll be starting where we left off in the previous chapter, *Chapter 6, Building a Content Management System*. For your convenience, a skeleton project has been included in the project resources folder for this chapter that contains the foundation that we'll be starting with. Begin by copying the source code over to a new folder, and make sure that it is available at a different URL. In this chapter, I'll be using `http://chapter7.example.com` as our example URL. After importing the database and updating the database configuration using the instructions provided in the previous chapter, you should see the home page of our blog:

Creating the module

Now that our application is set up, we can begin to create our module. We'll start by creating the basic folder structure within our protected/modules directory:

```
protected/
    [...]
    modules/
        /dashboard
            assets/
            components/
            config/
            controllers/
            views/
                layouts/
                user/
                category/
                filemanager/
                default/
```

As you can see, the basic structure of our module looks identical to that of our main application. With our folder structure in place, we now need to create the DashboardModule class that we'll later tell Yii about so that it knows what to load. The steps are as follows:

1. Start by creating a new file, called DashboardModule.php, within protected/modules/dashboard with the following definition:
   ```
   <?php class DashboardModule extends CWebModule {}
   ```

2. Then, create an init() method for the module:
   ```
   public function init() {}
   ```

3. Within the module, we'll want to set the layoutPath so that our module knows what layout to provide our views with:
   ```
   $this->layoutPath = Yii::getPathOfAlias('dashboard.views.layouts');
   ```

4. We'll also want to tell our module to automatically import the contents of the components directory in which we'll be storing classes later:
   ```
   $this->setImport(array(
       'dashboard.components.*',
   ));
   ```

   This will tell Yii's autoloader to automatically load classes in the components folder. This is the same behavior that is used within Yii to load the classes registered in the import section of our protected/config/main.php file.

5. Finally, we'll want to set a few custom components for our module—mainly the error handler—so that we can handle errors that occur within our module in a different manner from the errors that occur within our main application:

```
Yii::app()->setComponents(array(
    'errorHandler' => array(
        'errorAction'  => 'dashboard/default/error',
    )
));
```

We'll then need to create two new classes; the first will be a controller component that all controllers within our module will extend from, and the second will be the default controller that will be accessed when no routes are specified. Within `protected/modules/dashboard/components/`, create a new file called `DashboardController.php` with the following definition. We'll be adding more information to this component once we've registered our module with Yii:

```
<?php class DashboardController extends CMSController {}
```

Then, create `DefaultController.php` inside `protected/modules/dashboard/controllers`. We'll also specify our `actionIndex()` method so that, once we register our module with Yii, we can see something:

```
<?php class DefaultController extends DashboardController
{
    public function actionIndex()
    {
        echo "Hello World!";
    }
}
```

Registering the module with Yii

Before we can see anything in our module, we first need to tell Yii about our module. For this, we simply need to specify the module name within the modules section of our `main.php` file at `protected/config/`:

```
<?php return array(
    [...]
'modules' => array(
```

```
          'dashboard'
    ),
    [...]
);
```

Now, if you navigate to `http://chapter7.example.com/dashboard`, you should see the text **Hello World** displayed. This is the simplest way to register a module with Yii. Unfortunately, this method requires us to make a change to our configuration file every time we want to use a new module, which in turn means we have to change the application code every time we use a new module. Another method of loading our module is to create a `protected/config/modules.php` file that we register in the modules section, instead. This allows us to simply change a cache setting outside our application without having to modify the code within our configuration file.

For this, first change the modules section of `main.php` at `protected/config/` so that it looks as follows:

```
<?php return array(
[...]
'modules' => require_once __DIR__ . DIRECTORY_SEPARATOR . 'modules.php',
[...]
);
```

Then, create a `modules.php` file at `protected/config/`. We'll start by declaring where the `modules` directory is located, and the location where our generated configuration file should be cached:

```
<?php

// Set the scan directory
$directory = __DIR__ . DIRECTORY_SEPARATOR . '..' . DIRECTORY_SEPARATOR . 'modules';
$cachedConfig = __DIR__.DIRECTORY_SEPARATOR.'..'.DIRECTORY_SEPARATOR.'runtime'.DIRECTORY_SEPARATOR.'modules.config.php';
```

We'll then check to see whether a cached file already exists. If it does, we'll simply return it:

```
// Attempt to load the cached file if it exists
if (file_exists($cachedConfig))
    return require_once($cachedConfig);
```

Creating a Management Module for the CMS

If a cached file doesn't exist, we'll iterate through all the folders in the `protected/modules` directory to retrieve all the module names and push them to an array. Since some Yii modules require additional configuration, we'll tell our loader to inject anything in `main.php` at `protected/modules/<module>/config/` as options for the module to use. When we've compiled a list of all the modules we're going to load, we'll write that out as a serialized array to a file within our `protected/runtime` directory:

```
else
{
    // Otherwise generate one, and return it
    $response = array();

    // Find all the modules currently installed, and preload them
    foreach (new IteratorIterator(new DirectoryIterator($directory)) as $filename)
    {
        // Don't import dot files
        if (!$filename->isDot())
        {
            $path = $filename->getPathname();

            if (file_exists($path.DIRECTORY_SEPARATOR.'config'.DIRECTORY_SEPARATOR.'main.php'))
                $response[$filename->getFilename()] = require($path.DIRECTORY_SEPARATOR.'config'.DIRECTORY_SEPARATOR.'main.php');
            else
                array_push($response, $filename->getFilename());
        }
    }

    $encoded = serialize($response);
    file_put_contents($cachedConfig, '<?php return unserialize(\''.$encoded.'\');');

    // return the response
    return $response;
}
```

The resulting file that is generated then looks as follows and is returned all the way up to our `main.php` file at `protected/config/`:

```
<?php return unserialize('a:1:{i:0;s:9:"dashboard";}');
```

If we ever want to add a new module, we simply need to delete the `module.config.php` file at `protected/runtime/`. The first request to hit the system will immediately regenerate the updated file.

While slightly more expensive in terms of disk operation, this method of loading modules enables us to dynamically load modules with Yii just by adding them to the `modules` directory. It also eliminates any changes we need to make to our application in order to add a new module, which in turn means that we'll be less likely to introduce new behaviors or bugs to our main application while adding a new module.

Adding custom routes to a module

While Yii will perform a lot of module routing for free, we have to add our routes to our `CUrlManager` configuration in `main.php` at `protected/config/` in order for our module to have any custom routing. While it's easy to execute, this method does not keep our module and application configurations sufficiently separated. To get around this limitation in Yii, we need to modify the `CMSUrlManager` class that we created in the previous chapter in order to retrieve custom module routes that we define. This enables us to write routes as part of our module rather than as part of our application. The steps are as follows:

1. Start by creating a new file, `routes.php`, in `protected/modules/dashboard/config/`, that contains the following. For this module, we'll define a custom route for our save actions to be loaded from:

   ```
   <?php return array(
       '/dashboard/<controller:\w+>/save' => '/dashboard/<controller>/save',
   );
   ```

   > This example is purely to illustrate how to add custom routing to a module, since Yii does not support it natively.

2. With our custom route defined, we'll next update `CMSUrlManager` to automatically import these rules. Open `CMSUrlManager.php` at `protected/components/`, and add the following to the `if` block of the `processRules()` method:

   ```
   $this->rules = CMap::mergearray($this->addModuleRules(), $this->rules);
   ```

3. We'll finally define a `addModuleRules()` method that will search all of our installed modules for a `routes.php` file at `config/` and register them with Yii:

```php
private function addModuleRules()
{
    // Load the routes from cache
    $moduleRoutes = array();
    $directories = glob(Yii::getPathOfAlias('application.modules') . '/*' , GLOB_ONLYDIR);

    foreach ($directories as $dir)
    {
        $routePath = $dir .DS. 'config' .DS. 'routes.php';
        if (file_exists($routePath))
        {
            $routes = require_once($routePath);
            foreach ($routes as $k=>$v)
                $moduleRoutes[$k] = $v;
        }
    }

    return $moduleRoutes;
}
```

Now, our dashboard module will be able to handle nonstandard routes without having to update a configuration file within our main application.

Creating the controllers

Now that we have registered our application with Yii and defined our custom routes, we can start working on our controllers. First, we should work on our `DashboardController` component so that our controllers automatically inherit some common behaviors. The steps are as follows:

1. Within our `DashboardController.php` component, we should first define our `accessRules()` method. This will ensure that only administrators have access to the dashboard:

```php
public function filters()
{
   return array(
       'accessControl'
   );
```

```
}

    public function accessRules()
    {
       return array(
           array('allow',  // allow authenticated admins to perform any action
               'users'=>array('@'),
           ),
           array('deny',  // deny all users
               'users'=>array('*'),
               'deniedCallback' => array($this, 'actionError')
           ),
       );
    }
```

2. Next, we'll define the `default` layout that we'll want to use throughout the module:

   ```
   public $layout='default';
   ```

3. Then, we'll create a custom error action that will prevent both unauthenticated users and unauthorized users from accessing our module. By default, if Yii encounters an unauthorized error, it will simply return a 403 error. Our error action will improve the user experience by redirecting unauthenticated users to the login page with a next $_GET parameter so that they can be returned to the exact page they wanted to go to after they have been authenticated. If a user is simply unauthorized, on the other hand, it will display the appropriate error and deny them access:

   ```
   public function actionError()
   {
       if (Yii::app()->user->isGuest)
           return $this->redirect($this->createUrl('/site/login?next=' . Yii::app()->request->requestUri));

       if($error=Yii::app()->errorHandler->error)
       {
           if(Yii::app()->request->isAjaxRequest)
               echo $error['message'];
           else
               $this->render('error', array('error' => $error));
       }
   }
   ```

4. To complete this, redirect the $_GET parameter. We also need to make a change to our SiteController.php file at protected/controllers/ so that it knows how to handle the parameter. Simply replace the redirect with the following:

   ```
   $this->redirect(Yii::app()->request->getParam('next', $this->createAbsoluteUrl('content/index')));
   ```

5. Finally, we need to implement a way to manage our assets independently of our main application. Many module implementations simple add assets to a globally available assets folder. This implementation makes it very difficult to ensure that all traces of a module have been removed. An easier way of managing assets for modules is to create a folder for all of our module-specific assets to reside in, and then, publish that folder using CAssetManager independently of our application. This way, if we make any changes to our module assets, they won't affect our main application. In our SiteController, we should define the following method:

   ```
   public function getAsset()
   {
       return Yii::app()->assetManager->publish(YiiBase::getPathOfAlias('application.modules.dashboard.assets'), true, -1, YII_DEBUG);
   }
   ```

   Since this method is a getter and since it returns the path where the assets are published, we can call it from our layout file as follows (using the dashboard.css file that should be copied from the project resources folder to your module's assets folder):

   ```
   Yii::app()->clientScript->registerCssFile($this->getAsset().'/dashboard.css');
   ```

Migrating the functionality to the module

Now that our module is set up, we can start by moving the functionality from our application controllers and theme into our dashboard module. We'll go over everything that is needed for each model: Categories, Content, and Users.

Migrating content management

In this next section, we will migrate all of the management functionalities we built in the previous chapter into our new module:

1. Starting with our ContentController, we first want to remove the actionAdmin(), actionSave(), and actionDelete() methods from the ContentController.php file at protected/controllers/.

2. Next, we should remove the access control properties for the actions we just deleted from our `ContentController`. The restored `accessRules()` method should look as follows:

   ```
   public function accessRules()
   {
      return array(
         array('allow',
            'actions' => array('index', 'view', 'search'),
            'users' => array('*')
         ),
         array('deny',  // deny all users
            'users'=>array('*'),
         ),
      );
   }
   ```

3. With our `ContentController` stripped of our administrative behaviors, we can begin moving the functionality into our `DefaultController.php` file at `protected/modules/dashboard/controllers/`, which we'll be using as our `ContentController`. We'll start by adding our `accessRules()` method to our `DefaultController`. Since we want to inherit the rules defined in `DashboardController.php` at `components/`, we'll use `CMap::mergeArray()` to merge the parent rules with our newly defined rules:

   > Do the naming conventions have you confused? If you don't want to store the content-related functionality in `DefaultController`, you can set the `$defaultController` property in `DashboardModule` to `content`. This will override Yii's default behavior.

   ```
   public function accessRules()
   {
      return CMap::mergeArray(parent::accessRules(), array(
         array('allow',
            'actions' => array('index', 'save', 'delete'),
            'users'=>array('@'),
            'expression' => 'Yii::app()->user->role==2'
         ),
         array('deny',  // deny all users
            'users'=>array('*'),
         )
      ));
   }
   ```

4. Then, we'll redefine our `loadModel()` method:

```
private function loadModel($id=NULL)
{
    if ($id == NULL)
        throw new CHttpException(404, 'No category with that ID exists');

    $model = Content::model()->findByPk($id);

    if ($model == NULL)
        throw new CHttpException(404, 'No category with that ID exists');

    return $model;
}
```

5. Then, we'll define our `actionDelete()` method:

```
public function actionDelete($id)
{
    $this->loadModel($id)->delete();

    $this->redirect($this->createUrl('/dashboard'));
}
```

6. Then we'll write an index method to display all of the content entries on our database:

```
public function actionIndex()
{
    $model = new Content('search');
    $model->unsetAttributes();

    if (isset($_GET['Content']))
        $model->attributes = $_GET;

    $this->render('index', array(
        'model' => $model
    ));
}
```

7. Finally, we'll write a method to both create new content entries and edit existing content entries:

   ```
   public function actionSave($id=NULL)
   {
      if ($id == NULL)
         $model = new Content;
      else
         $model = $this->loadModel($id);

      if (isset($_POST['Content']))
      {
         $model->attributes = $_POST['Content'];
         $model->author_id = Yii::app()->user->id;

         if ($model->save())
         {
            Yii::app()->user->setFlash('info', 'The articles was saved');
            $this->redirect($this->createUrl('/dashboard'));
         }
      }

      $this->render('save', array(
         'model' => $model
      ));
   }
   ```

8. Next, we should copy our `save.php` file located at `protected/modules/dashboard/views/default/` from our project resources folder into our module. If you haven't done so already, copy the `default.php` layout file located at `protected/modules/dashboard/views/layouts/` into your project.

9. Finally, we need to make sure that our `index` view file is properly updated so that it links to the appropriate controller actions. If you were simply to copy the view from the theme file, you'd notice that none of the links work. To correct these links, we need to update our `createUrl` calls to point to the `save()` method our module's `DefaultController`, and update the `CButtonColumn` links to point to our module:

   ```
   <?php echo CHtml::link('Create New Post', $this->createUrl('/dashboard/default/save'), array('class' => 'btn btn-primary')); ?>
   ```

```php
<?php $this->widget('zii.widgets.grid.CGridView', array(
    'dataProvider'=>$model->search(),
    'htmlOptions' => array(
        'class' => 'table-responsive'
    ),
    'itemsCssClass' => 'table table-striped',
    'columns' => array(
        'id',
        'title',
        'published' => array(
            'name' => 'Published',
            'value' => '$data->published==1?"Yes":"No"'
        ),
        'author.username',
        array(
            'class'=>'CButtonColumn',
            'viewButtonUrl'=>'Yii::app()->createUrl("/".$data["slug"])',
            'deleteButtonUrl'=>'Yii::app()->createUrl("/dashboard/default/delete", array("id" =>  $data["id"]))',
            'updateButtonUrl'=>'Yii::app()->createUrl("/dashboard/default/save", array("id" =>  $data["id"]))',
        ),
    ),
    'pager' => array(
        'htmlOptions' => array(
            'class' => 'pager'
        ),
        'header' => '',
        'firstPageCssClass'=>'hide',
        'lastPageCssClass'=>'hide',
        'maxButtonCount' => 0
    )
));
```

Now that we're finished, we'll be able to view all the articles in our CMS, delete them, edit them, and navigate to the frontend view—all from a single interface, as shown in the following screenshot:

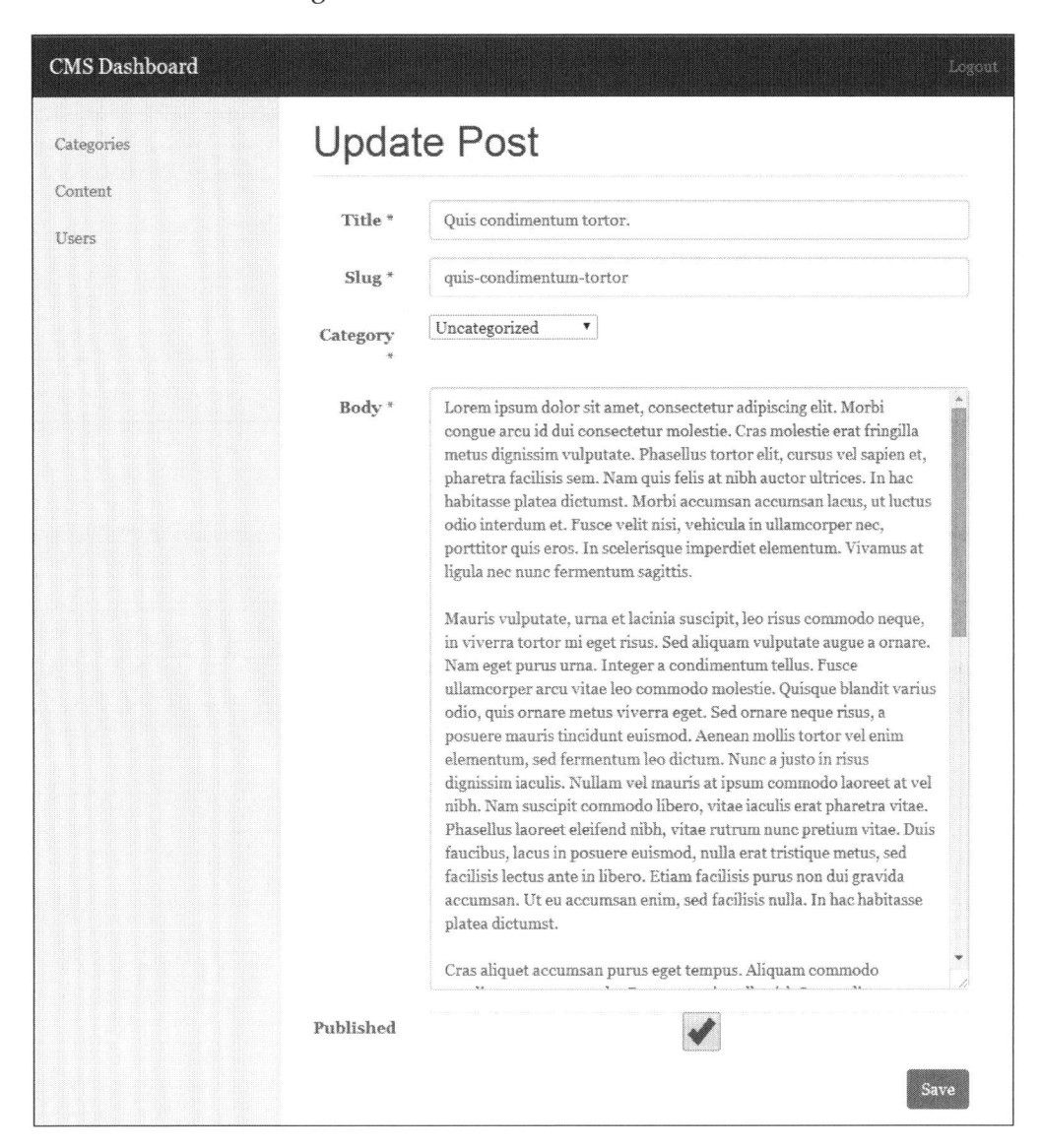

Migrating categories

The changes for our users and categories controllers are going to be very similar—let's work through them. The steps are as follows:

1. Starting with our `CategoryController`, we first want to remove the `actionAdmin()`, `actionSave()`, and `actionDelete()` methods from the `CategoryController.php` file at `protected/controllers/`.

2. Next, we should remove the access control properties for the actions we just deleted from our `CategoryController`. The restored `accessRules()` method should look as follows:

   ```
   public function accessRules()
   {
      return array(
         array('allow',
            'actions' => array('index', 'view', 'search'),
            'users' => array('*')
         ),
         array('deny',  // deny all users
            'users'=>array('*'),
         ),
      );
   }
   ```

3. Our new `accessRules()` method for our `CategoryController.php` file at `protected/modules/dashboard/controllers/` will then look as follows:

   ```
   public function accessRules()
   {
      return CMap::mergeArray(parent::accessRules(), array(
         array('allow',
            'actions' => array('index', 'save', 'delete'),
            'users'=>array('@'),
            'expression' => 'Yii::app()->user->role==2'
         ),
         array('deny',  // deny all users
            'users'=>array('*'),
         )
      ));
   }
   ```

Chapter 7

4. Next, we'll reimplement all of the management actions with updated redirects, starting with our `actionIndex()` method:

```
public function actionIndex()
{
    $model = new Category('search');
    $model->unsetAttributes();

    if (isset($_GET['Category']))
        $model->attributes = $_GET;

    $this->render('index', array(
        'model' => $model
    ));
}
```

5. We'll then re-implement the save method and modify it to work in our module:

```
public function actionSave($id=NULL)
{
    if ($id == NULL)
        $model = new Category;
    else
        $model = $this->loadModel($id);

    if (isset($_POST['Category']))
    {
        $model->attributes = $_POST['Category'];

        if ($model->save())
        {
            Yii::app()->user->setFlash('info', 'The category was saved');
            $this->redirect($this->createUrl('/dashboard/category'));
        }
    }

    $this->render('save', array(
        'model' => $model
    ));
}
```

6. We'll then reimplement the delete method in our module and update the redirects:

```
public function actionDelete($id)
{
   $this->loadModel($id)->delete();

   $this->redirect($this->createUrl('/dashboard/category'));
}
```

7. Finally, we'll update the `loadModel()` method so that it works without our module:

```
private function loadModel($id=NULL)
{
   if ($id == NULL)
       throw new CHttpException(404, 'No category with that ID exists');

   $model = Category::model()->findByPk($id);

   if ($model == NULL)
       throw new CHttpException(404, 'No category with that ID exists');

   return $model;
}
```

8. Then copy the view files' `index.php` located at `protected/modules/dashboard/views/category/` and `save.php` located at `protected/modules/dashboard/views/category/` from the project resources folder into our module.

9. Notice once again that we've updated our `CButtonColumn` links to point to our module rather than to the home page routes we had defined earlier:

```
array(
    'class'=>'CButtonColumn',
    'viewButtonUrl'=>'Yii::app()->createUrl("/".$data["slug"])',
    'deleteButtonUrl'=>'Yii::app()->createUrl("/dashboard/category/delete", array("id" => $data["id"]))',
    'updateButtonUrl'=>'Yii::app()->createUrl("/dashboard/category/save", array("id" => $data["id"]))',
),
```

Our final category management interface will look as follows and will behave identically to how our content management interface behaves:

Implementing user management

In the previous chapter, we didn't implement a UI for user management; let's go ahead and implement that functionality now so that our dashboard module fully encompasses all the management functionality. The steps are as follows:

1. Begin by creating a new controller, `UserController.php`, in `protected/modules/dashboard/controllers` with the following definition:

    ```php
    <?php class UserController extends DashboardController {}
    ```

2. Next, we'll define our `accessRules()` method for this controller:

    ```php
    public function accessRules()
    {
        return CMap::mergeArray(parent::accessRules(), array(
            array('allow',
                'actions' => array('index', 'save', 'delete'),
                'users'=>array('@'),
                'expression' => 'Yii::app()->user->role==2'
            ),
            array('deny',  // deny all users
                'users'=>array('*'),
            )
        ));
    }
    ```

Creating a Management Module for the CMS

3. Then, we'll implement a `loadModel()` utility method:

    ```
    private function loadModel($id=NULL)
    {
        if ($id == NULL)
            throw new CHttpException(404, 'No category with that ID exists');

        $model = User::model()->findByPk($id);

        if ($model == NULL)
            throw new CHttpException(404, 'No category with that ID exists');

        return $model;
    }
    ```

4. Next, we'll update our delete action so that it redirects properly within our module:

    ```
    public function actionDelete($id)
    {
        $this->loadModel($id)->delete();

        $this->redirect($this->createUrl('/dashboard/user'));
    }
    ```

5. Then we'll reimplement the index action to display a listing of all of our users:

    ```
    public function actionIndex()
    {
        $model = new User('search');
        $model->unsetAttributes();

        if (isset($_GET['User']))
            $model->attributes = $_GET;

        $this->render('index', array(
            'model' => $model
        ));
    }
    ```

6. Finally, we'll migrate our save method into our module. Since we've already implemented all the core functionality of how our users behave into our User model class, the implementation of our `actionSave()` method is straightforward:

[248]

```
public function actionSave($id=NULL)
{
    if ($id == NULL)
        $model = new User;
    else
        $model = $this->loadModel($id);

    if (isset($_POST['User']))
    {
        $model->attributes = $_POST['User'];

        if ($model->save())
        {
            Yii::app()->user->setFlash('info', 'The user was saved');
            $this->redirect($this->createUrl('/dashboard/user'));
        }
    }

    $this->render('save', array(
        'model' => $model
    ));
}
```

7. Finally, copy the index.php view file located at protected/modules/dashboard/views/user/ and the save.php view file located at protected/modules/dashboard/views/user/ from the project resources folder into your application. Once again, we're left with an interface that is identical to our content and category management interfaces:

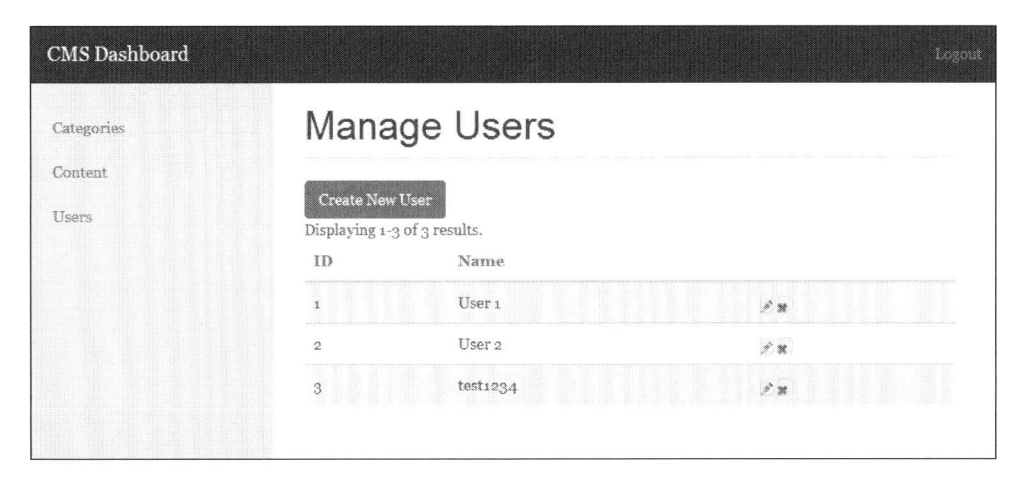

Uploading files

The final component that we'll be adding to our module is a file manager with file upload capabilities. For this component, we'll be creating a dedicated controller to view all of our uploaded files in paginated format, several new classes to handle the actual file upload, and a few view changes to our content save view so that we can associate files with a particular article.

Rather than bundling all of this functionality into our `FileController` that we'll be building, we'll start by building three different components to handle the various aspects of uploading a file. The first class `File` will represent a `$_FILES['file']` object and will provide the functionality for saving the file. The second class, `FileUpload`, will be our call point for uploading our file and will return the appropriate database to us. The final class, `FileUploader`, will handle the interactions between the `File` and `FileUpload` class. These three classes will ensure that our `FileController` class is clean and will make working with the file upload extremely easy.

Creating the File class

We'll start by creating the `File` class, a simple object that represents `$_FILES['file']`, that we'll be sending via a POST request. Create the `File.php` file in `protected/modules/dashboard/components/`:

```php
<?php

class File {
    public function save($path)
    {
        if (!move_uploaded_file($_FILES['file']['tmp_name'], $path))
            return false;

        return true;
    }

    public function __get($name)
    {
        if (isset($_FILES['file'][$name]))
            return $_FILES['file'][$name];

        return NULL;
    }
}
```

For simplicity, we'll be storing all of our files in the root directory of our main application called /uploads. Go ahead and create this folder now, and make sure that your web server has write access to it.

Creating the FileUploader class

The next class we'll be building out is the `FileUploader` class. This class will handle the validation and will call the `File` class that we just created in order to save the file to the uploads directory. The steps are as follows:

1. Start with the class definition in `FileUploader.php` located at protected/modules/dashboard/components/:

   ```
   <?php class FileUploader {}
   ```

2. Then, define some private attributes to be used as validators:

   ```
   private $allowedExtensions = array(
       'png',
       'jpeg',
       'jpg',
       'gif',
       'bmp'
   );

   private $sizeLimit = 10485760;

   private $file;
   ```

3. Next, we'll create a constructor for this new object that will set some basic variables for the validator later on and will also create the `File` object using the `$_FILES['file']` array:

   ```
   function __construct(array $allowedExtensions = array(), $sizeLimit = 10485760)
   {
       $allowedExtensions = array_map("strtolower", $allowedExtensions);

       If (!empty($allowedExtensions))
           $this->allowedExtensions = $allowedExtensions;
       $this->sizeLimit = $sizeLimit;

       $this->checkServerSettings();

       $this->file = false;
       if (isset($_FILES['file']))
           $this->file = new File();
   }
   ```

4. Next, we'll create the `checkServerSettings()` method that we defined earlier. This will ensure that we don't try to upload files that are larger than what is defined in our `php.ini` file:

```php
private function checkServerSettings()
{
    $postSize = $this->toBytes(ini_get('post_max_size'));
    $uploadSize = $this->toBytes(ini_get('upload_max_filesize'));

    if ($postSize < $this->sizeLimit || $uploadSize < $this->sizeLimit){
        $size = max(1, $this->sizeLimit / 1024 / 1024) . 'M';
        $json = CJSON::encode(array(
            'error' => 'increase post_max_size and upload_max_filesize'
        ));
        die($json);
    }
}
```

5. Finally, we'll create the validators that will validate that the file meets the restrictions we put in place earlier. This class will ultimately return an array to our `FileUpload` class that we'll be creating next:

```php
private function toBytes($str)
{
    $val = trim($str);
    $last = strtolower($str[strlen($str)-1]);
    switch($last)
    {
        case 'g': $val *= 1024;
        case 'm': $val *= 1024;
        case 'k': $val *= 1024;
    }
    return $val;
}


public function handleUpload($uploadDirectory, $replaceOldFile = FALSE)
{
    if (!is_writable($uploadDirectory))
```

```php
        return array('error' => "Server error. Upload directory isn't writable.");

    if (!$this->file)
        return array('error' => 'No files were uploaded.');

    $size = $this->file->size;

    if ($size == 0)
        return array('error' => 'File is empty');

    $pathinfo = pathinfo($this->file->name);
    $filename = $pathinfo['filename'];

    //$filename = md5(uniqid());
    $ext = $pathinfo['extension'];

    if(!in_array(strtolower($ext), $this->allowedExtensions))
    {
        $these = implode(', ', $this->allowedExtensions);
        return array('error' =>"File has an invalid extension");
    }

    $filename = 'upload-'.md5($filename);

   if(!$replaceOldFile)
    {
        /// don't overwrite previous files that were uploaded
        while (file_exists($uploadDirectory . $filename . '.' . $ext))
            $filename .= rand(10, 99);
    }

    if ($this->file->save($uploadDirectory . $filename . '.' . $ext))
        return array('success'=>true,'filename'=>$filename.'.'.$ext);
    else
        return array('error'=> 'Could not save uploaded file. The upload was cancelled, or server error encountered');
}
```

Creating the FileUpload class

The last component that we'll create is the `FileUpload` class that will act as an intermediary between our `FileUploader` class and our `FileController` class:

1. Begin by creating the `FileUpload.php` file in `protected/modules/dashboard/components/` with the following definition:

   ```
   <?php class FileUpload {}
   ```

2. Then, declare a few properties and the constructor:

   ```
   private $_id = NULL;

   private $_response = NULL;

   public $_result = array();

   public function __construct($id)
   {
      $this->_id = $id;
       $this->_uploadFile();
   }
   ```

3. We'll then create our `_uploadFile()` method that we called in our constructor. This method will instantiate a `FileUploader` object and will perform the upload before passing it off to our `ContentMetadata` object, where we'll store the reference to the file:

   ```
   private function _uploadFile()
   {
       $path = '/';
       $folder = Yii::app()->getBasePath() .'/../uploads' . $path;

       $sizeLimit = Yii::app()->params['max_fileupload_size'];
       $allowedExtensions = array('jpg', 'jpeg', 'png', 'gif', 'bmp');
       $uploader = new FileUploader($allowedExtensions, $sizeLimit);

       $this->_result = $uploader->handleUpload($folder);

       if (isset($this->_result['error']))
   ```

```
        throw new CHttpException(500, $this->_result['error']);
    return $this->_handleResourceUpload('/uploads/' . $this->_
result['filename']);
}
```

4. Finally, we'll create the _handleResourceUpload() method. This method will take the response object returned by the FileUploader object and, if the file was successfully uploaded, will store the filename of the uploaded file in our database so that we can manage it easily. It will also link a particular file to a given article:

```
private function _handleResourceUpload($value)
{
  if ($this->_result['success'] == true)
    {
        $meta = ContentMetadata::model()->findbyAttributes(array('content_id' => $this->_id, 'key' => $this->_result['filename']));

        if ($meta == NULL)
            $meta = new ContentMetadata;

        $meta->content_id = $this->_id;
        $meta->key = $this->_result['filename'];
        $meta->value = $value;
        if ($meta->save())
        {
            $this->_result['filepath'] = $value;
            return $this->_result;
        }
        else
            throw new CHttpException(400,  'Unable to save uploaded image.');
    }
    else
    {
        return htmlspecialchars(CJSON::encode($this->_result), ENT_NOQUOTES);
        throw new CHttpException(400, $this->_result['error']);
    }
}
```

Creating the controller for the file manager

Now that we have the functionality in place to upload a file, we need to create the controller actions to manage it. We'll be creating three separate actions: an `index` action where all files and their associations can be viewed; a `delete` action; and an `upload` action. The steps are as follows:

1. Begin by creating the `FileController` class in `protected/modules/dashboard/controllers` with the following definition:

   ```
   <?php class FileController extends DashboardController {}
   ```

2. We'll then define the `accessRules()` method:

   ```
   public function accessRules()
   {
       return CMap::mergeArray(parent::accessRules(), array(
           array('allow',
               'actions' => array('index', 'upload', 'delete'),
               'users'=>array('@'),
               'expression' => 'Yii::app()->user->role==2'
           ),
           array('deny',  // deny all users
               'users'=>array('*'),
           )
       ));
   }
   ```

3. Next, we'll define our `index` action that will allow us to view all files uploaded into our CMS. Since our `ContentMetadata` table might contain other attributes, we'll only be searching against items that have a key of upload:

   ```
   public function actionIndex()
   {
       $model = new ContentMetadata('search');
       $model->unsetAttributes();
       $model->key = 'upload';

       if (isset($_GET['ContentMetadata']))
           $model->attributes = $_GET;

       $this->render('index', array(
           'model' => $model
       ));
   }
   ```

4. Then, we'll create an upload action that will call our FileUpload class. After uploading the file or having an error, the action will redirect the user to where they came from with either the relative URI to the file, or a useful error message generated from our FileUploader class:

```
public function actionUpload($id = NULL)
{
   if ($id == NULL)
      throw new CHttpException(400, 'Missing ID');

   if (isset($_FILES['file']))
   {
      $file = new FileUpload($id);

      if ($file->_result['success'])
         Yii::app()->user->setFlash('info', 'The file uploaded to
' . $file->_result['filepath']);
      elseif ($file->_result['error'])
         Yii::app()->user->setFlash('error', 'Error: ' . $file->_
result['error']);

   }
   else
      Yii::app()->user->setFlash('error', 'No file detected');

   $this->redirect($this->createUrl('/dashboard/default/
save?id='.$id));
}
```

5. Then we'll create a loadModel() method and a delete action to remove files from our database:

```
public function actionDelete($id)
{
   if ($this->loadModel($id)->delete())
   {
      Yii::app()->user->setFlash('info', 'File has been deleted');
      $this->redirect($this->createUrl('/dashboard/file/index'));
   }

   throw new CHttpException(500, 'The server failed to delete the
requested file from the database. Please retry');
}

private function loadModel($id=NULL)
{
```

```
        if ($id == NULL)
            throw new CHttpException(400, 'Missing ID');

        $model = ContentMetadata::model()->findByAttributes(array('id'
=> $id));
        if ($model == NULL)
            throw new CHttpException(400, 'Object not found');

        return $model;
    }
```

6. We'll then move on to creating the views for our file manager. The first view we'll create will be an index view, which will consist of a CListView container that will allow us to easily browse through our images. Add the following to index.php located at protected/modules/dashboard/views/file/:

```
<?php $this->widget('zii.widgets.CListView', array(
    'dataProvider'=>$model->search(),
    'itemView'=>'_file',
));
```

7. We'll also create the corresponding itemView file called _file.php located at protected/modules/dashboard/views/file/:

```
<div class="file">
    <a href="<?php echo $data->value; ?>"><img src="<?php echo $data->value; ?>" style="width: 150px; height: 150px;"/></a>
    <?php echo CHtml::link('Article ID: '. $data->content_id, $this->createUrl('/dashboard/default/save', array('id' => $data->content_id))); ?>
    <?php echo CHtml::link('Delete', $this->createUrl('/dashboard/file/delete', array('id' => $data->id)), array('class' => 'btn btn-danger')); ?>
</div>
```

8. Finally, we'll need to update save.php at protected/modules/dashboard/views/default/ with a file upload form so that files can be uploaded:

```
<?php if (!$model->isNewRecord): ?>
    <hr />
    <?php $form=$this->beginWidget('CActiveForm', array(
        'id'=>'file-upload-form',
        'action' => $this->createUrl('/dashboard/file/upload', array('id' => $model->id)),
```

```
                'htmlOptions' => array(
                    'class' => 'form-horizontal',
                    'role' => 'form',
                    'enctype'=>'multipart/form-data'

                )
        )); ?>
            <div class="form-group">
                <div class="col-sm-10">
                    <input type="file" name="file" />
                </div>
            </div>

            <div class="row buttons">
                <?php echo CHtml::submitButton('Upload file',
    array('class' => 'btn btn-primary pull-right col-md-offset-1'));
    ?>
            </div>

        <?php $this->endWidget(); ?>
    <?php endif; ?>
```

Now, if you upload a file from the content save screen, the URL of the file will be returned back to you for you to add it to your article:

[259]

Additionally, if you want to view all files uploaded to the CMS, or if you want to delete a file, you can navigate to `http://chapter7.example.com/dashboard/files` in your web browser or add a link to the sidebar in your `default.php` file at `protected/modules/dashboard/views/layouts/`, as shown in the following screenshot:

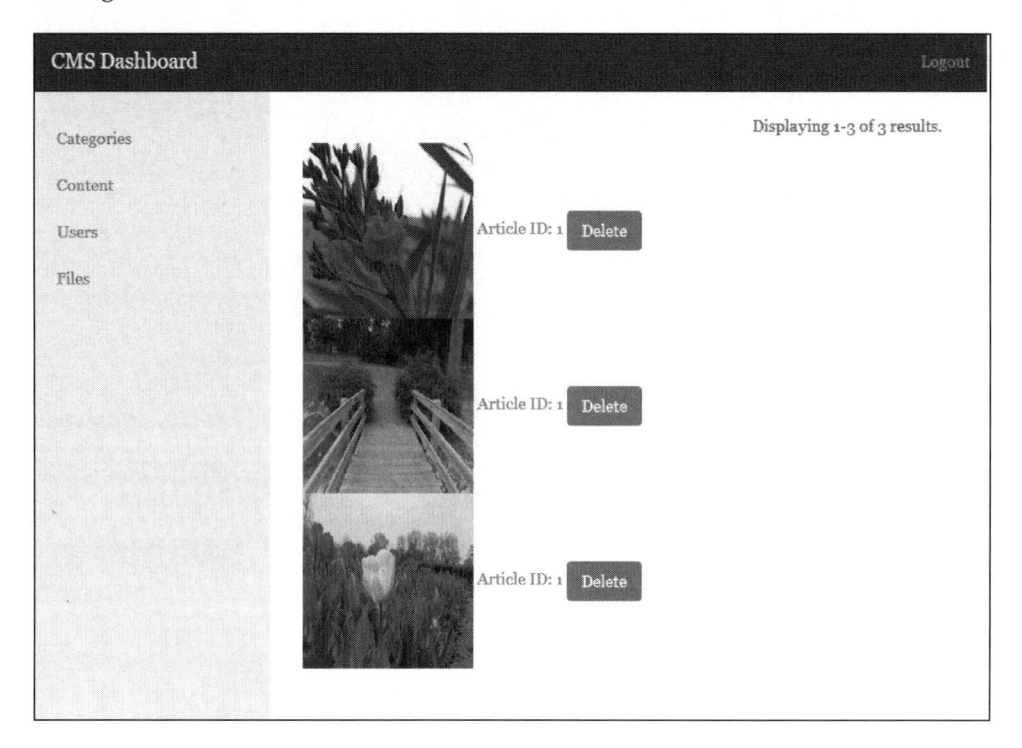

Strategies for deploying our application

The last topic we should discuss is how we want to deploy our new module alongside our application. There are several different deployment strategies that we can make use of, each of which has its own advantages and disadvantages. In the next section, we'll go over the benefits and downfalls of a few different strategies. When the time comes to deploy your module alongside your application, be sure to give careful thought to how you want your module and application to be integrated.

Deploying as the application

The simplest deployment strategy we can use is to simply commit our module's source code directly to our main application. When the time comes to deploy our application, our module is automatically included. While incredibly simple and basic, this strategy has several disadvantages.

First and foremost, it binds the state of our module to our application, which makes it more likely that we'll unintentionally introduce bugs or incomplete features when we deploy our application. The second disadvantage is that it tightly couples our module's state at any given time to our application. The final disadvantage is that it makes it very difficult to deploy a module update independently of our application.

Deploying as a submodule

The second deployment strategy is to commit our module code to a completely separate repository and include it in our project as a submodule. This method not only ensures that our project retrieves the latest code, but it also ensures that our module code and application code are properly separated. The alternative to using a submodule is to simply clone the module repository into the `protected/modules` directory every time we want to run a deployment. While this method is simple, it does increase the complexity of our application and requires us to have a detailed understanding of Git submodules. Additionally, it is difficult to automate while ensuring that deployments don't result in downtime.

Deploying as a Composer dependency

A third strategy is to create a completely separate repository for our module, include it into our project as a Composer dependency, and use the `composer/installers` package to ensure that the module is placed in the correct directory. While it is significantly more complex than the other strategies, this strategy has the advantage of ensuring that our module and application code remain separated. It also has the advantage of moving deployment-related tasks back to the application rather than the module.

Summary

We covered a lot of information on working with modules and overcoming some of the limitations that they have. We discussed how to create a module, how to integrate it with our application, how to handle custom routing for modules, how to migrate the management functionality from a regular Yii application into our module, and we also added a file manager and upload capabilities to our CMS. Additionally, we covered different strategies for deploying our module alongside our application.

In the next chapter, we will create an API module for our application that will allow for web services and native applications to connect to our CMS. We'll expand upon the topics covered in this chapter, and we'll also cover how we can override several core Yii components to make our API flexible and easy to develop with.

Before continuing to the next chapter, be sure to review the Yii Class Reference at `http://www.yiiframework.com/doc/api/` and review all the classes that we used in this chapter.

8
Building an API for the CMS

Throughout this book, we've covered the development of view-oriented applications—applications that the user can interact with directly. Our view-oriented approach, however, doesn't allow us to easily integrate with other services or provide functionalities for native applications. This view-oriented approach often leaves us with hardcoded functionality and makes integrations significantly more difficult. The Yii framework, however, is extremely adaptable and enables us to build API-driven applications rather than view-driven applications. An API reduces the amount of code we have to maintain; if executed properly, it reduces the amount of code that needs to change when we want to add a feature. Ultimately, this allows us to work faster and be more adaptable to changes.

Building an API-driven application also enables us to easily develop both web and native clients that work with our API, thus completely separating view-oriented logic from our application. In this chapter, we'll go over what we'll need to do in order to build an API-driven module for our content-management system that we created earlier. By fostering an ecosystem around our application, we can provide value to both developers and users, and increase the value of our application.

The following is the demonstration:

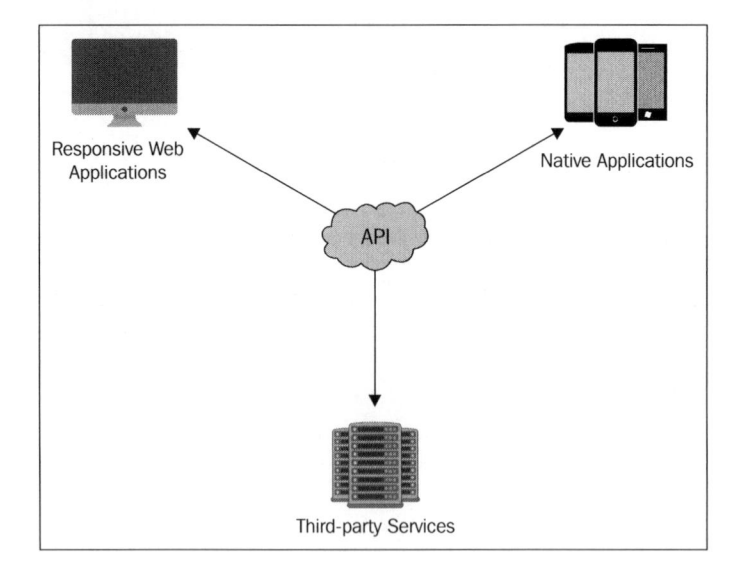

[Diagram: API in the center connecting to Responsive Web Applications, Native Applications, and Third-party Services]

In this chapter, we'll go over what we'll need to do to build an API-driven module for our content management system that we created earlier.

Prerequisites

Since we'll be expanding upon the work we did in *Chapter 7, Creating a Management Module for the CMS*, we'll need the completed source code from the previous chapter. You can either build the project yourself, or you can use the completed source code available in the project resources folder in the previous chapter. We'll also need a URL request client that will allow us to send GET, POST, and DELETE requests with JSON-encoded data to our application. You can either use cURL, or you can download a Google Chrome extension called **RESTClient** available at `https://chrome.google.com/webstore/detail/rest-console/cokgbflfommojglbmbpenpphppikmonn?hl=en`. The examples throughout this chapter will use RESTClient.

Describing the project

In this chapter, we'll be building an API module for our content-management system. The development of this module can be broken down into several pieces:

- Configuring the module
- Extending Yii to "RESTfully" render JSON or XML instead of a view file

- Handling data input
- Handling user authentication
- Handling exceptions and errors
- Specifying what data will be returned with each response
- Implementing authentication, deauthentication, and basic CRUD actions

Configuring the module

The first component of this project will consist of creating and configuring our module so that it integrates with our main application. Since we added the functionality that seamlessly integrates modules into our application in the previous chapter, the only work required for this section will be to clear out our module cache, initialize the module, and add in the necessary routes.

Extending Yii to render JSON or XML in a RESTful way

Since the Yii framework is designed to work with view files, we'll need to extend several components of the Yii framework in order to get it to output and render JSON or XML documentations. We'll also need to make several different changes to Yii so that it knows how to handle GET, POST, and DELETE actions independently of one another. To accomplish this, we'll create a new controller that will extend CMSController, which we created in the previous chapters. This will overload several key methods from CController, namely runAction(), filterAccessControl(), createAction(), and beforeAction(). We'll also extend several other classes— CInlineAction, CAccessControlFilter, and CAccessRule—to implement all the functionality we need. Finally, we'll also change the way the renderer works so that we can return data from our actions and have our base controller handle the output, thus reducing the amount of echoing we need to perform in each controller.

Handling data input

For any request that modifies data in our application, we'll need to handle the acceptance of that data to the RESTful endpoint. To keep things simple, we'll accept JSON-encoded data, or we'll accept data encoded with application/x-www-form-urlencoded or HTML form fields for our convenience. In our application, we'll turn either of these data sources into usable attributes that we can modify and work from in order to complete tasks.

Authenticating users to the API

In Yii, user authentication and identification are typically handled by our `UserIdentity` class and cookies. By convention, RESTful API's don't send or accept any cookies, which means that we'll have to change the way we perform authentication within our application. For this, we'll create a custom `AccessControlFilter` that will initially authenticate our users using their username and password. If a user successfully authenticates against our API, we'll return to them a unique token that the user will use for all future requests that require authentication. This token, and the user's email address will be sent via two custom headers, `X-Auth-Token` and `X-Auth-Email`, and will allow us to identify the user in our API without requiring them to resend their password information. This token will be stored alongside our user in the `user_metadata` table we created in the previous chapters.

Handling API exceptions

The next components we'll need to handle are errors and exceptions. These will range from errors that Yii will encounter naturally, such as 404 errors when an action isn't found, to exceptions that we throw within our application to notify clients interacting with our API of either an unexpected error or a warning that something has happened. Since we'll be changing the way rendering works within our application, we'll simply reroute our errors the same way we would for the response of any action.

Handling data responses

With every request, we'll return the HTTP status code, a message if an error occurred, and a mixed content response attribute that will contain all the information that we want to return to the client for consumption. The response will look as follows:

```
{
    "status": <integer::http_status_code>,
    "message": "<string::null_or_error_message>",
    "response": <mixed::boolean_string_or_array_response"
}
```

We'll also have our actions return a method that will allow us to define what attributes should be returned with each request. This will allow us to return only a limited amount of information, preventing accidental information disclosure, and will enable us to protect private information such as passwords or credentials.

Implementing actions

The last big part that we'll handle is the implementation of all of our controller actions. This will include our authentication endpoint, all the user actions such as registering and resetting their password, and the management of our three core data models: Users, Categories, and Content.

Initializing the project

For this project, we'll be starting where we left off in *Chapter 7, Creating a Management Module for the CMS*. The steps are as follows:

1. For your convenience, a skeleton project has been included in the project resources folder for this chapter that contains the foundation that we'll be starting with. Begin by copying the source code to a new folder, and make sure that it is available at a different URL from the one we used in the previous chapter. In this chapter, I'll be using `http://chapter8.example.com` as our example URL.

2. After importing the database and updating the database configuration using the instructions provided in the previous chapter, create a new folder called `api` in `protected/modules` and also create the following directory structure:

   ```
   api/
       components/
       config/
       controllers/
   ```

3. Next, create the `ApiModule` class, `ApiModule.php`, in `protected/modules/api/`, which will bootstrap our module:

   ```php
   <?php

   class ApiModule extends CWebModule
   {
       public function init()
       {
           // import the module-level models and components
           $this->setImport(array(
               'api.components.*',
           ));

           Yii::app()->log->routes[0]->enabled = false;
   ```

```
            Yii::app()->setComponents(array(
                'errorHandler' => array(
                    'errorAction'  => 'api/default/error',
                )
            ));
        }
    }
```

4. Next, create `routes.php` in `protected/modules/api/config/`, and populate it with the following information:

```
<?php return array(
    '/api/<controller:\w+>/<action:\w+>' => '/
api/<controller>/<action>',
    '/api/<controller:\w+>/<action:\w+>/<id:\w+>' => '/
api/<controller>/<action>'
);
```

Finally, remove `modules.config.php` in the `protected/runtime/` directory, and the contents of the `protected/runtime/cache` directory, to clear the modules cache that we implemented in the previous chapter. This will ensure that Yii recognizes and caches our new module. The next time we access Yii, this file will be regenerated and will contain the appropriate module configuration for our application.

Extending Yii to return data

There are two approaches to having Yii render the JSON or XML data. The first and the easiest approach is to create a JSON or XML view file and, from every action, call `$this->render('json')`. While this is simple, it forces us to store a lot of information and explicitly call the `render()` method in each action. If we're extending a class that modifies the `render()` method, this can be extremely problematic if we want to make changes later. Another issue with this approach is that it treats errors as separate response types. When throwing an error with this approach, Yii will want to render the error as HTML rather than JSON. Depending upon our logging and debug level, this can cause our API to return the wrong data to our client.

A more preferable approach is to simply return the data that we want to present to the client in each action and have our parent controller class handle the rendering and output. This approach makes it easier to identify what data is being presented from each action and ensures that our API consistently returns the right data format even when exceptions or errors happen.

1. To get this working, however, we need to extend a few classes from the Yii framework and modify them so that they return data instead of outputting it. The first class we need to extend is CInlineAction. CInlineAction. It represents the actual action method within our controllers and is called by the runAction() controller method. To make our API return data instead of outputting it, we first need to intercept the response of our actions by modifying the CInlineAction runWithParamsInternal() method, which we'll then return to the runAction() method in the parent controller.

2. We'll do this by creating a new class called ApiInlineAction that extends CInlineAction and overloads the runWithParamsInternal() method. For our convenience, we'll put this code in ApiInlineAction.php, located at protected/modules/api/components/:

```php
<?php
class ApiInlineAction extends CInlineAction
{
    protected function runWithParamsInternal($object, $method, $params)
    {
        $ps=array();
        foreach($method->getParameters() as $i=>$param)
        {
            $name=$param->getName();
            if(isset($params[$name]))
            {
                if($param->isArray())
                    $ps[]=is_array($params[$name]) ? $params[$name] : array($params[$name]);
                elseif(!is_array($params[$name]))
                    $ps[]=$params[$name];
                else
                    return false;
            }
            elseif($param->isDefaultValueAvailable())
                $ps[]=$param->getDefaultValue();
            else
                return false;
        }

        return $method->invokeArgs($object,$ps);
    }
}
```

3. Next, we'll need to create a base controller class that all of our API controllers will extend from. This parent class will be what ultimately class `runWithParamsInternal`. Begin by creating a new class in `protected/modules/api/components` called `ApiController.php` with the following definition:

   ```
   <?php class ApiController extends CMSController {}
   ```

4. Throughout this class, we'll be referencing the private `$_action` variable, which we'll need to redefine from the parent class. We'll define the status and message variables at this time as well. These variables will hold the HTTP status code as well as any error messages that we want to present to the client:

   ```
   private $_action;
   public $status = 200;
   public $message = null;
   ```

5. We'll then overload our `runAction()` method to call our output method instead of Yii's rendering methods:

   ```
   public function runAction($action)
   {
       $response = null;
        $priorAction=$this->_action;
        $this->_action=$action;

       if($this->beforeAction($action))
       {
           $response = $action->runWithParams($this->getActionParams());
            if($response===false)
                $this->invalidActionParams($action);
            else
                $this->afterAction($action);
       }

       $this->_action=$priorAction;

       $this->renderOutput($response);
   }
   ```

> Have questions about `CInlineAction`? Be sure to check out the class documentation at http://www.yiiframework.com/doc/api/1.1/CInlineAction.

Rendering data

The next part in outputting our data is to create the `renderOutput()` method that we called earlier:

1. We'll begin by defining the method. In order to make it as adaptable as possible, we'll want the ability to manually call this method with the status and message that we want to present:

   ```
   public function renderOutput($response = array(), $status=NULL,
   $message=NULL) {}
   ```

2. At this time, we'll define several response headers that will allow web clients to talk to our API and get the same-origin policy settings that modern web browsers have in place in order to protect users. Without these cross-origin resource-sharing headers (CORS, for short), web clients won't be able to talk to our API. This will also allow web browsers to send our API custom authentication headers that we'll define later:

   ```
   header("Access-Control-Allow-Origin: *");
   header("Access-Control-Allow-Headers: x-auth-token, x-auth-email");
   header('Access-Control-Allow-Methods: PUT, PATCH, DELETE, POST, GET, OPTIONS');
   ```

3. We'll then define our base data response:

   ```
   $data = array(
       'status' => $status != NULL ? $status : $this->status,
       'message' => $message != NULL ? $message : ($this->message == NULL ? 'Your request was successfully fulfilled' : $this->message),
       'response' => $response
   );
   ```

4. Then, we'll determine the data format in which we want to return our data from a GET parameter called `format` and render the data appropriately:

   ```
   $format = Yii::app()->request->getParam('format', 'json');
   if ($format == 'xml')
   {
       header ("Content-Type:text/xml");
       echo $this->renderXML($data);
   }
   else
       echo $this->renderJSON($data);
   Yii::app()->end();
   ```

5. To render JSON data, we'll simply take the data response that we built in the previous steps and output it with `CJSON::encode()`:

```
private function renderJSON($data)
{
    header('Content-Type: application/json');
    return CJSON::encode($data);
}
```

6. Rendering the XML data is slightly more involved but can easily be done with the following recursive method:

```
private function renderXML($array, $level=1)
{
    $xml = '';
    if ($level==1)
        $xml .= '<?xml version="1.0" encoding="ISO-8859-1"?>'."\n<data>\n";

    foreach ($array as $key=>$value)
    {
        $key = strtolower($key);
        if (is_array($value))
        {
            $multi_tags = false;
            foreach($value as $key2=>$value2)
            {
                if (is_array($value2))
                {
                    $xml .= str_repeat("\t",$level)."<$key>\n";
                    $xml .= $this->renderXML($value2, $level+1);
                    $xml .= str_repeat("\t",$level)."</$key>\n";
                    $multi_tags = true;
                }
                else
                {
                    if (trim($value2)!='')
                    {
                        if (htmlspecialchars($value2)!=$value2)
                            $xml .= str_repeat("\t",$level)."<$key><![CDATA[$value2]]>"."</$key>\n";
                        else
```

[272]

```
                                  $xml .= str_repeat("\t",$level)."<$key
>$value2</$key>\n";
                        }

                        $multi_tags = true;
                    }
                }

                if (!$multi_tags and count($value)>0)
                {
                    $xml .= str_repeat("\t",$level)."<$key>\n";
                    $xml .= $this->renderXML($value, $level+1);
                    $xml .= str_repeat("\t",$level)."</$key>\n";
                }

            }
            else
            {
                if (trim($value)!='')
                {
                    if (htmlspecialchars($value)!=$value)
                        $xml .= str_repeat("\t",$level)."<$key>"."<![C
DATA[$value]]></$key>\n";
                    else
                        $xml .= str_repeat("\t",$level)."<$key>$value<
/$key>\n";
                }
            }
        }

        if ($level==1)
            $xml .= "</data>\n";

        return $xml;
}
```

> Have questions about the methods we're extending from `CController`? Be sure to take a look at the guide for this class at http://www.yiiframework.com/doc/api/1.1/CController.

Calling actions in a RESTful way

In a RESTful API, a single endpoint might respond differently to different kinds of HTTP requests. For instance, the /api/user/index endpoint might return a list of users or a particular user if a GET request is called with an ID parameter. However, if a POST request is called, a new user will either be created or modified. If a DELETE request was called to that endpoint with an ID, it would delete a user from the system.

To emulate this behavior in Yii, we need to overload the createAction() method of our ApiController so that it calls the correct action. In our controllers, this will allow us to separate functionality by the request type. Internally, our API will be calling actions in the format of action<Name><Method>, with the default GET action hitting the raw action method (for example, actionIndex(), actionIndexPost() and actionIndexDelete()). This method will also call the ApiInlineAction class that we defined earlier instead of CInlineAction:

```
public function createAction($actionID)
{
    if($actionID==='')
        $actionID=$this->defaultAction;

    if (Yii::app()->request->getRequestType() != 'GET' && $actionID != 'error')
        $actionID .= Yii::app()->request->getRequestType();

    if(method_exists($this,'action'.$actionID) &&
strcasecmp($actionID,'s'))  // we have actions method
        return new ApiInlineAction($this,$actionID);
    else
    {
        $action=$this->createActionFromMap($this->actions(),$actionID,$actionID);
        if($action!==null && !method_exists($action,'run'))
            throw new CException(Yii::t('yii', 'Action class {class} must implement the "run" method.', array('{class}'=>get_class($action))));
        return $action;
    }
}
```

Authenticating users

Since RESTful APIs don't pass the cookie information between the API and the client, we need to make several modifications to our controller in order to separate authenticated users from unauthenticated users. For this, we'll overload CAccessControlFilter so that it operates against the user information that we'll populate in our controller:

1. We'll begin by adding a few more public properties to our `ApiController`. The `xauth` attributes will store the `X-Auth-Token` and `X-Auth-Email` headers that we'll send for authentication, and the `user` property will store the raw user model for the authenticated user. We'll pass this information down to the child controllers for authentication and also to our overloaded `CAccessControlFilter` class:

   ```
   public $xauthtoken = null;
   public $xauthemail = null;
   public $user = null;
   ```

2. Next, we'll load our `accessControl` filter. We'll also define another filter called `CHttpCacheFilter` that will tell clients not to cache the responses our API returns:

   ```
   public function filters()
   {
       return array(
           array(
               'CHttpCacheFilter',
               'cacheControl'=>'public, no-store, no-cache, must-revalidate',
           ),
           'accessControl'
       );
   }
   ```

3. We'll then define our base `accessRules()` that will deny access to any method other than our error action:

   ```
   public function accessRules()
   {
       return array(
           array('allow',
               'actions' => array('error')
           ),
           array('deny')
       );
   }
   ```

4. Next, we'll need to handle the authentication in our controller before passing it to `CInlineActionFilter`. We'll begin by overloading the `filterAccessControl()` method in our `ApiController`:

   ```
   public function filterAccessControl($filterChain) {}
   ```

Building an API for the CMS

5. We'll then retrieve the `X-Auth-Token` and `X-Auth-Email` headers:

   ```
   $this->xauthtoken = isset($_SERVER['HTTP_X_AUTH_TOKEN']) ? $_
   SERVER['HTTP_X_AUTH_TOKEN'] : NULL;
   $this->xauthemail =isset($_SERVER['HTTP_X_AUTH_EMAIL']) ? $_
   SERVER['HTTP_X_AUTH_EMAIL'] : NULL;
   ```

6. Now we'll validate these against our database. For this, we'll look up a user in our database with the `X-Auth-Email` address; if this is found, we'll then check for the API token that we'll generate later on in the `user_metadata` table. If an API token is found, we'll populate `$this->user` with the raw user model:

   ```
   if ($this->xauthemail != NULL)
   {
       // If a user exists with that email address
       $user = User::model()->findByAttributes(array('email' => $this->xauthemail));
       if ($user != NULL)
       {
           $q = new CDbCriteria();
           $q->addCondition('t.key LIKE :key');
           $q->addCondition('value = :value');
           $q->addCondition('user_id = :user_id');
           $q->params = array(
               ':user_id' => $user->id,
               ':value' => $this->xauthtoken,
               ':key' => 'api_key'
           );

           $meta = UserMetadata::model()->find($q);

           // And they have an active XAuthToken, set $this->user =
   the User object
           if ($meta != NULL)
               $this->user = $user;
       }
   }
   ```

7. Finally, we'll call our custom `CAccessControlFilter` class, pass the user to it, set rules, and call the filter:

   ```
   $filter=new ApiAccessControlFilter;
   $filter->user = $this->user;
   $filter->setRules($this->accessRules());
   $filter->filter($filterChain);
   ```

Overloading CAccessControlFilter

We need to create a new class called the `ApiAccessControl` filter within `protected/modules/api/components/` so that we can continue using the `accessRules` array in our controllers. This class will operate on the `user` object we passed to it from our controller and will make our `accessRules` array work with our new user object:

1. After creating the `ApiAccessControlFilter.php` file, define it as follows:

   ```
   <?php class ApiAccessControlFilter extends CAccessControlFilter {}
   ```

2. We'll then need to add the `user` attribute to store the user as passed from our controller and redefine the `private $_rules` property that the parent class operates on:

   ```
   public $user;
   private $_rules;
   ```

3. Since the `$_rules` array in the parent class is private, we'll need to redefine the getter and setter for the rules array as well as the `preFilter()` method that uses the private property. We'll start with the `preFilter()` method:

   ```
   protected function preFilter($filterChain)
   {
       $app=Yii::app();
       $request=$app->getRequest();
       $user=$this->user;
       $verb=$request->getRequestType();
       $ip=$request->getUserHostAddress();

       foreach($this->getRules() as $rule)
       {
           if(($allow=$rule->isUserAllowed($user,$filterChain->controller,$filterChain->action,$ip,$verb))>0) // allowed
               break;
           elseif($allow<0) // denied
           {
               if(isset($rule->deniedCallback))
                   call_user_func($rule->deniedCallback, $rule);
               else
                   $this->accessDenied($user,$this->resolveErrorMessage($rule));
               return false;
           }
       }

       return true;
   }
   ```

4. We'll then create both a getter and setter for our `rules` array:

```
public function getRules()
{
    return $this->_rules;
}

public function setRules($rules)
{
    foreach($rules as $rule)
    {
        if(is_array($rule) && isset($rule[0]))
        {
            $r=new ApiAccessRule;
            $r->allow=$rule[0]==='allow';
            foreach(array_slice($rule,1) as $name=>$value)
            {
                if($name==='expression' || $name==='roles' || $name==='message' || $name==='deniedCallback')
                    $r->$name=$value;
                else
                    $r->$name=array_map('strtolower',$value);
            }
            $this->_rules[]=$r;
        }
    }
}
```

5. At this time, we'll also want to redefine the `accessDenied` behavior that gets called when a user doesn't have access to a particular action. Here, we'll simply call the `renderOutput()` method of `ApiController`:

```
protected function accessDenied($user,$message=NULL)
{
    http_response_code(403);
    Yii::app()->controller->renderOutput(array(), 403, $message);
}
```

6. To follow the same convention as Yii, we will also add a second class, `ApiAccessRule`, that extends `CAccessRule` inside the same file. This is just a simple modification that ensures that our information is loaded instead of the information that is passed to `CAccessRule`:

```
class ApiAccessRule extends CAccessRule
{
```

[278]

```
        public function isUserAllowed($user,$controller,$action,$ip,$v
erb)
        {
            if($this->isActionMatched($action)
                && $this->isIpMatched($ip)
                && $this->isVerbMatched($verb)
                && $this->isControllerMatched($controller)
                && $this->isExpressionMatched($user))
                return $this->allow ? 1 : -1;
            else
                return 0;
        }
    }
```

> Want to learn more about `CAccessControlFilter`? Take a look at the class documentation at http://www.yiiframework.com/doc/api/1.1/CAccessControlFilter.

Processing the incoming data

Since our RESTful API will be returning JSON, it's only appropriate that it should accept JSON as well. For convenience, we'll configure our API to accept `application/x-www-form-urlencoded` from the data (data sent from a form), so that our web clients can simply POST directly to our API without having to perform data conversion.

To make our API accept this data, we'll overload the `beforeAction()` method in order to take the raw JSON body, if supplied, and populate it into our `$_POST` data if it is a valid JSON request. If invalid JSON is sent, we'll return an HTTP 400 error, indicating that something was wrong with the request. The error will hit our `actionError()` method and bubble up to our `runAction()` method, which will finally display the error:

```
    public function beforeAction($action)
    {
        // If content was sent as application/x-www-form-urlencoded,
use it. Otherwise, assume raw JSON was sent and convert it into
        // the $_POST variable for ease of use
        if (Yii::app()->request->rawBody != "" && empty($_POST))
        {
            // IF the rawBody is malformed, throw an HTTP 500 error.
Use json_encode so that we can get json_last_error
            $_POST = json_decode(Yii::app()->request->rawBody);
            if (json_last_error() != JSON_ERROR_NONE)
            {
```

```
            header('HTTP/1.1 400 Bad Request');
            $this->status = 400;
            $this->message = 'Request payload not properly formed
JSON.';
            return null;
        }

        $_POST = CJSON::decode(Yii::app()->request->rawBody);
    }

    return parent::beforeAction($action);
}
```

Handling errors

Before moving on to creating controllers, we need to make sure that our parent class can handle any errors that get sent to it. There are two types of errors we'll want to handle—the first being errors that Yii encounters either internally, or through exceptions we call, and the second being errors that we want to present to the user but that we don't want to send through an exception.

Exception handling

To handle exceptions that either we throw or that Yii throws internally, we'll define the base `actionError()` method as follows. The data set here will simply populate the `runAction()` method that we overloaded earlier and will ensure that the appropriate error is displayed in the correct format:

```
public function actionError()
{
    if($error=Yii::app()->errorHandler->error)
    {
        $this->status = $error['code'];
        $this->message = $error['message'];
    }
}
```

Custom error handling

Within our controllers, there will be situations that we'll want to return an error to the user without triggering an exception. A great example of this is a model validation error. We want to inform the user that something went wrong, but we want to return from the error gracefully without stalling our application. For this, we'll create a `returnError()` method that we'll call from our controller that will populate back up to the `runAction()` method we defined earlier:

```
public function returnError($status, $message = NULL, $response)
{
    header('HTTP/1.1 '. $status);
    $this->status = $status;

    if ($message === NULL)
        $this->message = 'Failed to set model attributes.';
    else
        $this->message = $message;

    return $response;
}
```

Testing whether everything works

Before we start creating other controllers and actions, let's create a very simple controller in order to verify that our API is working the way we want it to. For this, let's create a class called `DefaultController` in `protected/modules/api/controllers` with the following setup:

```
class DefaultController extends ApiController
{
    public function accessRules()
    {
        return array(
            array('allow',
                'actions' => array('index', 'error')
            ),
            array('deny')
        );
    }

    public function actionIndex()
    {
        return "test";
    }
}
```

If your API is set up correctly, you should be able to open your browser to `http://chapter8.example.com/api` and see the following displayed:

```
{
    "status":200,
    "message":"Your request was successfully fulfilled",
    "response":"test"
}
```

Building an API for the CMS

As you can see, whatever data we returned from our action is now in the response attribute of our JSON object. Additionally, if we want to render XML instead of JSON, we can add the `format=xml GET` parameter to the `http://chapter8.example.com/api?format=xml` URL as follows:

```
<data>
    <status>200</status>
    <message>Your request was successfully fulfilled</message>
    <response>test</response>
</data>
```

> Most load balancers and health-check services verify that endpoints return a 200 status. For this reason, it's recommended that you simply return true from this default method if you're going to add a health check to your API.

Authenticating users

Now that our API is functional, let's add the ability for users to be authenticated against our API. For this, we're going to create an endpoint that accepts the following JSON request body:

```
{
    "email": "user@example.com",
    "password": "<example_password>"
}
```

With this information, the API will be authenticated using `LoginForm`, which we worked on in previous chapters. If the user is valid, we'll generate a new API token that will be stored in the `user_metadata` table. This token will be returned to the client who is making the request and will be used to authenticate for all future requests:

1. To get started, create a new controller in `protected/modules/api/controllers/` called `UserController.php` with the following definition:

   ```
   <?php class UserController extends ApiController {}
   ```

2. Next, we'll need to define a default set of access rules so as to allow our authentication method to be used without authentication:

   ```
   public function accessRules()
   {
       return array(
   ```

```
        array('allow',
            'actions' => array('tokenPost'),
        ),
         array('deny')
    );
}
```

3. Since this is a POST endpoint, we'll define our new method as follows:

   ```
   public function actionTokenPost() {}
   ```

4. We'll then instantiate a new instance of LoginForm and retrieve our e-mail address and password from the JSON body. Remember that, in our ApiController class, we transformed the raw JSON body directly into our $_POST parameters in order to make things easier to work with:

   ```
   $model = new LoginForm;
   $model->username = Yii::app()->request->getParam('email', NULL);
   $model->password = Yii::app()->request->getParam('password', NULL);
   ```

5. After retrieving this information, we'll attempt to log in:

   ```
   if ($model->login()) {}
   ```

6. If successful, we'll load the user information:

   ```
   $user = User::model()->findByAttributes(array('email' => $model->username));
   ```

7. Try to either update an existing API token, or generate a new one:

   ```
   $token = UserMetadata::model()->findByAttributes(array(
       'user_id' => $user->id,
       'key' => 'api_key'
   ));

   if ($token == NULL)
       $token = new UserMetadata;

   $token->attributes = array(
      'user_id' => $user->id,
      'key' => 'api_key',
      'value' => $user->generateActivationKey() // Reuse this method for cryptlib
   );
   ```

[283]

8. If we are able to save the token to the database, we'll return it:
   ```
   if ($token->save())
       return $token->value;
   ```

9. Outside our `if ($model->login())` condition, we'll simply return an error to the user, indicating that something went wrong. Since this is an authentication method, we don't want to give away too much information in order to prevent people from attempting to brute-force our API endpoint:
   ```
   return $this->returnError(401, $model->getErrors(), null);
   ```

Testing the authentication

Before proceeding, let's make sure that our authentication endpoint works. To test this, we'll be using a Google Chrome extension called **RestConsole** and that can be downloaded from the Chrome App Store at `https://chrome.google.com/webstore/detail/rest-console/cokgbflfommojglbmbpenpphppikmonn?hl=en`. If you do not already have Google Chrome installed, you can download it from `https://www.google.com/intl/en-US/chrome/browser/`. After installing, navigate to the RestConsole download page and install the plugin. Once it's installed, you can click on the **Launch App** button in the Chrome App Store to load RestConsole. Once it's loaded, you'll see several different sections:

> A tool such as RestConsole will allow us to quickly test our API endpoints from a nice GUI interface. If you prefer, you can test the endpoints directly from your command line using the cURL utility, available through most package managers.

1. In the **Target** section, fill out the form as shown in the following screenshot. Be sure to adjust to your local environment. The key detail in this section is the **Request URI** field.

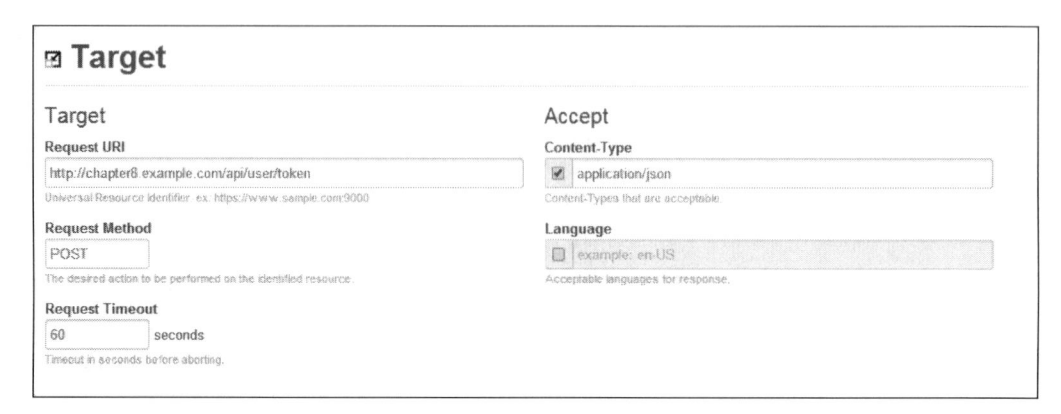

2. Then, scroll down to the **Body** section, and fill out the section as follows:

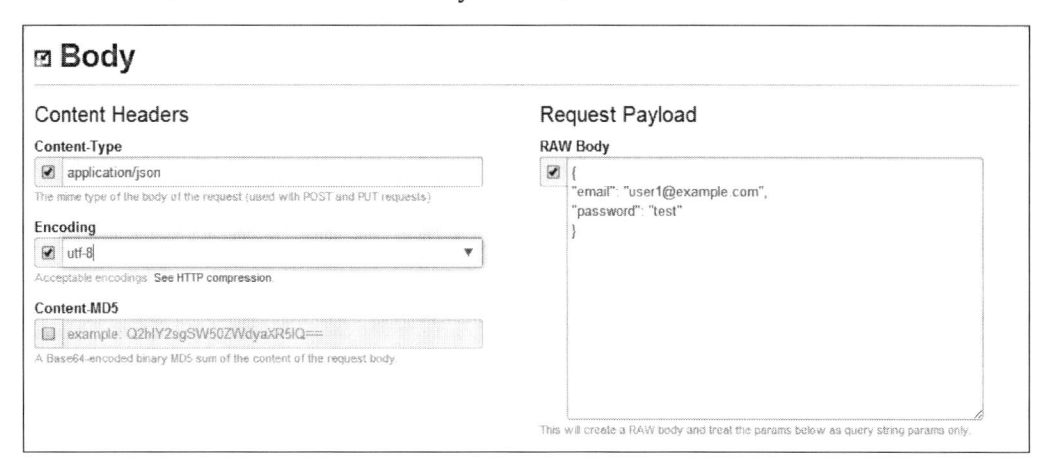

> The key part of this section is the **Request Payload** section. This is where you'll add the raw JSON body that will be sent to the server. In this example, we're using the credentials that we established in *Chapter 7, Creating a Management Module for the CMS*.

```
{
    "email": "user1@example.com",
    "password": "test"
}
```

If you've changed these credentials since then, be sure to change them in your JSON body.

3. Finally, click on the **Post** button at the bottom of the page. This will send the request to the server. If successful, you'll receive an HTTP 200 status code in response with your API token in the response body:

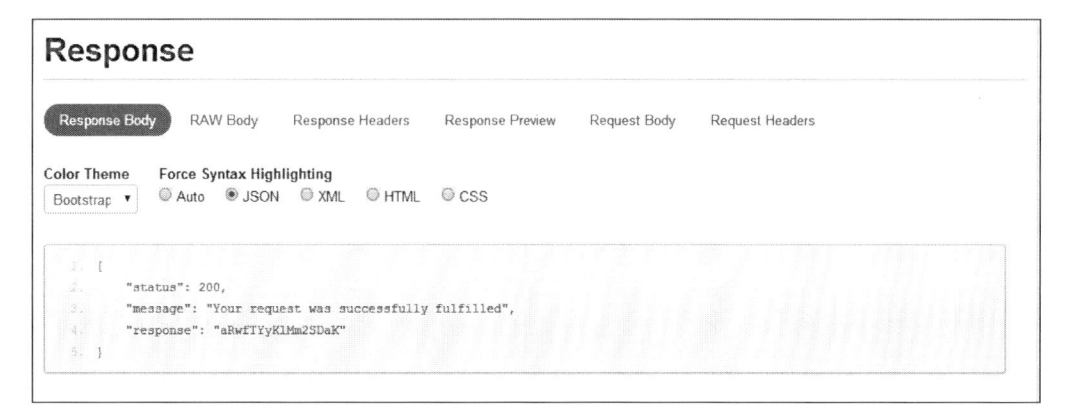

```
{
    "status": 200,
    "message": "Your request was successfully fulfilled",
    "response": "aRwfTYyKlMm2SDaK"
}
```

> Your response body will differ slightly as the API token is randomly generated on each authentication request.

Sending authenticated requests

Now that we can authenticate against our API, let's make sure that we can send authenticated requests. For this, we'll be creating an API endpoint in order to deauthenticate our user. This will accept the user's credentials and then delete the API token from the database in order to prevent future use:

1. Creating this endpoint consists of two parts. First, we need to add an item to our `accessRules` array that allows authenticated users to send a DELETE request to the token endpoint. We'll do this by adding the following to our `accessRules` array:

    ```
    array('allow',
        'actions' => array('tokenDelete'),
        'expression' => '$user!=NULL'
    )
    ```

2. Then we'll add the delete method for our token endpoint that will be available over the HTTP DELETE method:

    ```
    public function actionTokenDelete()
    {
        $model = UserMetadata::model()->findByAttributes(array('user_id' => $this->user->id, 'value' => $this->xauthtoken));

        if ($model === NULL)
            throw new CHttpException(500, 'An unexpected error occured while deleting the token. Please re-generate a new token for subsequent requests.');
        return $model->delete();
    }
    ```

Now that are endpoint is set up, return to RestConsole, remove the request body, and add the following custom headers to the **Custom Headers** section below the request body, as shown in the following screenshot:

```
X-Auth-Email: user1@example.com
X-Auth-Token: aRwfTYyKlMm2SDaK
```

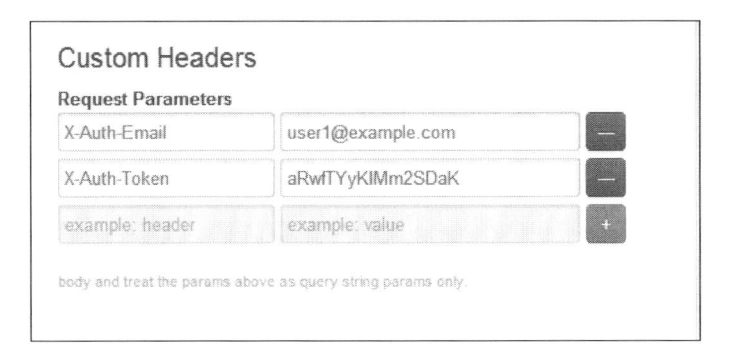

Then, hit the **Delete** button at the bottom of the page to send a `DELETE` request. You should receive the following response:

```
{
    "status": 200,
    "message": "Your request was successfully fulfilled",
    "response": true
}
```

We've now successfully tested user authentication and added the ability to deauthenticate from our API. Notice that, if you try to submit a `DELETE` request again, our `acccessRules` array will kick in and will block the request for us, thus returning the following response:

```
{
    "status": 403,
    "message": "You are not authorized to perform this action.",
    "response": []
}
```

Implementing CRUD actions

Now that we can authenticate and work with our API, we can work on implementing the four basic CRUD actions in a RESTful manner. The RESTful actions boil down to three main HTTP request types—`GET`, `POST`, and `DELETE`. We'll implement each one for our users.

The first method we need to implement is our `loadModel()` method. This method will be loaded in our User model and will throw the appropriate errors if something goes wrong:

```
private function loadModel($id=NULL)
{
    if ($id == NULL)
        throw new CHttpException(400, 'Missing ID');

    $model = User::model()->findByPk($id);

    if ($model == NULL)
        throw new CHttpException(400, 'User not found');

    return $model;
}
```

Deleting users

The first method that we'll implement is our DELETE method. Remember that, for each method, we'll be hitting a single endpoint, /api/user/index, with different HTTP request types:

1. The first change that we need to make is to our `accessRules`. We want only administrators to have the ability to delete a user. We'll do this by setting up an expression that checks whether the user is an admin:

   ```
   array('allow',
       'actions' => array('indexDelete'),
       'expression' => '$user!=NULL&&$user->role->id==2'
   )
   ```

2. Then, we'll implement the delete action. We want to make sure that users are not able to delete themselves:

   ```
   public function actionIndexDelete($id=NULL)
   {
       if ($id == $this->user->id)
           return $this->returnError(401, 'You cannot delete yourself', null);

       return $this->loadModel($id)->delete();
   }
   ```

Sending a DELETE request to /api/user/index/id/<user_id> will now delete a user with the given ID.

Retrieving users

The second method that we'll implement is a `GET` method that will either retrieve a single user if an ID is provided, or multiple users if a user is an administrator. In either case, we'll want to make sure that a user is authenticated:

1. The first change, once again, will be to our `accessRules` array. We'll check to see whether a user is an admin, or whether the given ID belongs to the currently authenticated users:

    ```
    array('allow',
        'actions' => array('index'),
        'expression' => '$user!=NULL&&($user->role->id==2||Yii::app()->request->getParam("id")==$user->id)'
    )
    ```

2. We'll then set up a `GET` method in our controller. Remember, we set up our `createAction()` method in our `ApiController` class so that `GET` requests don't require the HTTP verb at the end of the method:

    ```
    public function actionIndex($id=NULL) {}
    ```

3. Then, if an ID was provided, we'll simply load the requested user. If the user is not an admin and they requested another user, we'll throw an exception; otherwise, we'll return the appropriate data:

    ```
    array('allow',
        'actions' => array('index', 'indexPost'),
        'expression' => '$user!=NULL&&($user->role->id==2||Yii::app()->request->getParam("id")==$user->id)'
    if ($id !== NULL)
    {
        if ($this->user->role->id != 2 && $this->user->id != $id)
            throw new CHttpException(403, 'You do not have access to this resource');

        return $this->loadModel($id)->getApiAttributes(array('password'), array('role', 'metadata'));
    }
    ```

    If you recall, we made changes to our `CMSActiveRecord` model in order to add a `getApiAttributes()` method. Calling this method now allows us to exclude certain elements that we don't want to send in the request, such as the user password. This also allows us to return metadata about the user, such as the role and any metadata associated with the user.

Building an API for the CMS

4. Carrying on, if an ID was not specified, we'll make sure that the user is an admin:

   ```
   if ($this->user->role->id != 2)
       throw new CHttpException(403, 'You do not have access to this resource');
   ```

5. If so, we'll load up a search instance of our model. This extends our endpoint to allow for dynamic searching:

   ```
   $model = new User('search');
   $model->unsetAttributes();  // clear any default values
   if(isset($_GET['User']))
       $model->attributes = $_GET['User'];
   ```

6. To allow for pagination, we'll instance a copy of CActiveDataProvider from the $model->search() method and set the page variable to the GET parameter page. This will allow us to paginate through our users rather than dumping all of them in a single request:

   ```
   $dataProvider = $model->search();
   $dataProvider->pagination = array(
       'pageVar' => 'page'
   );
   ```

7. To handle pagination, we'll simply continue to display results until no results are found. When no results are found, we'll throw an HTTP 404 error. This will allow for infinite scrolling on the client side and will let our clients know when to stop asking for data:

   ```
   if ($dataProvider->totalItemCount == 0 || ($dataProvider->totalItemCount / ($dataProvider->itemCount * Yii::app()->request->getParam('page', 1))) < 1)
       throw new CHttpException(404, 'No results found');
   ```

8. We'll then iterate through our `dataProvider` using the `getData()` method and generate an array of all the user objects in the current page:

   ```
   $response = array();

   foreach ($dataProvider->getData() as $user)
       $response[] = $user->getAPIAttributes(array('password'), array('role', 'metadata'));
   ```

9. Finally, we'll return the entire response:

   ```
   return $response;
   ```

Now, make a few requests to the API endpoint in order to test everything out. You should be able to log in as an admin and view all users or any user. You should also be able to log in as a regular user and only retrieve information about yourself.

Creating and updating users

The last endpoint we'll need to implement is a POST method that will serve as an endpoint to both creating and updating existing users:

1. We'll begin by updating the `accessRules` array that we defined in the previous section in order to include `indexPost`:

   ```
   array('allow',
       'actions' => array('index', 'indexPost'),
       'expression' => '$user!=NULL&&($user->role->id==2||
   Yii::app()->request->getParam("id")==$user->id)'
   )
   ```

2. We'll then create a POST endpoint that will branch off into two separate methods—one that creates users and one that modifies users:

   ```
   public function actionIndexPost($id=NULL)
   {
       if ($id == NULL)
           return $this->createUser();
       else
           return $this->updateUser($id);
   }
   ```

3. Since all the information for creating users will be coming from a normal POST response, all we need to do to create a new user is verify that they are an admin, instantiate a new User model, validate it, and save it. If, for any reason, we encounter an error (such as an invalidate attribute), we'll simply return the errors from `$model->getErrors()` in the JSON response:

   ```
   private function createUser()
   {
       if ($this->user->role->id != 2)
           throw new CHttpException(403, 'You do not have access to this resource');

       $model = new User;
       $model->attributes = $_POST;

       if ($model->save())
           return User::model()->findByPk($model->id)-
   >getApiAttributes(array('password'), array('role', 'metadata'));
       else
           return $this->returnError(400, $model->getErrors(), null);
   }
   ```

4. As it turns out, updating users is as simple as loading an existing User model and doing the same thing as creating a new user. The only difference in this endpoint is that we need to make sure that the user is either an admin, or that they are trying to modify their own data:

```
private function updateUser($id=NULL)
{
    if ($this->user->role->id != 2 && $this->user->id != $id)
        throw new CHttpException(403, 'You do not have permission to modify this user');

    $model = $this->loadModel($id);

    $model->attributes = $_POST;

    if ($model->save())
        return User::model()->findByPk($model->id)->getApiAttributes(array('password'), array('role', 'metadata'));
    else
        return $this->returnError(400, $model->getErrors(), null);
}
```

At this point, go ahead and verify that you can create new users as an admin and that existing users can modify their own data.

Implementing other controller actions from the main application

At this point, we've created the basic CRUD interface for our User data model. While this takes care of a lot of the administrative tasks, there are a couple of other methods that we can move from the frontend of our application to our API. These methods include actions such as registration, account verification, and password reset requests. Moving these methods from our frontend and into our API immediately makes this functionality available to any consumer of our API, which makes our API more valuable to both web and native clients.

For example, we can easily adapt our registration action from our frontend to our API by simply replacing the render actions with either a Boolean value indicating that the registration was successful, or a list of errors generated by the model. Because all of our validation rules and verification checks are performed in the model, adapting the action is fairly simple, as shown:

```
public function actionRegisterPost()
{
    $form = new RegistrationForm;
    $form->attributes = $_POST;

    if ($form->save())
        return true;
    else
        return $this->returnError(400, $form->getErrors(), null);
}
```

Go ahead and try implementing the other actions from our frontend controller, such as `actionVerifyPost`, `actionActivate`, `actionForgotPost`, and `actionResetPasswordPost`.

Implementing categories and content API controllers

Our CMS is made up of more than user-related actions—we also have to manage content and categories. Once again, moving this functionality from our dashboard controllers to our API is fairly simple. We simply strip out the view-related functionality and return either Boolean values, or errors generated from the model. In the case of our GET method, we simply add in some pagination using the already provided pagination functionality of `CActiveDataProvider` and return the relevant results. Both of these controllers will look nearly identical to our `UserController`, as they work in the same way except with different data models. Go ahead and try to complete these controllers on your own.

> Remember that a fully completed application is included with the project resources. If you get stuck, take a look at the resources folder.

Documenting our API

While our API can be fun to work with and easy to integrate with, it means nothing to developers who want to work with our API if the available endpoints, details, and examples aren't documented clearly. Before sharing your API with the world, be sure to document what endpoints clients can access. It's also a good idea to thoroughly document what users need to do in order to authenticate against the API. Generally, this is done by providing detailed example requests and detailed example responses.

Summary

As shown throughout this book, the Yii framework is an extremely powerful, flexible, and easy PHP framework to work with. In this chapter, we completely overhauled how the Yii framework handles user authentication through JSON requests and adapts it to return both JSON and XML document types for an API that can be consumed by both web and native applications. In this chapter, we also covered what changes we needed to make in order to migrate functionality that was previously designed to be rendered directly to the client to our API to be rendered as JSON or XML. Finally, we adapted our API to respond to different types of HTTP requests on the same endpoint, allowing us to make a RESTful JSON API that is well documented.

Thank you for reading this book. Throughout this book, we've shown countless examples of how powerful and flexible Yii is. From working with third-party APIs to performing database-agnostic migrations and all the way to developing feature-complete applications complete with an API, the Yii framework enables us to quickly work, develop, and adapt our code to meet our objectives and end goals in a timely manner. I hope that you found the information contained within this book informative, useful, and fun. I also hope that you've learned how to use the Yii framework to do more than just create simple web applications.

On the about page of the Yii framework, Yii is described as an acronym for "Yes It Is" that answers some of the most basic questions asked about Yii. Is Yii fast? Is Yii secure? Is Yii professional? Is Yii right for your next project? I hope this book has shown you that the answer to those questions is a simple "Yes, it is".

Index

A

access rules
  used, for creating authentication system 34, 35
accessRules() method 34
actionDelete() method 112
actionIndex() method
  implementing 160
actionSave() method 112
actionSearch() method 120
actionView() method
  implementing 170
API
  building 264
  building, for CMS 263, 264
  CMS categories, implementing 293
  CMS content, implementing 293
  controller actions, implementing 267, 292
  data input, handling 265
  data responses, handling 266
  documenting 293
  exceptions handling 266
  initializing 267
  module, configuring 265
  prerequisites 264
  testing 281, 282
  URL, for documentation 59
  user authentication 266
  Yii extending, for rendering JSON/XML 265
API key
  generating 52, 53
  storing 53

authenticate() method 38
authentication system, task management application
  controller, creating 35
  creating 34
  creating, with access rules 34, 35
  creating, with filters 34, 35
  login layout, creating 36
  login model, creating 39, 40
  login view, creating 37
  users, identifying with UserIdentity CUserIdentity class 38

B

Bcrypt password
  hashing 78
beforeAction() method 279
beforeSave() method 20, 76
beforeValidate() method 78

C

CAccessControlFilter
  overloading 277, 278
  URL, for documentation 279
caching
  what's nearby application performance, optimizing with 63, 64
categories, CMS
  about 184
  entries, viewing 206
  entries, viewing with RSS feed 206-208
  implementing, to API 293
  managing 205-209
  viewing 205

CButtonColumn
  about 111
  URL 111
CConsoleCommand
  about 94
  reference link 51
CController class
  URL, for guide 273
CFormModel 142
CHtml::listData() method 61
CHttpRequest Class Reference
  reference link 203
CInlineAction class
  URL, for documentation 270
CMS
  about 181
  API, building for 263, 264
  components 183
  initializing 185, 186
  prerequisites 182
  social authentication, with HybridAuth 210
CMS, skeleton project
  custom UrlManager class, using 189-193
  custom validator, creating for
    slugs 187, 188
  exploring 186
  models, extending from common class 186
  themes, using 188
  truly dynamic routing 189
components, CMS
  categories 184
  content 184
  SEO 185
  users 183
components, issue tracking application
  e-mails 104-106
  issues 104, 105
  users 104, 105
components, scheduled reminders
  events 68, 69
  reminders 68-70
  task runner 68, 70
  users 68
components, task management application
  projects 7, 8
  tasks 7, 8

users 7, 8
Composer
  URL, for downloading 68, 104, 182
content, CMS
  about 184
  comments, adding with Disqus 199-202
  displaying 193
  displaying, with ID 197-199
  implementing, to API 293
  list view, displaying 196
  managing 193, 203-205
  searching 202, 203
  sitemap, rendering 194, 195
Content Distribution Network (CDN) 22
content management system. *See* CMS
controllers, CMS
  creating 236-238
controller, scheduled reminders
  creating, for user management 94
  user authentication, creating with
    Bcrypt 97-99
  user authentication, requiring 99
  users, creating 94, 95
  users, deleting 95
  users password, modifying 96, 97
createAction() method 274
CRUD actions
  implementing 287
  users, creating 291, 292
  users, deleting 288
  users, retrieving 289, 290
  users, updating 291, 292
CTimestampBehavior
  about 76
  reference link 76
custom error handling 280
custom routes
  adding, to modules 235, 236
custom UrlManager class
  URL 193
  using 189-193
custom validator
  creating, for slugs 187, 188
CWebUser object
  creating, from remote identity 216
  URL 79

D

database, scheduled reminders
  creating 73
  events migration 74, 75
  reminders migration 74, 75
  users migration 73, 74
database, task management application
  creating, SQLite used 10
  creating, with migration 14, 15
  overview 11
  projects table 9
  tasks table 8, 9
  users 10
database, what's nearby application
  creating 47
  designing 44
  locations table 44, 45
default route
  defining 41
Disqus
  about 182
  URL 182
  URL, for creating account 199
  used, for adding comments to CMS 199-202
DNS hosting service
  reference link 104
domain registrar
  reference link 103
down() method 75
dynamic routing 189

E

e-mail reminders
  sending 99-101
e-mails, issue tracking application
  about 104
  inbound e-mail parsing, handling 127
  issues, creating 129-131
  issues, updating 129-131
  receiving 106
  SendGrid Parse settings, adjusting 128
  sending, to SendGrid 127
error handling
  about 280
  custom error handling 280
  exception handling 280
events, scheduled reminders
  about 69
  controller, creating 81-83
  creating 91-93
  custom route, adding 81
  displaying 80, 81
  event list view, creating 87-90
  item view, creating 87
  layout, creating 85
  main view, creating 86, 87
  reminders controller, creating 83-85
  saving 91-93
  searching 80, 81
exception handling 266, 280

F

File class
  creating, for uploading files 250
files
  controller, creating 256-260
  File class, creating 250
  FileUpload class, creating 254, 255
  FileUploader class, creating 251, 252
  uploading 250
file upload capability
  adding, to modules 229
FileUpload class
  creating, for uploading files 254, 255
FileUploader class
  creating, for uploading files 251, 252
filters
  used, for creating authentication system 34, 35
find() method 100
functionality, CMS
  categories, migrating to modules 244-247
  content management, migrating to modules 238-243
  migrating, to modules 238
  user management, implementing to modules 247-249

G

generateRules() method 191
GET method 289

Gii
  about 16
  disabling 41
  models, creating with 16
Google API Console
  URL 51
Google APIs
  about 51
  API key, generating 52, 53
  API key, storing 53
  enabling 51
Google Chrome
  URL, for downloading 284
Google Maps
  interacting with 55
  what's nearby application, interacting with 55-58
Google Maps JavaScript API v3
  URL 58
Google Places API
  used, for creating what's nearby application 43

H

HybridAuth
  about 172
  additional providers, adding 224
  authenticating, with social identity 214, 215
  configuring 174, 175
  CWebUser object, creating from remote identity 216
  existing account, linking to social identity 212, 213
  implementing 217-224
  remote identities, validating 210
  remote registrations 211
  sharing, implementation 176-178
  social sign-on, implementing 176-178
  URL, for documentation 172, 210, 219
  used, for social authentication in CMS 210

I

initialization, API 267
initialization, CMS 185, 186
initialization, issue tracking application 107
initialization, modules 229, 230
initialization, scheduled reminders
  Composer dependencies, adding 72, 73
  database, creating 70
  MySQL user, creating 70
  parameters configuration file, creating 72
  Yii configuration file, creating 71
installation, MySQL 67
issues, issue tracking application
  about 104, 105
  creating 121, 122
  displaying, to users 119, 120
  e-mail views, creating 125, 126
  implementing 115
  Issues model 116-118
  Issues Update model 118
  searching 120, 121
  statuses 106
  updating 106, 123-125
  viewing 114, 115, 123-125
issue tracking application
  components 104
  creating 103
  initializing 107
  prerequisites 103, 104
  testing 127

L

loadModel() method 26, 112, 288
logging
  reference link 140

M

Main.js file 55
Markdown
  URL 124
microblogging platform
  creating 133
  description 135
  initializing 136, 137
  prerequisites 134, 135
  shares 136
  sharing on Twitter, with HybridAuth 172
  timeline of shares, viewing 160-162
  users 135
  Yii bootstrap file, modifying 137-139

microblogging platform, sharing on Twitter
   HybridAuth, configuring 174, 175
   HybridAuth sharing,
      implementation 176-178
   HybridAuth social sign-on,
      implementing 176-178
   Twitter application, setting up 172-174
migration
   about 14
   task management application database,
      creating with 14, 15
models
   creating, with Gii 16
   default validation rules, updating 17
   enhancing 16
   project metadata, retrieving 19
   relations, defining 18
   tasks, removing 19
   timestamp, setting 20
   timestamp, updating 20
models, scheduled reminders
   behaviors, adding 76
   creating 76
   Events model 79, 80
   Reminders model 78
   Users model 77
module, API
   configuring 265
modules
   about 228
   CMS categories, migrating to 244-247
   CMS functionality, migrating to 238
   content management, migrating to 238-243
   creating 231, 232
   custom routes, adding 235, 236
   deploying 230
   deploying, as application 261
   deploying, as Composer dependency 261
   deploying, as submodule 261
   deploying, with CMS 260
   file upload capability, adding 229
   initializing 229, 230
   management functionality,
      moving 229
   prerequisites 228
   registering, with Yii 232-234
   routing 229

URL, for guide 228
user management, implementing 247-249
MySQL
   installing 67
   URL, for downloading 67

P

PHP 5.5
   URL, for password functions 78
PHPMailer
   URL, for documentation 101
POST method 291
presentation layer, task management
      application
   creating 21
   projects, managing 21
   tasks, viewing 30
presentation layer, what's nearby
      application
   creating 53-55
   Google Maps, interacting with 55-58
   nearby locations, displaying on map 61-63
   nearby locations, searching 59, 60
   nearby locations, selecting 60
   performance, optimizing with
      caching 63, 64
processRules() method 190
projects
   about 8
   completion state, modifying 26
   creating 27-29
   deleting 27
   layout, creating 22, 23
   project index action, creating 24, 26
   updating 27-29
projects table
   about 9
   creating, SQLite used 10

R

relations() method 18
ReminderController 83
RemindersCommand 99
reminders, scheduled reminders 69, 70
renderItems() method 89

render() method 24
renderSorter() method 89
RESTClient
  URL 264
RestConsole
  about 284
  URL, for downloading 284
roles, issue tracking application users
  administrator 105
  customer 105
  supporter 105
routing
  with module 229
RSS feed
  used, for viewing entries in CMS categories 206-208
rules() method 17

S

scheduled reminders
  about 67, 68
  components 68
  database, creating 73
  e-mail reminders, sending 99-101
  initializing 70
  models, creating 76
  prerequisites 67, 68
search engine optimizations. *See* SEO
search() method 196
SendGrid
  e-mails, sending to 127
  Parse settings, adjusting 128
  URL, for creating developer account 104
  URL, for creating SMTP account 68
SendGrid Developer
  URL 182
SendGrid Parse API webhook
  URL 128
SEO 185
shares, microblogging platform
  about 136
  content, sharing 166
  liking 168
  resharing, implementation 167, 168
  retrieving 162-165

searching 171
timeline page, viewing 160-162
unliking 170
viewing 170
SQLite
  used, for creating projects table 10
  used, for creating task management application database 10
  used, for creating tasks table 10

T

task management application
  about 7
  authentication system, creating 34
  components 7
  database 8
  default route, defining 41
  extra routes, adding 41
  finishing 40
  Gii, disabling 41
  initializing 11-13
  presentation layer, creating 21
  unauthorized access, preventing 34
task runner, scheduled reminders 70
tasks
  about 8
  managing 31, 32
  viewing 30
tasks table
  about 8, 9
  creating, SQLite used 10
theme attribute
  reference link 189
themes
  using 188
Twitter application
  setting up 172
Twitter Bootstrap 22
Twitter Developer
  URL 182

U

user authentication, API
  about 266
  authenticated requests, sending 286, 287

CAccessControlFilter, overloading 277, 278
  creating 282, 283
  handling 274-276
  testing 284, 285
users, task management application 8
users, CMS 183
users, issue tracking application
  about 104, 105
  authentication, managing 108-110
  creating 112, 113
  deleting 112
  listing 110, 111
  managing 108
  roles 105
  roles, managing 108-110
  updating 112, 113
  viewing 114, 115
users, microblogging platform
  about 135
  e-mail address, verifying 158-160
  enabling, for managing
     information 140, 153-158
  followers 135
  forgotten password, resetting 151-153
  forgotten passwords, handling 149-151
  likes 136
  secure registration process,
     implementing 142-148
  user follow up, determining 142
  UserIdentity class, upgrading 140
  user relations, defining 141
Users model, scheduled reminders
  Bcrypt password, hashing 78
users, scheduled reminders 68

V

validate() method 17
Virtual Private Server (VPS)
  about 104
  reference link 182

W

what's nearby application
  about 43
  configuration file, creating 46
  creating, Google Places API used 43
  database, designing 44
  data feed, importing 49, 50
  initializing 45, 46
  locations, displaying 44
  locations, importing 44
  locations model, creating 48
  locations, storing 44
  nearby locations, searching 43
  presentation layer, creating 53-55
  sample data, retrieving 47

Y

Yii
  benefits 138
  extending, for error handling 280
  extending, for implementing controller
     actions 274
  extending, for processing incoming
     data 279
  extending, for rendering data 271-273
  extending, for rendering JSON/XML in
     RESTful way 265
  extending, for rendering JSON/XML
     data 268-270
  extending, for user authentication 274-276
  modules, registering with 232-234
  URL, for documentation 140
  URL, for loading view file 114
  URL, for official guide 11
  URL, for quick start guide 11
  URL, for valid column types 74
  URL, for validation rules 17
yiic command 73
yiic file 13
yiic tool 11

Thank you for buying
Yii Project Blueprints

About Packt Publishing

Packt, pronounced 'packed', published its first book "*Mastering phpMyAdmin for Effective MySQL Management*" in April 2004 and subsequently continued to specialize in publishing highly focused books on specific technologies and solutions.

Our books and publications share the experiences of your fellow IT professionals in adapting and customizing today's systems, applications, and frameworks. Our solution based books give you the knowledge and power to customize the software and technologies you're using to get the job done. Packt books are more specific and less general than the IT books you have seen in the past. Our unique business model allows us to bring you more focused information, giving you more of what you need to know, and less of what you don't.

Packt is a modern, yet unique publishing company, which focuses on producing quality, cutting-edge books for communities of developers, administrators, and newbies alike. For more information, please visit our website: www.packtpub.com.

About Packt Open Source

In 2010, Packt launched two new brands, Packt Open Source and Packt Enterprise, in order to continue its focus on specialization. This book is part of the Packt Open Source brand, home to books published on software built around Open Source licenses, and offering information to anybody from advanced developers to budding web designers. The Open Source brand also runs Packt's Open Source Royalty Scheme, by which Packt gives a royalty to each Open Source project about whose software a book is sold.

Writing for Packt

We welcome all inquiries from people who are interested in authoring. Book proposals should be sent to author@packtpub.com. If your book idea is still at an early stage and you would like to discuss it first before writing a formal book proposal, contact us; one of our commissioning editors will get in touch with you.

We're not just looking for published authors; if you have strong technical skills but no writing experience, our experienced editors can help you develop a writing career, or simply get some additional reward for your expertise.

Yii Application Development Cookbook
Second Edition

ISBN: 978-1-78216-310-7   Paperback: 408 pages

A Cookbook covering both practical Yii application development tips and the most important Yii features

1. Learn how to use Yii even more efficiently.
2. Full of practically useful solutions and concepts you can use in your application.
3. Both important Yii concept descriptions and practical recipes are inside.

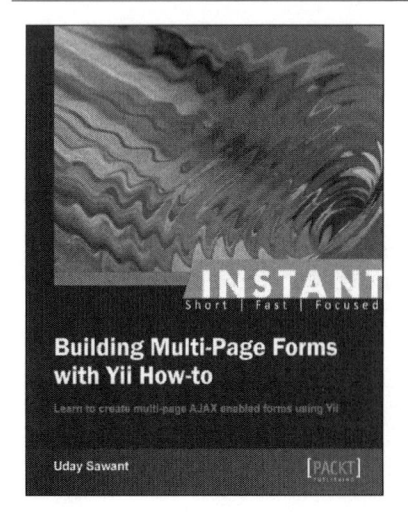

Instant Building Multi-Page Forms with Yii How-to

ISBN: 978-1-78216-642-9   Paperback: 50 pages

Learn to create multi-page AJAX enabled forms using Yii

1. Learn something new in an Instant! A short, fast, focused guide delivering immediate results.
2. Quick, easy-to-follow recipes with immediate results.
3. Filled with useful tasks to improve maintainability of web applications.

Please check **www.PacktPub.com** for information on our titles

Instant Yii 1.1 Application Development Starter

ISBN: 978-1-78216-168-4   Paperback: 62 pages

Get started with building attractive PHP web applications with the Yii framework

1. Learn something new in an Instant! A short, fast, focused guide delivering immediate results.
2. Set up your development environment and plan your application.
3. Use Yii's automatic code generators to scaffold routes, forms, and list views.

Web Application Development with Yii and PHP

Second Edition

ISBN: 978-1-84951-872-7   Paperback: 332 pages

Learn the Yii application development framework by taking a step-by-step approach to building a Web-based project task tracking system from conception through production deployment

1. A step-by-step guide to creating a modern Web application using PHP, MySQL, and Yii.
2. Build a real-world, user-based, database-driven project task management application using the Yii development framework.

Please check www.PacktPub.com for information on our titles

Printed in Great Britain
by Amazon